Yale Agrarian Studies Series

JAMES C. SCOTT, series editor

Children
of the
Northern Forest

Wild New England's History
from Glaciers to Global Warming

JAMIE SAYEN

Yale UNIVERSITY PRESS/NEW HAVEN & LONDON

Published with assistance from the foundation established in memory of
Amasa Stone Mather of the Class of 1907, Yale College.

Yale University Press books may be purchased in quantity for educational,
business, or promotional use. For information, please e-mail sales.press@yale.edu
(U.S. office) or sales@yaleup.co.uk (U.K. office).

Set in Minion type by Newgen North America.
Printed in the United States of America.

Library of Congress Control Number: 2023932567
ISBN 978-0-300-27057-0 (hardcover : alk. paper)
A catalogue record for this book is available from the British Library.

This paper meets the requirements of ANSI/NISO Z39.48-1992
(Permanence of Paper).

10 9 8 7 6 5 4 3 2 1

For Mitch Lansky
My alter ego

The criteria for appropriate forest policy should be that
practices qualify as ecologically sound, socially responsible,
economically viable, and sustainable.

Mitch Lansky

. . . and what I have been preparing to say is, that in Wildness is the preservation of the World. Every tree sends its fibres forth in search of the Wild. The cities import it at any price. Men plow and sail for it. From the forest and wilderness come the tonics and barks which brace mankind. Our ancestors were savages. The story of Romulus and Remus being suckled by a wolf is not a meaningless fable. The founders of every state which has risen to eminence have drawn their nourishment and vigor from a similar wild source. It was because the children of the Empire were not suckled by the wolf that they were conquered and displaced by the children of the northern forests who were.

Henry David Thoreau, *Walking*

Contents

Preface

Throughout the twentieth century the paper industry dominated the economy, politics, and land health of northern New England. A year after I moved to northern New Hampshire and took a job as a reporter at a local weekly newspaper, a French holding company placed nearly a million acres of timberland, formerly owned by Diamond International, on the market at a price double its timber value.

I advocated the public acquire the forty-thousand-acre Nash Stream watershed a few miles east of my log cabin and designate it as wilderness. Leading state conservationists called me a wilderness cultist and effectively excommunicated me from conservation circles.

I was bewildered. Scientists were sounding the alarm: conservation strategies had failed to conserve the full array of species native to a particular region. Why this hostility to wildlands? Why would conservationists oppose efforts to restore land health and the full complement of species native to a given place?

I quit my job and became a wildlands activist. Millions of acres of forestland in northern New England had been cut intensively in the previous two decades. I envisioned a rewilding of these abused forests on a grand scale. I became especially vocal about ending forest degradation by clear-cuts and other intensive logging practices. I quickly realized we need to transform our economic thinking and practices if we are to protect forest health.

Today, the once-dominant regional paper industry is a fading memory. In the quarter century after the Diamond land sale, US-based paper companies sold all eight million acres of undeveloped forestland in northern Maine, New Hampshire, and Vermont, and seventeen of the region's small, medium, and large paper mills ceased operation. In the mid-1980s northern New England's paper mills provided more than twenty thousand jobs; today they sustain fewer than five thousand. Logging jobs have suffered comparable declines. Mill towns and timber-dependent communities have yet to recover from the loss of their economic mainstay.

In the 1990s, as most regional conservationists embraced conservation science, hostile political and economic powers pressured them to compromise its teachings. Policy often mitigated some of the symptoms but rarely confronted the root causes of the crisis in our forests.

I hope *Children of the Northern Forest* helps communities and conservationists transform the conventional "jobs versus environment" argument into a "jobs *and* environment" conversation focused upon developing and implementing strategies to revive local economies and restore ecosystem integrity in an age of rapid climate change.

Children of the Northern Forest asks: *Why have our democratic institutions failed to address existential threats to life on earth?* It offers a case study of northern New England. To understand our relationship with nature, we need to view life from the perspective of nonhuman species and the unborn—the ecological Golden Rule, and to recognize that wild nature is our most important teacher.

Too many voices in our communities remain marginalized: loggers; millworkers; residents of poor communities suffering from contaminated air, water, and soils; and nonhuman species.

We need a coherent New England conservation strategy that acknowledges the striking differences between northern and southern New England. The economies of southern and central New England are diverse and generally robust. An affluent populace generously supports conservation and land trust organizations. Development and overcrowding in southern and some parts of central New England limit the potential for large wildlands reserves.

Sparsely populated northern New England, however, offers the promise of wildlands and carbon capture on a scale unimaginable in most of the United States. Southern New England can provide political and financial support for the acquisition of former paper company lands and preservation of them as wildlands. Southern New England offers markets that can help transform the struggling northern forest economy from low-value commodity markets into a diversified producer of low-impact, high value-added products and services. A rewilded northern New England that enjoys a frugal prosperity can inspire communities throughout the world.

Children of the Northern Forest offers a fresh perspective for addressing intractable questions about humankind's relationship with wild nature. I invite those who wish to protect the rights of all citizens and the needs and rights of nonhuman species and unborn generations to join the conversation.

Children of the Northern Forest

(Copyright © Jon Luoma)

The Education of a Tree-Hugger

Whoever degrades another degrades me.

WALT WHITMAN

I fell in love with the wild terrain of northern New Hampshire in the mid-1980s. I bought a remote log cabin a few miles from the Connecticut River, and then, to celebrate, I headed to the White Mountain National Forest to hike a portion of the Appalachian Trail. To distract myself on this raw, socked-in, early October day, I meditated upon the paucity of wilderness in the East.

A global extinction crisis alarmed conservation scientists. Most public land reserves, they warned, including designated wilderness areas and the largest US national parks, were too small to support viable populations of many native species such as wolves, cougars, and grizzly bears. The loss of biological diversity was greatest in smaller parks, but species were disappearing even from the two-million-acre Yellowstone National Park. In 1975 biologist Jared Diamond had urged conservation scientists to design networks of large reserves connected to other protected lands, rather than continue to protect small, isolated tracts.[1]

It occurred to me that the Appalachian Trail could connect wildlands from Georgia to Maine along an Appalachian "wilderness backbone." A widened trail corridor could link protected landscapes on existing—and future—public lands in its vicinity. Hundreds of roads crisscrossed the landscape, and private landowners might not immediately warm to the idea. These obstacles did not discourage me because, I reasoned, if there is merit in an idea, broadcast it. *Earth First!* published my proposal in the spring of 1987.[2]

I took possession of the log cabin and thirty-seven acres on New Year's Eve 1986. My land was rocky, wet, and sloped to the southwest. A year earlier, the former owners, no longer dwelling there, had hired a local, unsupervised logger to cut some wood. He cleared away three-quarters of the land, leaving the occasional paper birch standing. The edge between my clear-cut land and trees belonging to Diamond International formed the western property line. Trees on my neighbor's land to the south constituted the southern line. The road served as the eastern boundary, and an unkempt stone wall marked the northern bound.

I spent $100 on a cord of split, dry firewood that lasted less than a month in the homemade basement furnace I inherited. Then the pipes froze. I spent the rest of the winter cutting blown-down paper birch and sledding logs uphill to burn the following day. My leaky wood cookstove sputtered to keep the green wood burning as I shivered beside it.

I opened a crude path on Diamond lands to the brook through a swampy softwood stand composed mostly of balsam fir but also some red spruce and a few hemlock. The riffles, easy meanders, and cascading whitewater passed through stands of yellow birch, white ash, diseased American beech, sugar maple, and poplar, with a mixture of fir, spruce, hemlock, and the occasional white pine. Polypores grew on standing and downed deadwood. In winter, I encountered tracks of bobcats, mink, coyotes, snowshoe hare, red squirrels, deer, and moose.

In the mid-nineteenth century, a few small sawmills and some isolated hardscrabble farms had operated along the larger brooks in the neighborhood. Sam Stone, my neighbor, told me my land had been a field during his childhood; the logging operation in the mid-1980s had cut a very young forest.

I could see Mount Lafayette and the ski trails on Cannon Mountain in Franconia Notch an hour's drive south. Today, a young forest obstructs the view. Clear-cuts take the better part of a lifetime to recover enough to sustain decent-paying logging jobs. It will take several more decades before a logger might cut high-value sawlogs on our land.

Over the years, as the forest slowly recovered, wildlife sightings have changed. One or more bats occupied the cabin in the first years. Flying squirrels floated from a spruce outside the kitchen window to the side of the cabin. Woodchucks frustrated my early attempts at growing vegetables. But bats are now rare; I haven't seen a flying squirrel near the cabin in decades; and woodchucks have moved off the premises. Marsh hawks—northern harriers—hunted in the clearing until the trees grew back.

A chorus of spring peepers, attracted to a vernal pool in an old skidder rut, heralds the arrival of spring. As the weather warms, chipping and white-throated sparrows visit our lawn and gardens, phoebes nest in the garage or under the eaves of our cabin, and hornets build nests in our woodshed and above the porch on our rustic sauna. Fox occasionally visit our compost pile. Mice, voles, and shrews abound outside—and inside—our cabin, and moles build tunnels in the lawn.

In autumn, bears visit our feral apple orchard and deposit their pulpy scat along the trail to our upper garden. Moose pass through, often visiting the small pool below the outlet pipe of our spring-fed well. I once photographed a saucy raccoon eating the rotting Halloween pumpkin on our porch.

Wild turkeys saunter down the long driveway to visit our garden; chipmunks steal our strawberry harvest; ruffed and spruce grouse spend the winter on the premises; coyotes howl nearby; and a variety of woodpeckers—black-backed, pileated, hairy, and yellow-bellied sapsuckers—drill our trees and, on occasion, our sheet metal roof.

One New Year's Day, a barred owl we named Bardy took up residence on a branch of a young yellow birch or atop the sauna roof for a week, swooping down upon voles and other small rodents. Snakes also feast on rodents and sun themselves near the wood pile. In the spring, I discover several shed skins in the stacked firewood.

Routinely, high winds topple trees, especially balsam fir. One memorable storm around Halloween 2017 deposited six softwoods across the driveway.

We are three-and-a-half miles from the Connecticut River to the southwest and about five miles west of the Percy Peaks in the Nash

Stream watershed. The paper mill in Groveton was eight miles south. Berlin is approximately thirty miles to the southeast. Mount Washington and the Presidential Range are an hour's drive to the south.

Vermont's Northeast Kingdom is just across the Connecticut River. Western Maine lies a few miles east of Berlin, and the Quebec–Vermont–New Hampshire confluence is thirty-five miles to the north. Our cabin is situated roughly at the midpoint between Baxter State Park and the Adirondack Park.

In May 1987, editor-publisher John Harrigan offered me a job reporting for the weekly *Coös County Democrat*—provided I passed a test. If I could deliver a photo of a Stratford dairy farmer crossing Route 3 to his barn with his one-legged milking stool already strapped to his derriere, I had a job. Fortunately, the dairy farmer was a kind man, and when I explained my predicament, he graciously agreed to pose for a goofy picture.

The *Democrat* is still housed in a rickety old downtown Lancaster building where laughter routinely drowned out the clacking of typewriters—no computers until 1988. We reported on the *human and natural* communities of northern New Hampshire and northeastern Vermont. Harrigan loved to celebrate cougar sightings and other wildlife news. In the fall of 1987, a front-page headline read, "Two Giants of the Forest, Locked in Death's Embrace." A hunter had stumbled upon the skeletons of two lovesick bull moose whose massive palmate antlers had become entangled jousting for the affections of a cow. A year later, another page-one headline proclaimed, "Beaver Fells Tree; 3 Towns Lose Power." An industrious *Castor canadensis* had dropped a poplar ("popple" in local vernacular) across a power line in a swamp near a small airport in the shadow of the White Mountains. Darkness descended upon eight hundred households in Jefferson, Randolph, and Whitefield, New Hampshire.[3]

The *Democrat* covered fires, feuds over water rights, and the weekly police blotter. I wrote features about black flies, acid rain, and comical human-bear interactions. Harrigan was pleased with my efforts, and after a month, he increased my hourly wage by $1. Because I produced too much copy for the paper to handle, he cut my hours from forty to thirty a week. My pay raise cost me $60 a fortnight.

On a frigid evening in February 1988, I attended a meeting introducing the state's new conservation program, the Trust for New Hampshire Lands, a privately funded initiative whose agents evaluated conservation lands with an eye toward acquisition. Henry Whittemore was endeavoring to explain how the trust could preserve managed farmland and forestland by acquiring a tract's development rights via a "conservation easement." His agitated audience kept interrupting: "Was the Nash Stream for sale?" Eventually, Whittemore yielded. Yes, ninety thousand acres in northern New Hampshire and northeastern Vermont owned by the Groveton Papers mill for most of the century were indeed for sale.

In most of the United States, the public has little, if any, right to tread on private property. Since colonial times, the public has enjoyed unfettered access to northern New England's private and corporate lands. This began to change in the 1980s when Great Northern Nekoosa, owners of two million acres in Maine, imposed access fees.

Generations of current and former Groveton paper mill workers and their families had leased land from the mill for a nominal sum and constructed rude hunting and fishing camps in this sportsman's paradise. These camp owners had been spooked by rumors of the sale. Would they lose their camps? Would "No Trespassing" signs close off public access to absentee-owned timberland? Would the new owner enclose this last vestige of the tradition of common lands?

When the meeting concluded, I asked Whittemore what the fuss was about. He invited me to his office in Lancaster the following day where he produced maps of the Diamond lands and explained the terms of the sale.

The forty-thousand-acre Nash Stream watershed was the jewel of the Diamond holdings. The Nash Stream flows south through a valley, about a dozen miles northeast of the village of Groveton. Timber cutters in the late nineteenth century had impounded the Nash Bog to store water for log drives to two Groveton sawmills. The paper mill had bought much of the Nash Stream watershed early in the twentieth century. The earthworks beside Nash Bog dam had blown out during a spring flood in 1969 and shut down the mill for a month. The mill never rebuilt the dam, and the bog has gradually reverted to wetlands and forest. Hikers who scale Mount Sugarloaf (3,701 feet in elevation) and North Percy

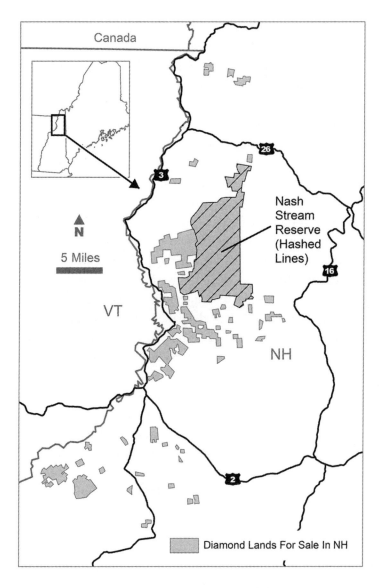

Map of Nash Stream and Diamond's other New Hampshire holdings. In the winter of 1988 a French holding company offered for sale ninety thousand acres of former Diamond International lands in northern New Hampshire (sixty-seven thousand acres) and Vermont's Northeast Kingdom (twenty-three thousand acres that are not shown here). The forty-thousand-acre Nash Stream tract was the jewel of the New Hampshire lands. In 1989 it became the Nash Stream State Forest (indicated by the hashed lines). (Map by Brian Hall)

Nash Stream and North and South Percy Peaks. (Photo by author)

Peak (3,400 feet) enjoy panoramic views of Coös County and Vermont's Northeast Kingdom.

I asked our congressman, later governor and senator, Judd Gregg whether federal funds could be used to add the Nash Stream to the White Mountain National Forest (WMNF). He replied there was a "very, very slim chance" that Congress would appropriate any federal money to buy these lands because they lay outside of the WMNF purchase boundary set by Congress.[4]

My story appeared in the February 24 edition of the *Coös County Democrat.* The following day, New Hampshire's largest newspaper, the *Manchester Union-Leader,* ran a page-one story on the sale, and the day after, US Senator Gordon Humphrey announced a March 10 emergency conservation summit meeting in Concord at the headquarters of the Society for the Protection of New Hampshire Forests (commonly known as the Forest Society). I managed to wangle an invitation because I had broken the story, I lived in the town with the most acreage for sale, and my property abutted a ninety-acre tract of Diamond lands.

At the summit, Ed Spencer of The Nature Conservancy outlined a bid his organization had submitted two weeks earlier to LandVest, the real estate firm handling the sale. The conservancy planned to protect the most ecologically important sites. It would resell the remainder of the lands to state, federal, or private buyers after protecting rare species and assuring public access.

Executive Councilor Ray Burton, who represented the northern part of the state, raised the jobs mantra and opposed the use of funds from the Trust for New Hampshire Lands to purchase the Nash Stream watershed. A North Country planner worried that wilderness designation would jeopardize the "fragile" economy of the region and deny towns the timber yield tax: "You take that [tax] away, and they've got nothing." Our Coös County state senator was "deeply distressed" by the pending sale. He feared 170,000 acres in the Connecticut Lakes region were also available.

Paul Bofinger, president/forester of the Forest Society, urged: "Let's keep the status quo, which is good managed forest lands. We are trying to keep it the way it is." Bofinger feared developers could remove the land from the state's timber base. Hank Swan, president of Wagner Woodlands and an astute timberlands investor, assessed its timber value at only about $100 an acre due to past cutting.[5]

When invited to speak, I acknowledged concerns about fiber procurement, jobs, and taxes before asking, "Who speaks for the land?" I proposed that the public acquire the entire Nash Stream watershed and designate it as wilderness. In time, a maturing forest ecosystem might provide habitat for extirpated or rare native species such as cougars, American marten, and wolves. Northern New England boasted relatively little designated wilderness; this was a wonderful opportunity to begin the restoration of our wildland heritage.

A stunned silence.

Senator Humphrey gamely steered the meeting back on track. More talk of jobs, taxes, and fiber. Moments later, my friend Jeff Elliott, a high school biology teacher, who had accompanied me to Concord, declared: "[We have a] chance to preserve a unique watershed. . . . We can do something that is morally and politically right." More stony silence. Bofinger, citing Reagan-era deficits and hostility to public land acquisition among powerful interests, dismissed any hopes of federal financial assistance. Later that spring, he warned: "The days of going to Congress and requesting large sums for acreage like this are over. We've got to try something new."[6]

The *Manchester Union-Leader*'s coverage of the emergency summit dwelled upon economic issues and maintaining the status quo. It failed to mention the ecological concerns Jeff and I had raised. I believed a fair accounting of the meeting ought to mention our remarks. To my surprise, Harrigan urged me to include our statements in my report. In doing so, I felt my position on the *Democrat* had become untenable— reporters ought not participate in events they cover.

On a beautiful late winter morning a couple of days after the summit, my phone rang. A local politician, concerned by my performance in Concord, warned me that I risked losing my "credibility" and "seat at the table" if I did not rethink my proposals for public land acquisition and wilderness designation. He said I was "politically unrealistic," "close-minded," and "selfish" for suggesting the needs of the land be considered. Bewildered by his message, I blurted that I cared about retaining my credibility with the bears.

I explained that ecological reality—not political expediency or sentimental attachment to a failing status quo—determined my position. I suggested that politicians can strike a compromise deal on political issues, but they can't compromise away natural laws and ecological limits. Later, I understood I had lost my credibility because of my unwillingness to play by the rules of *their* game: economics and politics define the terms of conservation. After the summit, an employee of a conservation organization said he would agree with me over a glass of beer, but he dared not say so publicly. Kind words for wilderness were politically incorrect in New Hampshire—and a career-killer.

A few days after notification of my excommunication from New Hampshire conservation circles, I happened upon a draft of John Harrigan's next editorial, "Wilderness Is Fine, but You Can't Eat It." It appeared the following week under the revised title of "We Must Be Realistic About our North Country Woodlands." Harrigan supported "wise use" over "lock it up." He wrote: "some of the passionate arguments being advanced by the unbending proponents of the wilderness ethic bother us. . . . When we hear strident calls for leaving the forest entirely alone, in deference to an image of the wilderness or a romantic wish for all wildlife to be here as it once was, we have to ask where the paychecks are going to come from for all those families that now make up the fabric of the North Country."[7] I decided to quit the *Democrat* and defend the inedible.

Organizers of the April Diamond lands meeting excluded Jeff and me. At the May meeting, shortly after we appeared, Paul Bofinger entered and delivered a lecture against people who promoted wilderness protection as a kind of religion. There's no way, he warned, of getting funding to create "just another wilderness." Bofinger's assistant ruled Jeff out of order when he attempted to respond. We were *personae non gratae.*

Earlier in May, a consortium of state conservation groups led by the Forest Society released a statement: "[T]here is little public support in Northern New Hampshire for substantially expanding the traditional pattern of federal land ownership and management."[8] In mid-May, Diamond's realtor, LandVest, rejected The Nature Conservancy's bid to purchase some of the lands; it would entertain only a bid to buy all ninety thousand acres at the full asking price.

On Memorial Day weekend, Claude Rancourt, an unknown French-Canadian construction worker turned developer from Nashua, acquired the New Hampshire and Vermont Diamond lands for the asking price of $19 million.

Jeff and I had inadvertently hit upon the fundamental conflict dividing the conservation movement. Mainstream conservationists feared that developers threatened the viability of the regional timber industry. Preservationists believed that industrial forest practices degraded wildlife habitat and compromised ecosystem integrity.

When conservation elites banished me to the proverbial wilderness, I faced a choice: give up and go away, or advocate for conservation science, rather than support career-saving, politically calibrated conservation orthodoxy. The loss of my seat at the table liberated me to dream of taboo subjects. You have nothing to lose when you acknowledge reality and take pains to speak the truth. You automatically lose when you concede to others veto power over your words, work, and self-respect.

I believed that good-faith engagement among differing viewpoints could create conservation policies vastly superior to those agreed upon by insiders and vested interests. If I could participate in such a process, I would be delighted. If elites insisted upon blacklisting me, I would still be heard.

Gradually, I began to understand the "logic" of the decaying timber empire of northern New England—a magical wonderland where Alice and Orwell would feel at home. To maintain one's credibility in the industrial forest conversation, one must accept certain teachings on faith:

- *Wilderness is bad.* Resource exploiters claim that wilderness "locks up" the wealth of the land and private ownership is necessary to create wealth. To them, wilderness is useless; to most plant and animal species, wilderness is their life support system.

- *Private property rights are supreme:* Wilderness-bashers maintain that we need to perpetuate private land ownership. In Maine, the privately owned industrial forests are severely degraded.

- *Elites are entitled to control the agenda of public policy that affects their interests:* In a healthy democracy, all affected parties enjoy an equal right to determine the agenda. Undemocratic agendas have not served the region well. Efforts to appease large landowners fail to protect natural or human communities; subsidizing elites without requiring ecologically and socially responsible behavior is unsound public policy.

- *To create jobs and prosperity, it is necessary to degrade land, air, waters, and wildlife habitat.* This embodies a dangerous assumption: There are no consequences for ignoring natural limits.

• *There is no wilderness in New England.* Resource-oriented conservationists asserted that there was no wilderness because *their ancestors had destroyed it centuries ago.* I was about to learn otherwise.

The day after Claude Rancourt bought the Diamond lands, I joined a group of activists to paddle up the Connecticut River in imitation of spawning runs of anadromous Atlantic salmon. Since the construction of a dam at Turners Falls, Massachusetts, in 1798, salmon had been unable to reach upstream spawning beds. To the casual observer, the river had been severely degraded by marinas in southern Connecticut,

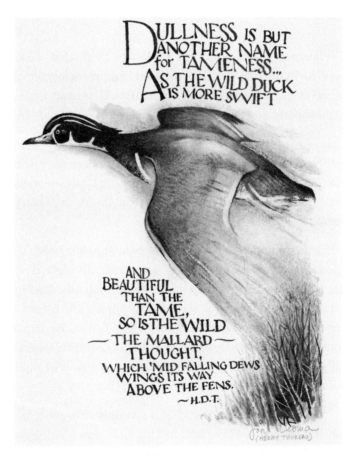

DULLNESS IS BUT ANOTHER NAME for TAMENESS... AS THE WILD DUCK IS MORE SWIFT

AND BEAUTIFUL THAN THE TAME, SO IS THE WILD — THE MALLARD — THOUGHT, WHICH 'MID FALLING DEWS WINGS ITS WAY ABOVE THE FENS. ~ H.D.T.

(Copyright © Jon Luoma)

agricultural runoff, major cities such as Hartford and Springfield, two nuclear reactors (now both decommissioned), numerous bridges, and many large hydropower dams. Before passage of the clean water acts of the 1960s and 1970s, municipal waste discharges into the Connecticut had earned it the title of "The Most Beautiful Sewer in America."

Rhythmic paddling, the cooling breezes, the wildlife, and the absence of artificial light at night helped dissolve the boundaries between our civilized lives and the wild river ecosystem. As we gradually became attuned to its wildness, the Connecticut River taught me: *Wildness survives even in the most abused lands; the moment we protect lands, the healing begins.*

T • W • O

A Force Not Bound to Be Kind to Man

The Northern Forest occupies a special place in the hearts of Americans
all over the nation. . . . [I]t includes many places that are beautiful and
awe inspiring, holding the power to touch the soul and humble the
beholder. The scarcity of such beauty, in a place so close to millions,
makes its existence all the more precious.

Northern Forest Lands Study, 1990

The undeveloped forests of northern New England are a world
apart from the urbanized and suburbanized northeast United
States. In 1936, Robert Marshall, a founder of The Wilderness
Society, collaborated with Althea Dobbins to assemble an inventory of the largest remaining roadless areas in the lower forty-eight
states. The 2.8-million-acre Aroostook-Allagash region of Maine topped
the list; the neighboring Upper Saint John River watershed, encompassing another 1.3 million acres, ranked eighth. Motorized vehicles still had
not penetrated more than four million acres of northernmost Maine.[1]

Today, eight million acres of industrial forest in northern Maine
remain free of year-round habitation. This is the largest uninhabited
area in the lower forty-eight states. Just to the west, northern Vermont and New Hampshire boast an additional eight hundred thousand acres of undeveloped forestlands. Their rivers and streams, lakes
and ponds, mountains and rolling landscape are an untapped national
treasure.

The origin story of the northern forests of New England—the largest intact broadleaf temperate forest in the world—goes back to the Pleistocene. For one hundred thousand years, a mile-thick blanket of ice covered Maine and most of New England. Around twenty-five thousand years before the present (BP), glaciers reached their maximum southern advance to about forty-one degrees north latitude (southern Connecticut). The North American coast extended as much as 180 miles eastward to Georges Bank as sea levels dropped 350 feet lower than today. A natural climate change event commenced around 21,000 BP, as the southern extent of the glaciers began to retreat north (and westward along the Atlantic coast). By about 13,000 BP, cold, strong winds buffeted ice-free northern Maine. Atmospheric carbon dioxide concentrations increased steadily from 200 parts per million to about 280 parts per million by 11,000 BP. They remained relatively stable until the advent of the industrial age.

The healing powers of wild nature soon began to transform this barren landscape. Lichens extracted minerals from rocks. Mosses spread. Pioneer plants trapped airborne silt. As plants died and decomposed, brown humus formed slowly, and seedlings of the first trees began to germinate. Vines and roots gradually stitched together soils and rocks. The earliest postglacial vegetative cover resembled northern Labrador's treeless tundra. Sedges and grasses, dwarf willows, birch, and alder shrubs, some ferns and club mosses, true mosses, and scattered growths of spruce, fir, larch, and beech covered the open country. After one or two millennia, aspen, spruce, and paper birch formed open woodlands. Mastodons, mammoths, caribou, and marine mammals flourished. There is a Paleo-American caribou hunting site dating back approximately twelve thousand years in Jefferson, New Hampshire, two dozen miles south of our cabin.

Vegetation dispersed north into the deglaciated landscape in fits and starts, advances and retreats. Plant and animal species recolonized at different rates, reflecting a variety of factors, including the migratory abilities of each species, the location of species' refugia during the most recent glacial period, competing vegetation, and changing climate. Red spruce moved north from the mid-Atlantic states and now-submerged coastal sites, reaching central Maine by about 12,500 BP and northern

Maine between 11,000 and 10,000 BP. Warm and dry conditions from around 11,000 to 8,000 BP pushed black and white spruce—cool, moisture-loving species—out of New England and into Canada by 9,000 BP. White pine and maples reached central Maine around this time.[2]

The Acadian forest today extends into Ontario, Quebec, and New Brunswick. It is a blend of the northern hardwood forests to the south and the boreal forests farther north. The dominant trees of the Acadian forest canopy are long-lived, shade-tolerant species: red spruce can survive 400 years, beech about 350 years, and sugar maple 300 years. Red spruce is a relative newcomer, having gained prominence only about 1,500 years ago as the climate moistened and cooled. It grows on relatively poor or thin soils and poorly drained lower elevation flats. Other shade-tolerant Acadian species—American beech, sugar maple, and white ash—grow on warmer, drier, higher fertility soils. Black spruce and tamarack are abundant in low-fertility soils, and yellow birch grows on moderately moist, mid- to high-fertility soils.

Once ubiquitous, old growth forests today cover only 0.4 percent of the northeastern United States. Most of the surviving examples of untrammeled Acadian forests grew on less productive soils or at inaccessible sites, such as above cliffs. Though they are too small and too few to express the full range of variation and diversity of natural forest conditions in the pre-European forest, they are indispensable to our understanding of forest conditions before the arrival of European colonists and nineteenth-century lumberjacks.[3] The largest old growth stand in northern Maine is the five-thousand-acre Big Reed Pond Reserve north of Baxter State Park.

Old growth forests are composed of a mixture of all age classes in a mosaic of live and dead trees. They sustain a rich diversity of habitats, from the canopies of large old trees to cool forest floors covered by a deep litter of leaves, needles, and smaller woody debris. Blackburnian warblers, magnolia warblers, Swainson's thrushes, solitary vireos, brown creepers, and black-throated green warblers flourish under old growth conditions. Secondary, managed forests provide these species inferior nesting habitat.

The profusion of mosses, lichens, fungi, and wildflowers, characteristic of the old growth forest, is less common or altogether missing
in cutover stands. The colder climate of the Acadian forest region slows
decomposition and allows litter to build up. Invertebrate decomposers,
abundant in older forests, are often extirpated from intensively managed forests.

Downed trees retard soil erosion and provide important wildlife
habitat and cover. Logs, stumps, limbs, and upturned roots are important for nutrient retention and cycling. Fungi, beetles, grubs, and ants
decompose dead and downed trees and branches. Rodents, shrews, sal-
amanders, snakes, and turtles rely on coarse woody debris for habitat.
Black bears, woodpeckers, rodents, and shrews feed at these sites, and a
number of species, from deer mouse to bear, den in or under downed
logs. Larger downed logs are especially valuable. Debris in streams cre-
ates pools and riffles that provide habitat for fish, nesting locations for
turtles and waterfowl, and dens for mink and otter.

Standing dead trees and live trees with cavities—often the result
of branches broken off by ice or wind—provide critical habitat for a
wide variety of wildlife. Woodpeckers, chickadees, and red-breasted
nuthatches are important cavity excavators in northern New England.
Cavity dwellers include wrens, tufted titmouse, bluebirds, flying squirrels, ermines, several species of bats, owls, ducks, fishers, long-tailed
weasels, gray fox, black bears, and raccoons. American martens, never
abundant, require large old trees.[4]

Old forests store the greatest amount of carbon. As trees age, they
grow larger, spread their roots ever wider, and increase the soil organic
pool. Dead leaves, twigs, and branches add carbon to the litter pool.
Deadwood, killed by insects, disease, wind, ice storms, and competition,
continues to store abundant carbon for long periods, and as it decom-
poses, it adds carbon to soils as well as releasing carbon to the atmosphere. Old growth stands store approximately 100 to 120 tons of carbon per acre. A one-hundred-year-old northern hardwood forest stores
roughly 60 to 80 tons of carbon per acre. It adds around 0.4 tons per
acre per year and will require another century to approach old growth
carbon storage levels.[5]

Earth's soils store more carbon than all the carbon in the atmosphere and all carbon stored in living and dead plants and animals. A major portion of soil organic carbon is tied up in fungal hyphae networks that connect the root systems of trees. Older trees develop many more fungal connections than younger trees, and older, undisturbed forests sustain much more complex networks. Hyphae, thin tubes ranging from two to twenty microns in diameter, transport water and nutrients between fungi and trees. Fungi extract minerals from rocks, soils, and decomposing plant and animal material. They share these nutrients with trees' root tips, and in return, they receive sugars and lipids from photosynthesizing plants. The availability of nitrogen and phosphorus limits plant and tree growth, and fungi can supply trees with 80 percent of the nitrogen and 100 percent of the phosphorus they require. Fungi also supply zinc and copper to trees.

Forest ecologists have made great strides in mapping and understanding the important role mycorrhizal fungi play in maintaining healthy and productive forests. Protecting older trees and forest stands maintains vital mycorrhizal fungal networks. Intensive forest management, including high-grading older trees, clear-cutting, and whole-tree harvesting, can cause these complex networks to unravel.

Ecologist Craig Lorimer studied early nineteenth-century government land surveys of the upper Penobscot and Aroostook River Valleys to reconstruct the pre-European forest in what would become the heart of Maine's industrial forest. Most of the hardwoods grew on well-drained, relatively rock-free upland slopes, while conifers dominated soils in stony flats, upper mountain slopes, and wetlands. In mixed forests, hardwoods claimed the better soils, and conifers were more abundant on poorer soils.

The relatively stable Acadian forest experienced few stand-replacing disturbance events. Lorimer estimated that major windstorms recurred about once every 1,150 years, and stand-replacing fires occurred at intervals of 800 to 1,900 years. He determined that older stands dominated the all-aged, presettlement forest:

• Because of recent fires and large windfalls, 2 percent of the
pre-European forest was younger than ten years of age;

- the birch-aspen forest, or young regrowth following a windfall between ten and seventy-five years old, covered 14 percent;

- a quarter of the forest had not experienced a major disturbance in 75 to 150 years;

- one-third of the forest was mature and uneven-aged (150 to 300 years old); and

- all-aged forest stands, where no major disturbance had occurred for at least three hundred years, covered 27 percent of the study area.[6]

Occasional large disturbances do not uniformly flatten the forested landscape. Even the largest events—ice storms and windstorms—will leave a mosaic of conditions, with less damaged or nearly untouched patches scattered within the matrix of the disturbed area. Even the most intense storms inflict "a pulse of damage . . . followed by a period of recovery."[7] A forest ecologist told me large disturbances "are superb for the forest!" They create a rich diversity of conditions and habitats that reinvigorate the affected stand.

Three millennia ago, Eastern Abenaki populations occupied the forests and coastal areas of Maine. The Western Abenaki maintained settlements along Lake Champlain and in the river valleys of Vermont and New Hampshire. They utilized the inland and upland forests primarily for hunting and passage between Canada, Lake Champlain, and the seacoast.

The Abenaki spent most of the year in family-oriented bands. Seasonal mobility helped maintain small populations and assured that demand for food, shelter, clothing, and fuel remained well below local carrying capacity. They established no permanent villages and moved their encampments regularly in response to the seasonal availability of food, extreme weather conditions, and diminishing local food sources. Because they had to carry all possessions, as well as infants, from place to place, they did not develop notions of property or theft.

The culture of the indigenous peoples of New England slowly evolved as conditions changed. Trade enhanced quality of life but was not an economic means to wealth. The exchange of surplus goods between tribes enabled Native groups to enjoy access to a greater variety of economic goods and sacred objects. Trade also played an important political and cultural role in expressing friendship through elaborate gift giving and the promotion of peaceful diplomatic relations between neighboring bands.

Low population densities and limited material desires promoted generally peaceful relations with neighbors. Historians William Haviland and Marjory Power suggest that the Abenaki of Vermont were not notably warlike: "[They] seem to have believed that one could not operate successfully in someone else's territory, since one didn't control the necessary supernatural powers. Furthermore, operating far below carrying capacity, they had no need to go after the resources of others." According to poet Gary Snyder, neighboring tribes in the Sierra Nevada were not tempted to occupy someone else's territory "because their skills were specific to their own area, and they could go hungry in an unfamiliar biome. It takes a long education to know the edible plants, where to find them, and how to prepare them."[8] Nomadic, indigenous North Americans did not view plants, trees, and animals as resources or commodities but as fellow peoples with whom they shared the land.

Anthropologist Marshall Sahlins has called the indigenous lifestyle "the original affluent society." Affluence can be achieved by producing much or desiring little. Contemporary nomadic cultures can generally satisfy the basic food needs of the group in a few hours a day, leaving abundant time for leisure. Because nomads maintained low populations, moved when local food sources began to give out, and accepted Earth's bounties instead of trying to engineer nature, abundant food supplies awaited them at their next destination. The lack of possessions brought them freedom, not poverty. Sahlins believed that when wants are few, there is no poverty. Poverty is "the invention of civilization."[9]

European traders were astounded by the plentitude of fish, forests, and furs in what they called the New World. The Eastern Abenaki of Maine soon grew wary of gift-bearing foreigners, who occasionally kidnapped indigenous people to display in European courts. When Giovanni da Verrazzano traded along Maine's coast in 1524, the Abenaki would not permit his sailors to come ashore. Upon completion of the transactions, the Natives mooned the departing traders.

Early visitors from Europe carried the germs of infectious diseases such as typhus, smallpox, plague, diphtheria, influenza, measles, yellow fever, and tuberculosis. On occasion, the population of entire villages perished. Epidemics caused famine. Survivors lost faith in their spirit guides and the healing powers of shamans. The population decline in eastern New England during the Contact Period may have been as high as 90 percent.

Global trading and trapping disrupted Native relationships with the land and each other. Long before the establishment of permanent European settlements, knives, pots, clothes, tools, guns, and alcohol ensnared Native peoples in the global economy. The traders gave little consideration to the rights and wishes of the people, the forests, or their denizens. The profits from trade accrued to investors on another continent; local communities bore the costs. Historian John F. Richards has written: "Indian ethnic groups drawn into trading furs suffered the fate of all human groups who gain a livelihood by extraction of natural resources for the world economy. In responding to market signals, the Indians necessarily changed their patterns of hunting in order to obtain the specialized products most in demand."[10] Hunters had less time for other food-procurement practices, and indigenous peoples became more dependent upon the fur trade to provide food. The practice of traditional craft skills, essential to their independent lifestyle, declined.

In the early decades of the seventeenth century, the remote Western Abenaki began feeling pressure from Dutch traders in the Albany region, French in the Saint Lawrence, and English moving up the Connecticut River and inland from the Maine coast. The insatiable European demand for the furs of otter, muskrat, moose, fox, raccoon, sable, mink, fisher, bobcat, and especially beaver transformed indigenous seasonal subsistence hunting into year-round market hunting.

Beavers act as important agents of disturbance that influence landscape diversity, complexity, and dynamics. The small, continually changing openings created by beaver dams, usually on second-, third-, and fourth-order streams, help maintain the patchy character of forests, increase available beaver habitat, increase their food supply, and protect against predators, particularly wolves. An adult beaver cuts a ton of aspen and birch within about three hundred feet of a pond annually. Alder and hazel exploit the openings created by beavers.

Beaver impoundments create and maintain small, wet meadows and early successional forest patches wherever there is running water. Dams trap sediment, and meadows slow seasonal flooding. Beaver engineering modifies nutrient cycling and influences the character of downstream water. Decomposition rates of organic matter are much slower in beaver ponds than in riffles. As a stream is transformed, pond invertebrates, such as mosquitoes and predaceous dragonflies, replace black flies and other running-water invertebrates.[11]

As the beaver pond fills with silt, the forest encroaches on the meadow, and the beaver's preferred foods near the shore diminish. Beavers abandon maturing sites and move upstream, downstream, or cross-country to establish a new impoundment. Migration exposes the beaver to predation by bobcat, lynx, bear, or wolf. The abandoned beaver dam falls into disrepair. Meadow grasses and forbs replace aquatic plants. Insects, voles, woodchucks, mice, herons, hawks, warblers, ribbon snakes, and white tail deer move in. The meadow eventually yields to shrubs and trees. In time, conditions become favorable for the return of beavers, and the cycle repeats.[12]

Beaver reproductive rates are low, and their habits are predictable. They rarely venture more than about three hundred feet from a pond's shore into the surrounding forest. They were easy prey for experienced Indian trappers. Before European contact, North American beaver populations are estimated to have been at least sixty million, perhaps as high as four hundred million. In the decade following the arrival of the Pilgrims, Connecticut and Massachusetts trappers took ten thousand beavers annually. By 1900, beavers were almost extinct in North America.[13] Today, beaver populations have recovered to an estimated fifteen million.

Beaver dams created a variety of habitats other species exploited. In the spring, drumming grouse performed upon logs felled by beavers. Wood ducks nested in the cavities of trees killed by beaver flooding.

Black ducks, ring-necked ducks, hooded mergansers, and goldeneyes bred on beaver ponds. Otters and muskrats required stable pond levels. Moose and deer browsed on aquatic plants. Moose sought refuge in the ponds in summer to escape the black flies. Deer, rabbits, and hare consumed tasty leaves on sprouts growing from stumps. As beavers vanished from the landscape during colonial times, species dependent upon habitats created by these industrious engineers declined.

William Bradford saw a "hideous and desolate wilderness full of wild beasts and wild men" when he set foot on the sands of Cape Cod in November 1620.[14] Since the late fifteenth century, England had suffered an acute shortage of timber for masts for the navy and beams for construction. As this wood shortage posed a threat to national security and England's colonial ambitions, the forests and wildlife the English colonists encountered were a godsend.

Throughout the seventeenth and first half of the eighteenth centuries, English settlements spread along the coasts from Long Island Sound to the Gulf of Maine, up rivers, and eventually inland. Upon settling a township, colonists established a central village and assigned the most productive lands to individual families, usually in lots of twenty-five to fifty acres. Few farmers owned in excess of five hundred acres. English colonists, viewing the presettlement forests as an obstruction to their economic needs, immediately began to transform them into fields and pastures. In the process, they wasted three-quarters of the wood they cut.[15]

As settlers cleared away forested habitat, white-tailed deer, wild turkeys, and other game animals disappeared. Native American hunters adjusted by killing free-roaming domestic animals. They believed animals, whether wild or domestic, belonged to no one until a hunter, following proper rituals, killed a particular animal. English courts routinely fined Native hunters for killing domestic animals. Colonials who violated Native rights, however, rarely faced discipline.[16] Some frontier communities established the death penalty for wolves and Native Americans convicted of stealing livestock.

Toward the end of the seventeenth century one early Connecticut settler expressed frontier attitudes toward wolves:

After the redskins the great terror of our lives at Wethers-
field . . . was the wolves. Catamounts were bad enough, and
so was the bears, but it was the wolves that was the worst. The
noise of their howlings was enough to curdle the blood of the
stoutest, and I have never seen the man that did not shiver
at the sound of a pack of 'em. What with the way we hated
'em, and the good money that was offered for their heads, we
do not hear 'em now so much, but when I do I feel again the
young hatred rising in my blood, and it is not a sin because
God made 'em to be hated.[17]

(Copyright © Jon Luoma)

In medieval times, peasant farmers did not own a particular parcel of land. Instead, they enjoyed the right to utilize the local commons, provided they discharged their responsibilities to protect and sustain common resources. Life may have been difficult, but the commons generally assured peasants could subsist.

Common lands ensured the fundamental economic rights of landless peasants to utilize a specific set of fields and forest. The welfare of the individual depended upon the sustainable management of the commons by the entire community. In return for the right to grow crops, graze domestic animals, collect firewood and building materials, procure fish and game, and gather nuts, berries, and medicinal herbs, the peasant contributed labor to maintain fences, to tend the common herd, to monitor the activities of others using the commons, and to participate in the politics of setting rules for usage and maintenance. The commons promoted a strong and healthy relationship between society and local ecology.

In the century before the Pilgrims arrived, England's ruling class, with the assistance of local courts, began the centuries-long process of enclosing, or privatizing, the commons. Enclosure brought great wealth to the lords, while landless peasants faced starvation or forced emigration to a town or city in search of wage labor.

The opportunity to own a piece of land inspired landless seventeenth-century individuals and families to risk the terrifying Atlantic crossing. The poor and middling settlers could become lords of their own land once they had removed the Native populations. Ownership of land signified their newfound liberty.

English colonists believed the Natives squandered the bounty of the land because they didn't engage in intensive, European-style agriculture. Most settlers presumed the indigenous peoples lived as wild animals and enjoyed no greater claim to permanent possession of the lands than wolves or bears. John Winthrop, the leader of the Puritans who migrated to New England in the 1630s to escape the persecutions of Charles I, believed Christians had an obligation to "improve" land. He justified land seizure because Native peoples "enclose no land, neither have they any settled habitation nor any tame cattle to improve the land by."[18]

The English failed to appreciate that the Natives had everything they needed to pursue happiness, and game abounded because Natives killed only what they required for sustenance. Native peoples responded to the character and rhythms of the land by moving with the seasons. They required access to territory, not an exclusive claim to a particular parcel of land. They respected the traditional territorial range of neighboring tribes but viewed land as unbounded.

As the English appropriated lands to establish new towns, they enclosed a de facto indigenous commons and dispossessed its commoners. When Native peoples permitted the English to use their land, they intended to share hunting and fishing rights with the settlers, not permanently transfer the land to a particular individual. They viewed such land transactions as a political negotiation between two sovereign peoples. Gary Snyder has written, "The place-based stories the people tell, and the naming they've done, is their archaeology, architecture, and *title* to the land." The colonists only recognized the sovereignty of the Natives to sell their land. They viewed land sales with Native peoples as economic transactions governed by English property law.[19]

Seventeenth-century English settlers cherished both private property and the Old World tradition of the commons. Less productive, unsettled lands were often held for the common use of all. Access to common lands was open to only citizens of the town. All citizens participated in deliberations over the regulation and management of the commons. Remote, less productive lands could confer significant economic benefits to groups of individuals who shared the capital costs and labor of managing and stewarding common lands. The poorest farmers especially benefited because they enjoyed the same access to the commons as their more affluent neighbors, provided they fulfilled their communal obligations.

Seventeenth-century New Englanders were not guided by current notions of ecological sustainability, but they did regulate flagrant, unsustainable, and inequitable activities on common lands. Poachers who cut down the most valuable oak and pine on common lands or farmers who sent too many head of cattle onto the commons paid fines and endured reproaches from their vigilant neighbors.[20]

The commons system promoted common social action and challenged citizens to consider the needs and welfare of the entire community. When the commons system worked well, it promoted positive reciprocal relations between generations. Sustainability is an acknowledgment of responsibilities to future generations; it challenges us to develop an economy that complements local ecology.

By the end of the seventeenth century, most common lands in southern and central New England had been privatized. As European colonists imposed Eurasian culture upon the North American wilderness, they objectified trees and game animals and viewed as "worthless" non-resources such as old forests and wolves. Global trade opportunities rewarded the commodification of beaver, timber, and market-oriented farming. European racism rationalized land seizure, genocide, and slavery. Racism and resource exploitation meant exploitation of, not membership in, the biotic community.

At the end of August 1846, Henry David Thoreau embarked on his first excursion into the north Maine woods. At the time, only 10.5 percent of Thoreau's hometown, Concord, Massachusetts, remained forested, and all of the presettlement forests had been cleared away.[21] In the wilds of Maine, Thoreau gained a sense of what had been lost: "What is most striking in the Maine wilderness is, the continuousness of the forest, with fewer open intervals or glades than you had imagined," he wrote in *The Maine Woods*. "[T]he forest is uninterrupted. It is even more grim and wild than you had anticipated, a damp and intricate wilderness, in the spring everywhere wet and miry." After his final trek in 1857 he observed: "It is all mossy and *moosey*. In some of those dense fir and spruce woods there is hardly room for the smoke to go up. The trees are a *standing* night, and every fir and spruce which you fell is a plume plucked from night's raven wing. Then at night the general stillness is more impressive than any sound, but occasionally you hear the note of an owl further or nearer in the woods, and if near a lake, the semi-human cry of the loons at their unearthly revels."[22]

He marveled at the contrast between the Maine wilderness and southern New England's remnant woodlots:

[The forest of Concord] has lost its wild, damp, and shaggy look, the countless fallen and decaying trees are gone, and consequently that thick coat of moss which lived on them is gone too. The earth is comparatively bare and smooth and dry. The most primitive places left with us are the swamps, where the spruce still grows shaggy with usnea. The surface of the ground in the Maine woods is everywhere spongy and saturated with moisture. I noticed that the plants which cover the forest floor there are such as are commonly confined to swamps with us. . . .[23]

As forest habitat disappeared, Thoreau lamented that much of the wildlife native to Massachusetts had also vanished. On March 23, 1856, he wrote in his journal:

[When I consider] that the nobler animals have been exterminated here,—the cougar, panther, lynx, wolverene, wolf, bear, moose, deer, the beaver, the turkey, etc., etc.,—I cannot but feel as if I lived in a tamed, and, as it were, emasculated country. . . . I listen to [a] concert in which so many parts are wanting. Many of those animal migrations and other phenomena by which the Indians marked the season are no longer to be observed. I seek acquaintance with Nature,—to know her moods and manners. Primitive nature is the most interesting to me. I take infinite pains to know all the phenomena of the spring, for instance, thinking that I have here the entire poem, and then, to my chagrin, I hear that it is but an imperfect copy that I possess and have read, that my ancestors have torn out many of the first leaves and grandest passages, and mutilated it in many places.[24]

Descending Mount Katahdin in 1846, Thoreau encountered the raw indifference of wild nature:

Perhaps I most fully realized that this was primeval, untamed, and forever untamable *Nature,* or whatever else men call it,

(Copyright © Jon Luoma)

while coming down this part of the mountain. . . . It is difficult to conceive of a region uninhabited by man. We habitu-
ally presume his presence and influence everywhere. And yet
we have not seen pure Nature, unless we have seen her thus
vast, and drear, and inhuman, though in the midst of cities.
Nature was here something savage and awful, though beautiful. . . . There was there felt the presence of a force not bound
to be kind to man.[25]

T • H • R • E • E

Over the Hump

... there are few who, on entering a beautiful native forest, would not
experience delight. The varieties of trees set out by the hand of Nature,
their graceful forms and spreading branches interlocked with neighborly
affection and recognition; the harmonious confusion of undergrowth;
the beautiful mosses; the ever-varying surfaces—old age, manhood, and
youth, childhood and infancy—massive trunks and little sprouts; the
towering Pine and creeping Winter-green, intermingled by the artless
genii of these wild retreats. . . .

JOHN SPRINGER, 1851

Timber has been a mainstay of the New England economy since the earliest colonial days. As southern New England colonists cleared away forests for farms and pastureland, they quickly exhausted local supplies of timber. When Massachusetts ran out of timber, it cast its eye to the Maine wilderness, where timber supplies appeared to be inexhaustible. The first Maine sawmill, erected in Berwick in 1634, was a short-lived operation; but other mills, financed by Massachusetts capital, soon followed.[1] When Civil War broke out in England in 1640, New Englanders began to build ocean-going vessels to export fish, farm produce, and lumber to the West Indies in exchange for cotton, sugar, and rum. The African slave trade, an integral part of this global network, enriched many New England investors.

In the mid-seventeenth century, Parliament's Acts of Navigation obligated the colonies to export their most important raw materials to Great Britain where its merchants could realize great profits by re-exporting manufactured products. The acts suppressed local manufacture and drained profits and hard currency from the colonies, forcing the colonists to intensify exploitation of furs and lumber. Yankee merchants responded by developing a profitable illegal trade with the West Indies. After the 1660s, New England routinely violated London's trade policies.

To maintain England's status as the world's greatest sea power, the British required a reliable supply of naval masts. The first shipment of New England masts to England occurred in 1634. When England's main source for masts—the Baltic states—became unreliable during the First Dutch War from 1652 to 1654, the British turned to New England white pine, the only tree known to Europeans capable of producing masts 120 feet tall with a base of forty inches in diameter from a single tree. The best pine grew in New Hampshire and the sparsely populated District of Maine. Regular shipments of white pine from Portsmouth, New Hampshire, began in 1653 and continued until the American Revolution. The Royal Navy also needed tar, pitch, and turpentine from the colonies.

The lumber industry dominated northern New England's economy after 1675. Northern Massachusetts, New Hampshire, and Maine boasted about fifty sawmills located along rivers and streams that produced between five hundred and one thousand board feet of white pine boards per day. The largest white pine approached two hundred feet in height, with a diameter at breast height of seven to eight feet. Giant white pine routinely exceeded one hundred feet in height and three feet in diameter at breast height. In 1687 Samuel Sewall recorded in his diary that one New Hampshire mast tree had required seventy-two oxen (thirty-two yoke before and four yoke on the sides) to pull it from the forest.[2]

The Massachusetts Bay Colony claimed Maine's vast forests in the middle of the seventeenth century. In 1691, King William and Queen Mary formally acknowledged Massachusetts's dominion over the District of Maine. For the next eighty-five years, Maine was the colony of a colony, and from 1776 to 1820, it was a colony of the Commonwealth of Massachusetts.

The 1691 charter claimed for the Crown all white pine with a diameter at breast height greater than twenty-four inches growing on land not previously granted. After 1704, agents of the Crown marked its pines by three cuts of an axe resembling an arrowhead or a crow's foot. The fine for cutting trees marked with the "Broad Arrow" amounted to 50 pounds sterling, with half going to the Crown and half to the informant. In 1722 the White Pine Act reserved for the navy all pine, regardless of size, growing on land not yet surveyed into townships.

Frontier lumbermen viewed unrestricted logging as an inalienable right. Good masts fetched 100–150 pounds in London. Colonial loggers earned the same price for lumber or mast trees, and since the domestic market for pine boards exceeded that of ship masts, woodsmen generally opted to supply the local mills. On occasion, they shipped mast pines to the French, Spanish, and Dutch West Indies. Some woodsmen viewed the Broad Arrow marking as a guide to the best pine. Others would mark trees with a counterfeit Broad Arrow to reserve trees for later cutting. Sometimes they set fires to ruin the great pines as masts, but not as lumber. Mills evaded the statute by limiting the width of pine boards to twenty-three inches.

After 1705, feckless London officials attempted to prosecute violators of the Broad Arrow law, but mill operators routinely received alerts before deputies paid inspection visits. Judges, with investments in the local timber industry, quashed cases of theft brought before them.[3] The Broad Arrow is the grandfather of all detested forestry regulations in New England. Woodsmen objected that it benefited economic interests in England at the expense of local farmers and entrepreneurs. Resentment over the act fueled a "woodland rebellion" and contributed to New Hampshire's revolutionary fervor in the 1770s.

Inland forests, distant from northern New England's major rivers, remained unsettled and unlogged until the nineteenth century. The British Crown had disposed of a few million acres of southern and central Maine to royal cronies and speculators in colonial times, but the rocky soils and short growing seasons in the interior lured few farmers. In the 1760s, Massachusetts attempted to reduce the debt it had incurred during the late French War by encouraging veterans to relocate to Maine as payment for their war service. Few responded, and most of them were poor, landless farmers, who quickly discovered Maine was no agricultural paradise.

After the Revolutionary War, Massachusetts again tried to reduce its debt by granting soldiers free farmland in the unsettled interior of Maine. With the fertile soils of the Ohio River Valley beckoning, few veterans responded, and Massachusetts soon began to sell off large tracts to absentee speculators. President George Washington's secretary of war, Henry Knox, along with a partner, purchased two million acres for 10 cents per acre in 1791. When farmers still failed to materialize, the proprietors and the government sold lands to timbermen.

By 1820, when Maine achieved statehood as part of the Missouri Compromise, Massachusetts had sold 5.5 million acres for $924,000 — about 17 cents an acre. The Bay State retained about 5 million acres in the north because frugal Maine legislators refused to pay it about 4 cents an acre. The new state used its vast public land base to finance schools and colleges, the clergy, public works, and the construction of the statehouse in Augusta. From 1820 to 1826, Maine sold its lands for about 14.5 cents per acre. For the next three years, prices jumped to around 44.5 cents per acre.

In June 1835 the *Niles Register* reported, "Land which was sold by the states of Maine and Massachusetts ten years ago at 6, 12, and 14 cents, will now readily command 8 and ten dollars an acre!" After 1835, the Maine Land Office again attempted to lure farmers to the state's interior, but land sales declined significantly. In 1844 the state reversed course and sold more than three million acres to timbermen during the following decade. By 1870, Maine had disposed of most of its undeveloped public lands for pennies to the acre. Speculators and timber investors, not Revolutionary soldiers, owned about half of Maine.[4]

The industrial revolution transformed New England's agrarian economy early in the nineteenth century. By this time, the primeval forests of southern and central Maine had been reduced to woodlots and swamps. To satisfy the hunger for lumber, the woodsmen headed up the great, wild rivers of Maine in search of white pine. When pine gave out, they set about clearing away the smaller, but much more abundant, red spruce.

At mid-century, one of the earliest Maine woodsmen, John Springer, published a lively account of his logging experiences in eastern Maine: "I was reared among the noble Pines of Maine, nestled in my cradle beneath their giant forms, and often has the sighing wind made music that has calmed me to repose as it gently played through their tasseled boughs. Often have I been filled with awe as I gazed upon their massive trunks and raised my eye to their cloud-swept tops."[5]

Springer would gladly trade city life "for those wilderness solitudes whose delightful valleys and swelling ridges give me nature uncontaminated—I had almost said, uncursed, fresh from the hand of the Creator." On spring mornings, his "ears were saluted with the wild notes of a thousand feathered songsters, whose sweet warblings lent a peculiar enchantment to the woodland scenery which skirted the shores of the lake." He caught trout weighing three to four pounds. He observed a black bear destroy a canoe in search of balsam pitch. Often, he encountered "a track of uncommon size and appearance" of "a dangerous specimen of the feline species, known by woodsmen as the Indian Devil." The catamount's track, he reported, "was round, and about the size of a hat crown."[6]

On one occasion, the intrepid woodsman witnessed a pack of wolves harass three teams of oxen hauling a log. The wolves "were of unusually large size, manifesting a most singular boldness, and even familiarity, without the usual appearance of ferocity so characteristic of the animal." They jumped on the log and rode it a while, gradually approaching the oxen: "There was something so cool and impudent in their conduct."[7]

The early lumbermen dubbed white pine the "whale of the forest." Individual trees routinely produced more than two thousand board feet. A few pines in the 1840s yielded eight thousand board feet. Springer once cut a pine 144 feet tall that had a six-foot diameter at breast height and was limb-free for the first 65 feet: "My heart palpitated as I occasionally raised my eye to its pinnacle to catch the first indications of

(Copyright © Jon Luoma)

its fall. It came down at length with a crash which seemed to shake a
hundred acres, while the loud echo rang through the forest, dying away
among the distant hills."[8]

Pine is strong and light; its straight grain makes it versatile and
easy to work. It produced the widest, most knot-free boards of any softwood. Uses for white pine in the mid-nineteenth century included large
beams and posts, framing for houses and bridges, clapboards, shingles,
flooring, and roofing. Its clearness and beauty made it ideal for panels and frames of doors and windows, for wainscotings, dormers, and
moldings.

In the 1820s, Springer recalled, "large tracts of country were covered principally with Pine-trees. Those tracts seemed purposely located
in the vicinity of lakes, large streams and rivers. . . . But the woodmen's
ax, together with the destructive fires which have swept over large

districts from time to time, have . . . driven this tree far back into the interior wilderness. In fact, the Pine seems doomed by the avarice and enterprise of the white man, gradually to disappear from the borders of civilization."[9]

As the most accessible pine disappeared, lumbermen penetrated deeper into the northern Maine wilderness along the Androscoggin, Kennebec, and Penobscot Rivers. They required increasing sums of capital to undertake and sustain large-scale, protracted logging operations far from settled communities. The capitalists, who gained control of most of the land and dominated Maine's timber industry, favored concentrated ownerships.

A nineteenth-century timber operation typically began in June or July, when timber cruisers set out to locate the best timber for the least expense. As Springer and his fellow cruisers hacked a path through the wilderness, "the blood-thirsty millions of [black] flies who swarm and triumph over these sanguinary fields" assailed them. At night, he added, "the mosquito lancers take up the action," and the no-see-um, who "insinuates himself under the collar, the wristband, and through the texture of the garments," added to their misery. When woodsmen arrived later in the fall, the cold had replaced these native insect torturers with fleas and lice in the camps.[10]

Once cruisers had located the stands to cut, they selected a site for the logging camp with ample supplies of wood and water as well as proximity to the log landing and major roads. They constructed camp buildings of red spruce. A covering of boughs insulated roofs of pine, spruce, or cedar shingles.[11]

Primitive early logging camps, with buildings lacking windows and floors, housed the loggers and the kitchen. A sand and rock fire pit in the center of the room heated the building and cooked the meals. A hole in the roof permitted most of the smoke to escape. The stench of wet clothing and the snoring of exhausted loggers, sleeping on hemlock boughs or hay, made these smoky camps memorable, if not comfortable, abodes. Many teamsters preferred to bed down with their oxen where they could sleep on clean straw. By 1860, windows, floors, bunks, and a cast iron box stove added a measure of comfort to the loggers'

sleeping quarters. A separate building housed the kitchen and din-
ing room.

Farm boys, whose families did not require their labor during the
winter months, filled the early logging camps. They were skilled with
both axe and saw and experienced teamsters with basic veterinarian
skills. However, logging exhausted work animals; woods work often
conflicted with plowing and planting season, and as commercial markets opened, farmers were less dependent on logging for cash income.[12]

Gradually, the timber barons employed a growing class of landless men whom they paid about a dollar a day throughout most of the
century. No insurance compensated loggers or their families for injury
or death. Smallpox occasionally visited the camps.

Loggers began arriving in October and November. An early
nineteenth-century logging camp might have forty to sixty oxen. Eventually, nimble, quicker horses replaced the slow beasts. The care and
attention that oxen and horses required consumed all the hours of a
teamster's day. In the 1840s, the better-capitalized operations established
farms in the north woods to produce hay for work animals and potatoes
for the woodsmen.

Loggers worked six days a week from before sunrise until after sun-
set in six-man crews: a swamper cleared underbrush to improve working conditions; two choppers, facing each other, felled trees with axes; a
knotter, wielding a sharp axe, delimbed the fallen trees; and a teamster
and yard roller transported the logs to yards where they awaited the
spring drive.

Loggers devoured three gigantic meals a day. Before mid-century,
loggers took turns at the cookstove. Soon, a full-time cook became
one of the most important members of a crew and a powerful recruit-
ing tool for a camp boss. The standard menu in early camps included
pickled beef, baked codfish, sourdough biscuits, flapjacks, and strong
tea. Cooks baked bread, beans, and pies in large Dutch ovens. Robert
Pike quoted one unnamed French-Canadian chef: "For me, I'll take
the prune. It makes even better apple pie than the peach."[13] The cook
and dishwasher strictly enforced the interdiction of conversation during dinner. Idle chatter prolonged the meal, offered opportunities for

men to comment unfavorably upon the fare, and could precipitate an outburst of fisticuffs.

On Sundays the loggers rested, mended clothing, washed laundry, sharpened tools, told stories, danced to camp fiddlers, and gambled. Some hunted deer, moose, bear, hare, and "partridge" (grouse). Others trapped marten. A few even tried to kill time and vermin with a hot bath. Traveling clergy and priests visited to offer services to the more devout. Ladies of questionable repute occasionally offered services of a different kind. To pass the time in the woods or resting in camp, loggers sang songs of their own composition. Consider this verse from "Boys of the Island":

> The lumberman's life, 'tis of short duration,
> It's mingled with sorrow, hard work and bad rum;
> If the hereafter is according to Scripture
> The worst of our days are yet to come.[14]

In March the entire crew moved the logs from the yard to a landing at the edge of a stream or lake to await ice-out. The drivers often waited several weeks for the river ice to melt. In the 1810s loggers began sending large shipments of loose logs downriver, replacing the earlier practice of lashing logs together as rafts.

To avoid financial ruin, the lumbermen dammed lakes, streams, and rivers to assure an adequate spring runoff to drive their logs to market. A removable gate released water from the small dams as needed. On larger bodies of water, dams required extensive investment and relentless maintenance. On Chesuncook Lake in 1840, a forty-foot-wide, two-hundred-foot-long sluice gate permitted the logs to pass through a five-hundred-foot dam for a toll.

Loggers did not enter the Upper Saint John region and its tributary, the Allagash, until the 1840s. The headwaters region of the Saint John River lacked the large lakes needed to store water for successful spring drives, and the Penobscot lumbermen were unhappy that the four-hundred-mile-long Saint John took Maine timber to mills in New Brunswick, Canada. They constructed the eight-hundred-foot-long

Telos Canal to divert water from the Allagash watershed to Webster Lake and thence to the East Branch of the Penobscot. Furious Saint John lumbermen destroyed the canal. Penobscot men promptly rebuilt it. A few years later, Thoreau contemptuously remarked, "They have thus dammed all the larger lakes, raising their broad surfaces many feet . . . thus turning the forces of nature against herself, that they might float their spoils out of the country."[15]

The drive began in spring with the breakup of ice, an event some-times hastened by dynamite. Loggers had to drive the feeder streams early when water was sufficient. Depending on the length of the river and the amount of available water, drives could last weeks or months. Springer described an early drive on the Mattawamkeag River in eastern Maine. It began on March 25, and fifty days later the logs from Baskahegan Stream and Lake had reached the main river. The 130-mile drive suffered several major jams before reaching the mills three months later.[16]

Moosehead Lake usually became ice-free by mid-May; April 30, 1889, was the earliest ice-out, and May 29, 1878, the latest. In today's warming climate, it is ice-free on average nine days earlier than a cen-tury and a half ago. As snow cover declines over northern New England and April air temperatures warm, ice-out dates will continue to advance, and stream flows will diminish much earlier than a century ago.[17] Under today's climate conditions, many historical river drives would have been hung up long before logs reached the mills.

On lakes, the drivers would gather the logs together in a bag boom—logs chained together encircling a large number of logs. They set a capstan upon a raft, rowed it ahead of the boom, and dropped an anchor. A gang of drivers turned the capstan to draw the boom to-ward the raft. A tailwind made the job relatively easy, but a headwind stopped the operation in its tracks, forcing the drivers to work at night after the wind had died down. Booming logs down the twenty-two-mile Chesuncook Lake required three days and three nights.

River drivers were a special breed of men. They had to be strong, agile, and decisive. They were always wet and cold, often having to stand in freezing water to move logs over shallow ledges. The *wangan*, or cook's wagon, followed the drive on rudimentary trails along the shore.

The cook provided four massive meals per day for the cold, wet drivers. Failure to calculate correctly the location of the drive at mealtime and at the end of the day could turn hungry drivers surly.

Logjams, the bane of the drivers' existence, occurred wherever there were falls and dangerous rapids, or when water was in short supply. Jams in the center of the river were more dangerous and difficult to clear than wing jams near the shore. The drivers often cleared the jam from a bateau; sometimes they had to climb onto the pile to pry loose the logs causing the jam. When all else failed, they used dynamite. Because death stalked them at every spin of a log and bend in the river, an often-reckless bravado animated their work, and they soon became a part of American folklore—part hero, part forest destroyer. "The Jam at Gerry's Rock" was a popular song among river drivers:

> It was on Sunday morning as you will quickly hear,
> Our logs were piled up mountains high, we could not keep
>   them clear.
> Our foreman said, "Turn out brave boys, with heart devoid
>   of fear
> We'll break the jam on Gerry's Rock and for Eganstown we'll
>   steer."
>
> Now some of them were willing while others they were not,
> For to work on jams on Sunday they did not think we ought;
> But six of our Canadian boys did volunteer to go
> And break the jam on Gerry's Rock with the foreman, young
>   Monroe.
>
> They had not rolled off many logs when they heard his clear
>   voice say:
> "I'd have you boys be on your guard for the jam will soon
>   give way."
> These words were scarcely spoken when the mass did break
>   and go,
> And it carried off those six brave youths and their foreman,
>   Jack Monroe.[18]

The drive was a time of stress for the lumberman. He could not recoup his investment until his logs reached the sawmill, so a premature spring thaw, a snowless winter, a dry spring, or a major jam spelled disaster. Too much rain washed the boom out to sea. As much as 10 percent of the logs sank. Prices tumbled when there was a glut of lumber or a depression.

Thoreau visited the northern Maine woods during the glory years of the timber industry. Moving north from Bangor along the Penobscot River in 1846, he observed lumber mills built "directly over and across the river." In 1837, 250 sawmills along the Penobscot and its tributaries sawed two hundred million board feet annually. At these mills, he sourly observed, the "once green tree . . . becomes lumber merely." He heard stories of sea vessels "becalmed off our coast, being surrounded a week at a time by floating lumber from the Maine woods."[19] Sawmills befouled rivers with sawdust, edgings, and refuse.

John Springer presciently observed that Bangor, the world's largest sawtimber producer in the 1840s, failed to capture the true economic value of Maine's majestic pines: "Of one great disadvantage, which must retard her progress, mention may be made, viz., capitalists abroad own too much of the territory on her river. A judicious policy in business must be steadily pursued, else she may only prove the mere outlet through which the wealth of her territory shall pass to other hands, leaving her with the bitter inheritance of one day becoming possessed of the knowledge, when too late, of what she might have been."[20]

Around 1845, as the great pines disappeared along the Penobscot, loggers began cutting red spruce. This smaller softwood makes excellent boards. Red spruce logs, much more abundant than white pine, exceeded the cut of pine for the first time in 1861. The nineteenth-century lumbermen rarely cut a spruce less than fifteen inches in diameter, and as old growth spruce disappeared, Maine's relative importance in the national timber economy faded as the century waned.[21]

Maine loggers enlisted in the Union Army in 1861, so lumbermen began to import Canadian loggers, especially farm boys from Prince Edward Island, to get out the cut and drive logs to the mills. Canadians, willing to work for lower wages, have been a controversial mainstay of the Maine timber industry ever since. Maine loggers blamed them for taking scarce jobs from Yankees and for depressing already low wages. The *Portland Argus* editorialized in 1883, "It is a question whether we can afford to have our forests destroyed for the sake of protecting such labor."[22]

Timber prices fell in the 1870s and 1880s as western railroads and the Erie Canal moved lakes states' timber into eastern markets, and new sources of wood became available in the south. Maine, with dwindling supplies of old growth; small, aging mills; and a precarious transportation infrastructure could no longer compete with the Midwest for investors' capital.

When Maine's white pine supply gave out, loggers and timber investors who scorned cutting spruce followed their manifest destiny to cut down the next frontier forest. Stewart Holbrook claimed you couldn't enter a Great Lakes logging camp without encountering Bangor Tigers, and when they had exhausted the pine in the Midwest, the Maine boys headed to the Pacific Northwest.[23] In the vernacular of the woodsmen, they went "over the hump." The timber barons had exercised their property right to mine the forest as a resource for maximal profits. They viewed lands shorn of trees as a tax burden to be sold or abandoned.

Throughout American history, the wildlands over the hump and beyond the frontier have served as a safety valve for unaddressed ecological and social problems. Farmers could temporarily *evade* natural limits by heading to the frontier when they had depleted soil productivity. Historian Patricia Nelson Limerick suggested that farming practices developed *over time* in crowded Europe with its excess of labor and scarcity of land. Gradually, farmers learned the secrets of the local soils, weather, and ecosystems to develop distinctive, local cultures. In the sparsely populated United States, however, blessed with a seemingly infinite expanse of land available for the taking from its indigenous inhabitants, land stewardship developed *in space* rather than time.[24] Farmers abandoned worked-over lands long before they understood how to work *with* the land.

By the time of Thoreau's 1853 trip to Maine, the best pine had become scarce: "At this rate," he railed, "we shall all be obliged to let our beards grow at least, if only to hide the nakedness of the land and make a sylvan appearance." He noted:

> how base or coarse are the motives which commonly carry men into the wilderness. . . . For one that comes with a pencil to sketch or sing, a thousand come with an axe or rifle. . . .
>
> Strange that so few ever come to the woods to see how the pine lives and grows and spires, lifting its evergreen arms to the light,—to see its perfect success; but most are content to behold it in the shape of many broad boards brought to market, and deem *that* its true success! . . .
>
> Is it the lumberman, then, who is the friend and lover of the pine . . . ? No! no! it is the poet; he it is who makes the truest use of the pine . . .[25]

On his final trip in 1857, Thoreau fumed:

> The Anglo-American can indeed cut down, and grub up all this waving forest, and make a stump speech, and vote for Buchanan on its ruins, but he cannot converse with the spirit of the tree he fells, he cannot read the poetry and mythology which retire as he advances. He ignorantly erases mythological tablets in order to print his handbills and town-meeting warrants on them. Before he has learned his a b c in the beautiful but mystic lore of the wilderness . . . , he cuts it down, coins a *pine-tree* shilling (as if to signify the pine's value to him), puts up a *dee*strict school-house, and introduces Webster's spelling-book.[26]

Four years earlier, Thoreau had proposed the preservation of some of wild northern Maine:

> The kings of England formerly had their forests "to hold the king's game," for sport or food, sometimes destroying

villages to create or extend them; and I think they were im-
pelled by a true instinct. Why should not we, who have re-
nounced the king's authority, have our national preserves,
where no villages need be destroyed, in which the bear and
panther, and some even of the hunter race, may still exist,
and not be "civilized off the face of the earth,"—our forests,
not to hold the king's game merely, but to hold and preserve
the king himself also, the lord of creation,—not for idle sport
or food, but for inspiration and our own true recreation? or
shall we, like the villains, grub them all up, poaching on our
own national domains?[27]

A Marriage of Morality and Capability

This forest philosophy is the philosophy of American democracy.

FREDERICK JACKSON TURNER, 1896

E uro-Americans radically transformed wild North America before they had had time to sink roots deep into the soil of their new home. Old World immigrants imposed an alien culture upon the so-called New World: Near Eastern religion, Eurasian agriculture, English property law, and global trade. Colonists seized land from Natives and purchased citizens of Africa abducted by slavers to grow commodities such as cotton, sugar, rice, and tobacco. They viewed nonhuman species as "resources" to be exploited, and old growth forests and wolves as "non-resources" to be removed.

In the late eighteenth century, they established the first modern democracy. Frederick Jackson Turner, in his celebrated essay "The Significance of the Frontier in American History," theorized democracy had been forged on the anvil of the receding frontier: "the most important effect of the frontier has been in the promotion of democracy here and in Europe." He defined the frontier as "the meeting point between savagery and civilization," adding, "The existence of an area of free land, its continuous recession, and the advance of American settlement westward, explain American development."[1]

Turner's essays on the frontier are spiced with rapturous statements: "The forest clearings have been the seed plots of American character. . . . This forest philosophy is the philosophy of American democracy." American democracy "came out of the American forest, and it gained new strength each time it touched a new frontier. Not the constitution, but free land and an abundance of natural resources open to a fit people, made the democratic type of society in America."[2]

The "free land" was the indigenous commons that sustained Native cultures for millennia. The advancing frontier meant loss of their land and culture; it brought disease, war, death. For passenger pigeons, bison, wolves, and salmon the diminishing wilderness caused extirpation and extinction.

If we view the frontier as a machine that consumes the raw material of wilderness to produce democracy, what fuels the engine of democracy when this fuel is exhausted? A decade after his seminal essay on the closing of the frontier, Turner wrote: "The free lands are gone. The material forces that gave vitality to Western democracy are passing away." The ideals of unrestrained individualism and democracy "had elements of mutual hostility and contained the seeds of its dissolution." Rugged frontier individualists may have arrived first, but in time, railroads, timber barons, ranchers, and mining corporations appropriated the wild, common lands. Turner believed frontier democracy was premised upon "equality of opportunity"—*at least for the enfranchised.* Frontier settlers "resented the conception that opportunity under competition should result in the hopeless inequality, or rule of class."[3]

The rise of conservation coincided with the closing of the frontier. Nineteenth-century conservationists reacted to the failure of democracy to protect land from exploitation. The emerging conservation movement began to reverse the North American enclosure movement, and it signaled the dawning of a more natural conception of democracy.

In the decades preceding the Civil War, artists, writers, poets, scientists, and adventurers, including Thoreau, popularized New Hampshire's White Mountain attractions such as Crawford Notch, Mount Washington, and the Old Man of the Mountain. Wealthy tourists, seeking escape from the heat, congestion, smells, and diseases of early industrial cities, flocked to boarding houses and rustic hotels with stunning views. After 1875, grand hotels accommodated thousands of pilgrims annually. The tourism industry became a powerful political actor.

Many visitors, scornful of the pampered life at the grand hotels, preferred hiking to mountain summits and searching out remote forest wonders. Hikers, who relished the rigorous climbs, the sublime sights, and a sense of self-renewal, anticipated the twentieth-century preservationist movement.[4]

In 1867 New Hampshire unburdened itself of the last of its public lands, selling 172,000 acres, including Mount Washington, for about 15 cents an acre. This paltry sum purportedly benefited the state's chronically underfunded public schools. Timbermen had previously avoided the forests of the White Mountains because the rivers draining the region were inhospitable to log drives. But after the railroads connected these old forests with markets in Boston, Portland, and New York around 1870, the heavy cutting began.

James Everell "Ev" Henry, a sour old Yankee, dominated logging in the heart of the Whites from 1880 until his death in 1912. He reputedly said, "I never see the tree yit, that didn't mean a damned sight more to me goin' under the saw than it did standin' on a mountain." His son George, who oversaw the woods operations, added, "There's no secret about this business of ours; we own the land and the timber and we're making every dollar out of it we can."[5]

Henry built a spur railroad off the Boston and Maine line south into the Zealand River Valley. In July 1886, five months after the Zealand line began operations, one of its trains threw a spark that ignited a fire in the lower Zealand Valley. It burned twelve thousand acres before rain extinguished it a week later. Thin mountain soils, scorched by the intense heat, washed away in the rains. The fire came at the height of the tourist season. Vacationers, appalled by the unsightly high-elevation fire scars, reviled Henry as a "woods butcher," and some began to clamor for restraints on the activities of men of his ilk. But he kept on cutting until his woodsmen had depleted the old growth.

In August 1892 Henry moved his operations a few miles south to gain access to timber he had acquired on the East Branch of the Pemigewasset River. When workers, laying out the streets of the new town of Lincoln, left shade trees standing along its main street, Henry ordered them cut down, reckoning they had more value as timber than as shade.[6] He owned Lincoln's hotel, bank, and company store and leased all the

Late nineteenth-century loggers cutting old growth spruce in the White Mountains. (Used by permission from Upper Pemigewasset Historical Society, Lincoln, NH)

houses to his employees. He and his sons, or trusted employees, held all local political positions.

To transport wood to their Lincoln sawmill, the Henrys constructed the East Branch and Lincoln Railroad. Over the next two decades, they laid more than fifty miles of tracks in what is now the White Mountain National Forest and kept four or five camps going each winter, employing as many as five hundred men. Two trains hauled two or three loads of logs a day.

Most of the loggers were Irish or French-Canadian; a few were Russians or Poles. No union ever successfully organized Henry's men. On one occasion, Henry, accompanied by a gang of loggers, informed a labor organizer to get out of town fast—or else. Larry Gorman, a celebrated Maine woodsman-minstrel, made the mistake of hiring out to the Henrys one winter. He immortalized his ordeal in a song, "Henry's Concern":

> Every month with pen and ink they'll figure up the cost;
> The crew is held responsible for all things broke or lost—
> An axe, a handle, or a spade, a cant-dog, or a chain—
> They'd call us fools to stand such rules in the good old State
>   of Maine.
>
> The meat and fish is poorly cooked, the bread is sour and
>   cold,
> The beans are dry and musty, and doughnuts hard and old;
> If you were to eat one it would give your jaws great pain—
> The grub we oft times have's a change, in the good old State
>   of Maine.[7]

Trees roughly twenty-five to thirty inches in diameter at breast height, without branches for at least twenty feet, dominated virgin red spruce stands. The best spruce grew on the north and northwest facing slopes on the East Branch between one thousand and twenty-eight hundred feet of elevation. Sometimes Henry's crews cut as much as eighty cords an acre. On a logging operation at Cedar Brook the spruce averaged about 275 years of age—seedlings when the Pilgrims landed.

Loggers felled the hardwoods first, then cut the spruce and rolled them downhill over the hardwoods left behind to rot in the woods. Henry sent smaller softwoods to the pulp mills he built in Lincoln in 1898 and Livermore Falls in 1899. He sold the pulp to paper mills along the Merrimack River until 1901–1902 when he constructed his own mill in Lincoln that produced fifty tons of paper a day.

When the big spruce were gone by 1908, the Henrys shut down their sawmill to concentrate on the more profitable pulp and paper business. After old man Henry died in 1912, his sons continued to skin the land for another five years. In 1917, they sold out to Parker-Young for $3 million and moved away from New Hampshire.

As a youth, George Perkins Marsh had witnessed a flood of mud washing down the streets of Woodstock, Vermont, after a clear-cut on Mount Tom. In his pioneering work on forest conservation, *Man and Nature,* published in 1864, Marsh warned: "The face of the earth is no longer a sponge, but a dust heap, and the floods which the waters of the sky pour over it hurry swiftly along its slopes, carrying in suspension vast quantities of earthy particles which increase the abrading power and mechanical force of the current. . . . The washing of the soil from the mountains leaves bare ridges of sterile rock, and the rich organic mould which covered them, now swept down into the dank low grounds." Marsh wrote that "man is everywhere a disturbing agent," and his wanton destruction of forests and rivers destroyed the balance between organic and inorganic nature.[8]

Joseph Walker, a prominent Concord lawyer, had fallen in love with the forests of the White Mountains after tromping around old growth near Franconia for several days in 1838. Inspired by *Man and Nature,* and increasingly alarmed by the liquidation of beloved forests, Walker pushed for the creation of a New Hampshire Forest Commission. In 1885, the commission issued a shocking report: the original, dense forest cover of New Hampshire had long since disappeared. The report quoted "an old resident" of Lancaster: "Instead of cutting timber that is matured, everything is cut to the size of five or six inches in diameter, and what remains is cut into fire-wood, or burned at once, leaving a dreary waste. In Lancaster the timber and wood are nearly all gone, and the mountains are being stripped to their summits."[9]

After the timber barons had cut old growth forests between Twin Mountain House and Fabyan's in the western shadow of Mount Washington, Walker, in an 1894 address to the American Forestry Association, reported:

> [The lumberman] swept away the forests which had made it one of the most pleasing localities in the mountains. He brought with him the sawmill, and defiled the clear waters of the streams with sawdust and worthless edgings. The work of destruction then commenced passed into the grand old woods then lining the road from Fabyan's to the Crawford House, and extending westward therefrom to the base of Mount Washington.
>
> Ere long, fire followed in the footsteps of the lumberman and swept away in its fury whatever he had spared. An abomination of desolation, as lugubrious as that spoken of by Daniel the prophet, succeeded the fire.
>
> This great tract of charred soil, dotted all over with blackened stumps . . . arrested the attention of every visitor. Universal regret, with much indignation, was freely expressed on account of the great injury thus done to one of the finest portions of the whole mountain region. Public opinion was aroused to activity.[10]

The Forest Commission report lamented in 1893: "all the mountain forests in New Hampshire are private property, and . . . we have no more control over their owners' treatment of them than we have over the condition of life on the moons of Mars."[11] The commission's report appealed to a diverse audience, including rural dwellers worried about dwindling supplies for local sawmills, farmers, hunters and anglers, and resort owners and their wealthy, influential clientele. Articles in leading magazines such as *The Atlantic Monthly, Harper's,* and *The Nation* alerted a wider audience to the growing crisis.

In 1899, A. H. Carter, an executive with Berlin Mills Company in Berlin, New Hampshire, expressed the industry's contempt for conservationists: "I have no patience with these theorists who are continually talking about the destruction of the forests and urging the preservation of the timberlands for future generations. . . . [T]he argument for saving the trees for future ages, is most absurd. As long as Americans remain as they are at present, they'll not be so considerate for the welfare of future inhabitants, as to cease money making and close down industries. They'll run the thing as long as there is any money in it."[12]

A group of wealthy forest lovers from New Hampshire and Massachusetts formed the Society for the Protection of New Hampshire Forests (the Forest Society) on February 6, 1901. The following year they hired Philip Ayers to lead the society's campaign to protect the White Mountains. In the summer of 1903 Ayers wrote that logging on high or steep forested slopes "is not profitable except to cut clean." He added, "Such timber should be cut only by a conservative use of the selective method, and this can probably be done only when the government takes control." He regretted the New Hampshire Legislature's defeat of a bill that would have prohibited cutting smaller diameter trees: "This principle appears to be contrary to American independence, curtailing a man's right to do what he will with his own."[13] The legislature responded by authorizing the US Bureau of Forestry, the predecessor of the US Forest Service, to examine the forestlands of the White Mountains.

Alfred K. Chittenden, an assistant forest inspector at the bureau and a member of the Yale School of Forestry's first graduating class in 1902, conducted the study and wrote the report. He discovered that the best spruce land sold for $20–$30 per acre, but rapidly vanishing virgin forests covered only about 12 percent of the region. North of Squam Lake, heavily cutover forests were worth only $2–$4 an acre.[14]

In late spring 1903, during a fifty-two-day drought, 554 fires burned more than eighty-four thousand acres in the White Mountains.[15] Chittenden reported that fires on newly cleared stands had destroyed softwood seedlings and fostered conditions favorable to the light-winged seeds of birch, aspen, and wild red cherry. The fires rarely impacted the old growth spruce, and those in old hardwood stands were "usually of the light surface type." Where human-caused fires burned hottest, Chittenden wrote, they destroyed the "intricate network of fine rootlets"— the part of the humus critical for retaining soil moisture and other organic matter. Following heavy rains, the parched soils washed away, leaving bedrock. Liquidation logging, followed by intense fire, had set the stand back to the time of the glacial retreat.[16]

Chittenden warned, "Unfortunately the owner of lands severely cutover usually has not, or thinks he has not, a sufficient financial interest at stake to provide for this. This circumstance and the fact that the State has the greatest interest in the protection of the land for the production of crops which shall be harvested by a succeeding generation, point to the desirability of its providing such patrol, toward defraying the expense of which taxes on timberlands may well be made to contribute." Taxes on timber, he noted, were "generally low." The Chittenden report concluded with a call for public acquisition of cutover lands for inclusion in a national forest reserve.[17]

In the early years of the twentieth century, timber industry trade associations supported legislation to establish eastern national forests because they hoped public lands, removed from commercial logging, could reduce overproduction and increase lumber prices. The timber lobby expected to continue to enjoy the "right" to log public forests and gain relief from the obligation to pay property taxes on the land. Congressional opposition to federal acquisition of private forestlands came from western, southern, and midwestern members of Congress who viewed this as an unprecedented usurpation of state powers by the national government.[18]

In 1906 New England conservationists joined with proponents of forest protection in the southern Appalachians to pass a bill to authorize the federal government to acquire private timberlands and establish eastern national forests in the southern and northern Appalachians. House Speaker Joseph Cannon, who notoriously pledged "not one cent for scenery," blocked the legislation. In 1907, the House Judiciary Committee ruled that the Appalachia bill was unconstitutional, except insofar as it protected watersheds for navigable rivers.[19] That year, John Weeks, a Massachusetts congressman born in Lancaster, New Hampshire, urged the speaker to stop blocking the forest bill. Cannon respected successful financiers such as Weeks, and he appointed him to the Agriculture Committee, promising to support a bill if business leaders endorsed it.

T. Jefferson Coolidge, treasurer of the Amoskeag Manufacturing Company in Manchester, New Hampshire, the largest textile mill in the United States, published a booklet designed to build support in Congress for forest protection. A dozen years earlier, spring floods on the Merrimack had shut down Amoskeag. Summer drought followed, and towns along the Merrimack had to ration water use to keep their textile mills open. The owners blamed logging at the headwaters of the Pemigewasset. Coolidge, complaining of the havoc alternating drought and flood played with mills, wrote, "One freshet, a few years ago cost the Amoskeag Company more than one hundred thousand dollars."[20]

In 1909 Weeks introduced a bill to appropriate funds that enabled the federal government to "purchase forestlands to protect forests containing the headwaters of rivers and streams used for navigation and water power."[21] He cited Chittenden's report on the impact of deforestation on New England's rivers. Women's clubs, granges, hunters, anglers, tourists, and locals fed up with Ev Henry and his ilk enthusiastically supported the Weeks bill. The House passed it in 1910, and the Senate approved it seven months later. President William Howard Taft signed the Weeks Act into law on March 1, 1911.

The Weeks Act enabled Congress to establish national forests east of the Mississippi, including the White Mountain National Forest. Between 1914 and 1937, the Forest Service purchased 540,000 acres for the WMNF at an average price of $10 an acre, the equivalent of about $200 in 2022. In July 1912, George Henry wrote his woods boss about the coming winter's logging operations at Ethan Pond and Mount Willey, the most remote tracts the Henrys had logged. The costs would be higher than usual, and Henry wanted his men to cut it hard: "I think we ought to plan to pull all we can from 21A [the camp at Ethan Pond] this winter as the time is soon coming when we will have to sell to the government probably our logged over lands, and if we get it clean it will sell for just as much as if we left lots of logs. Please don't leave this letter laying around and least said the better." A few years later the Henrys sold the cutover forest to the WMNF for $6 an acre.[22]

Wealthy New Yorkers had fallen in love with the wild lakes, rivers, mountains, and forests of the Adirondacks before intensive logging began in the 1860s. In the 1870s and 1880s, forest fires engulfed denuded, eroding hillsides, and deforestation's adverse effects on transportation on the Erie Canal and the Hudson River threatened commerce. As a result, a powerful political constituency of New York industrialists and affluent Adirondack camp owners raised alarms about reckless cutting.

In 1883 New York terminated all further sales of land in the Adirondacks. Two years later, it designated its scattered holdings a "Forest Reserve." To strengthen the vague 1885 decree, the state established the Adirondack Park on May 20, 1892. The park, then, as now, was a mix of private timberlands under active management; large estates of the ultra-rich; small, poor hamlets; and protected state forest.

In 1894, New York's constitutional convention adopted Article VII, Section 7: "The lands of the state, now owned or hereafter acquired, constituting the forest preserve as now fixed by law, shall be forever kept as wild forest lands. They shall not be leased, sold or exchanged, or be taken by any corporation, public or private, nor shall the timber thereon be sold, removed or destroyed." Today, the "Forever Wild" clause, subsequently renamed Article XIV, assures that 2.8 million acres of forestland in the 6-million-acre Adirondack Park are some of the best protected lands on Earth.

Maine failed to mount a public land acquisition and protection campaign during the Progressive Era. Historian Richard Judd observed that Maine differed from New Hampshire in important respects. Towns and villages ringed the White Mountains, but destructive logging in remote northern Maine went largely unobserved. Maine is less mountainous, and cutting in the headwaters of its great rivers caused fewer disastrous floods. Forest ownerships in Maine were much larger. The great landowners controlled the state government and conservation commissions. They thwarted regulation of destructive logging practices and maintained the focus of conservation on fire control and low taxes.[23]

An effective late nineteenth-century land preservation movement in Maine never developed because of the lack of economic diversity in its unsettled northern forests. In New York and New Hampshire, powerful economic interests, tourism, and well-connected summer residents successfully challenged the timbermen and won great conservation victories.

The Weeks Act stands as a landmark event in US conservation history. For the first time, the federal government could purchase forestlands from private owners for conservation purposes. It bucked the trend toward privatization of land beginning with the enclosure of indigenous New England commons three centuries earlier. Successful public land campaigns during the Progressive Era shared several characteristics, especially

- public outrage at the destruction of beloved forests;

- an understanding of the need to educate the public and media, coupled with outreach to foresters, hunters, anglers, nature lovers, farmers, women's clubs, and industries negatively impacted by destructive logging;

- economic diversity to counter unrestrained exploitation; and

- a respectful collaboration between visionaries and pragmatic insiders—a "marriage of morality and capability"— to earn support of the public and sympathetic politicians.[24]

The twentieth-century conservation movement has struggled to reconcile a century-long schism between political horse-trading and the obligation to protect the rights of nonhumans and abide by natural limits. The story of preservationist John Muir and political conservationist Gifford Pinchot sheds light on how the two conservation philosophies might rediscover their common ancestry. In 1896–1897, Muir, founder of the Sierra Club, and Pinchot, who later was appointed the first chief of the US Forest Service, became good friends when they collaborated to protect western federal lands from the worst depredations of timber operators, miners, and livestock grazing. Thereafter, however, their philosophies increasingly clashed.

Theodore Roosevelt, America's greatest conservation president, was ascending Mount Marcy, the highest peak in the Adirondack Park, when he learned of the death of William McKinley and his elevation to the office of president in September 1901. After a camping trip with Muir in 1903, Roosevelt proclaimed, "There is nothing more practical . . . than the preservation of beauty."[25] Roosevelt, however, chose Pinchot as his most trusted political advisor on conservation matters.

Pinchot opposed designating the Adirondacks as "Forever Wild" and expanding the national park system. He believed people faced a choice between wise and wasteful use: "The first duty of the human race on the material side is to control the use of the earth and all that therein is. Conservation means the wise use of the earth and its resources for the lasting good of men." It aimed "for the greatest good of the greatest number for the longest time." In 1904, he wrote, "no lands will be permanently reserves which can serve the people better in any other way."[26]

Muir's all-embracing love for *nature as it is* conflicted with Pinchot's belief that his experts could improve nature. "The world, we are told, was made especially for man—a presumption not supported by all the facts," Muir wrote. "Now, it never seems to occur to these farseeing teachers that Nature's object in making animals and plants might possibly be first of all the happiness of each one of them, not the creation of all for the happiness of one. . . . The universe would be incomplete without man; but it would also be incomplete without the smallest transmicroscopic creature that dwells beyond our conceitful eyes and knowledge."[27]

Pinchot funded the 1908 Conference of Governors on natural resources. He excluded Muir from the invitation list. Only three of nearly a hundred presentations at the conference, addressed by President Roosevelt, mentioned nonutilitarian issues such as wilderness preservation.[28]

Restoring the wilderness *commons* can help teach us to accept limits upon our material appetites, a goal of Pinchot. Simultaneously, in the spirit of Muir, we must dedicate ourselves to the welfare of others—the plant people, the animal people, unborn generations, and victims of environmental racism. Progressive Era conservationists rejected the crazy notion that property rights come without responsibilities to the land, its native species, and the future. They embraced the social compact: with *rights* to temporary ownership of land come *responsibilities* to protect the land whether or not it is useful to our economic and political aspirations. They took the first steps toward including the nonhuman world in democratic conversations.

The author of *Walden* and *The Maine Woods,* a prophet of the American conservation movement, also served the cause of abolitionism and acted as a conductor on the Underground Railroad. Late in July 1846, the midpoint of Thoreau's sojourn at Walden Pond and a month before he embarked on his first excursion into the north Maine woods, he spent a night in jail for refusing to pay a tax to support the war on Mexico. President James K. Polk, who traded slaves from the White House, invaded Mexico for the purpose of expanding the young nation's slave territories.

Sometime after his jailing, Thoreau penned the essay "Civil Disobedience." In it he asked: "Can there not be a government in which majorities do not virtually decide right and wrong, but conscience?—in which majorities decide only those questions to which the rule of expediency is applicable? Must the citizen even for a moment, or in the least degree, resign his conscience to the legislator? Why has every man a conscience, then? I think that we should be men first, and subjects afterward." He continued: "[There are cases] to which the rule of expediency does not apply, in which a people, as well as an individual, must do justice, cost what it may."[29]

In "Civil Disobedience," Thoreau offered an audacious interpretation of democracy: "any man more right than his neighbors, constitutes a majority of one already."[30] Plebiscites cannot determine whether or not to abide by moral laws. Citing the New Testament and the Declaration of Independence, abolitionists based the emancipation campaign on the power of democracy and free speech to incite a moral revolution to sweep away forces they could not defeat politically.

James Forten Jr., son of a free-born abolitionist, declared that slavery denied its victims their natural rights—"the right to the produce of our own labour, to our own limbs, life, liberty, and property—perfect rights, not human institutions, but Divine ordinations." He added, "It is not by the force of arms that Abolitionists expect to remove one of the greatest curses that ever afflicted or disgraced humanity; but by the majesty of moral power."[31]

The pope could excommunicate Galileo, but he could not place Earth at the center of the solar system. Climate science deniers possess the power to sabotage policies designed to reduce carbon emissions and atmospheric carbon levels, but they are powerless to evade the consequences of denialism. Surviving climate change, the sixth extinction event, and political insurrection requires the majesty of moral power aligned with the irresistible powers of wild nature.

Freedom requires a free people and a wild landscape. This requires a moral campaign that envisions an economy and a politics circumscribed by natural laws and limits. Any person who abides by nonnegotiable natural limits constitutes a majority of one already.

The Paper Plantation

We think it a settled principle, growing out of the nature of a well-ordered
society, that every holder of property, however absolute and unqualified may
be his title, holds it under the implied liability that his use of it shall be so
regulated that it shall not be injurious . . . to the rights of the Community.

Maine Supreme Judicial Court, 1908

The timber industry did not grant the Acadian forests a respite
after the barons and Bunyans went over the hump. In 1867,
scientists discovered how to make paper out of wood fiber.
Northern New England's forests abounded in the smaller
diameter softwoods desired by the new mills built along the region's
rivers. Papermakers especially valued the long fibers of red spruce for
pulping—the mechanical grinding or pressurized chemical cooking
processes that prepare wood fiber for papermaking.

Maine's great rivers offered cheap log transport, hydroelectric
power for the mills, abundant water for papermaking, and a convenient
dump for the mills' toxic sludge. In 1889, Maine's commissioner of Fish
and Game, E. M. Stilwell, blamed the collapse of the Atlantic salmon
population on pollution and the many dams between the ocean and
the salmons' spawning grounds. "No manufacturer of any kind whatever," he declared, "should be allowed to throw its waste into a river any
more than into our highways. No argument or demonstration is necessary here."[1] The state did not act, however; the salmon disappeared, and

paper mills externalized the costs of pollution onto the rivers, the fish, and the people of Maine. Jobs and profits prevailed over healthy rivers and public health.

Overproduction and falling prices plagued the era's undercapitalized paper mills. S. D. Warren's mill in Westbrook, Maine, outside of Portland, succeeded where others failed, adopting the latest technological advances at a steady, prudent pace. In 1873 Warren began to experiment with a chemical pulping process for papermaking. Four years later he had seven paper machines producing sixteen tons per day. After the depression of the 1870s, when its millworkers suffered two pay cuts, the S. D. Warren Company flourished. By 1880 the Westbrook mill was the largest of its kind in the world, employing eight hundred workers. It converted from water to steam power, and seven years later it began the conversion to hydroelectricity.

Warren built housing and community centers for his millworkers. But his paternalism came at a price: he and his successors kept the Warren mills nonunion until 1967; his managers dominated local and state politics; and Maine's seven-person Executive Council (a colonial-era body abolished in the 1970s) reserved a seat for the S. D. Warren mill. For decades, Maine governors vetoed any legislation the Warren interests deemed undesirable.[2]

Modernizers in the industry solved the problem of undercapitalization and disastrous price wars by consolidating many smaller firms. Hugh Chisholm, backed by Wall Street investors, merged twenty mills in Maine, New Hampshire, Vermont, New York, and Massachusetts to form International Paper in 1897–1898. The new conglomerate soon controlled 90 percent of the newsprint production in the eastern United States and turned a profit of nearly $3 million in its first year. Through careful investment and mill improvements, the company soon became the largest paper company in the world, a position it still enjoys.[3]

Garrett Schenck, Chisholm's right-hand man and an original member of International Paper's board, resigned to create a rival company, Great Northern. Schenck realized that a one-hundred-foot drop on the West Branch of the Penobscot provided an ideal location for a world-class pulp and paper mill. Construction of the town of Millinocket, a

dam on Millinocket Stream, and the Great Northern paper mill began
in March 1899. The mill began to produce paper in the fall of 1900, con-
suming 275 cords of pulpwood per day.[4]

Wall Street investors insisted the new corporations acquire vast
tracts of timberland to assure adequate supplies of pulpwood for their
mills. The timber barons happily unloaded their overcut forests. In
1899–1900, Great Northern acquired 252,000 acres in the West Branch
watershed for an average price of $4.14 an acre. By 1906, it owned
600,000 acres, and in 1929 the company controlled 1,354,513 acres in
the Penobscot and Kennebec watersheds. Eventually, Great Northern,
with 2.3 million acres, and International Paper, with another 1.5 million
acres, owned nearly one-fifth of Maine.[5]

Forester Philip Coolidge explained the logic behind these vast timberland holdings: "The companies found it expedient to own lands of
their own, if only to be in a position to bargain in buying wood. Often
it would cost more to conduct their own operations on their own lands,
but the fact that they could do this has enabled them to keep prices of
purchased wood within reason."[6] If smaller woodlot owners balked at
the low stumpage offered by the mill, the paper companies simply increased the cut on their own lands until the holdouts capitulated.

The paper companies quickly appropriated the timber barons'
veto power over Maine's legislature. They made certain that any legislation concerning taxes, rivers, and forest management benefited their
own interests—and those of their Wall Street investors. From 1920 to
1960 Maine led the nation in paper production.[7]

In 1903 forest fires burned almost 270,000 acres in Maine, including 220,000 acres in the industrial forest. Forest Commissioner Edgar
Ring, a timberman, turned the focus of the Forest Commission away
from controversies over unsustainable forestry and toward firefighting.
Farmers, urban dwellers, and manufacturers had long complained that
the timber owners were "tax dodgers" who did not pay their fair share
of taxes. They objected to increased state subsidies for fire prevention to
a private industry that would pocket the profits and continue to enjoy
special tax treatment. In 1906 the timberland owners delivered an "ul-
timatum"; they would agree to a wildlands tax surcharge, provided the
state dedicated it entirely to the suppression of forest fires.

(Copyright © Jon Luoma)

In 1909, the legislature abandoned nineteenth-century laissez-faire policies, established the Maine Forestry District, and redefined "conservation" in Maine to mean "fire-suppression."[8] State intervention in timber policymaking meant greater subsidies and lower taxes for the large landowners and paper mills, the defeat of popular proposals to regulate forest practices and mill pollution, and no public land acquisition.

Maine farmers had called for the regulation of reckless logging back in 1869: "We are but tenants of this beautiful earth, not owners in perpetuity." They argued that healthy forests were a public—common—right. George F. Talbot, an eastern Maine lumberman, warned, "to expect of men whose prudent judgement has led them to fortune, to make investments in enterprises, from which no substantial return is to be expected until after the lapse of a century, is making too large a demand upon the disinterestedness of human nature."[9] The legislature took no action.

In 1907 a muckraker blamed the large landowners for most of Maine's industrial problems. The state's forests, he wrote, were "held in the greedy grasp of an insolent and unscrupulous landed aristocracy."[10] Holman Day's 1908 novel *King Spruce* portrayed fictional barons such as "Stumpage John" Barrett and "The Honorable" Pulaski Britt as bullies who had stolen millions of acres of land from the public.

When conservationists introduced a bill to impose a minimum twelve-inch-diameter limit on pine and spruce cut, opponents howled that "the bill is unscientific; it is improperly and loosely drawn; it is freak legislation."[11] The legislature requested the Supreme Judicial Court's opinion on the bill's constitutionality. On March 10, 1908, the court ruled that Maine had the right to regulate cutting to prevent drought, protect soils, and preserve the water supply:

> We think it a settled principle, growing out of the nature of a well-ordered society, that every holder of property, however absolute and unqualified may be his title, holds it under the implied liability that his use of it shall be so regulated that it shall not be injurious to equal enjoyment of others having an equal right to the enjoyment of their property, nor injurious to the rights of the Community.
>
> While it might restrict the owner of wild and unculti-vated lands in the use of them, might delay his anticipated profits, and even thereby cause him some loss of profit, it would nevertheless leave his lands, their product and in-crease, untouched and without diminution of title, estate or quantity. He would still have large measure of control and large opportunity to realize values. He might suffer delay but not deprivation.[12]

For the next decade, legislators faithfully submitted bills to limit destructive forestry. The legislature rejected them all. To this day, despite the court's ruling, the state has passed no meaningful regulations to re-strict cut to less than growth—a basic measure of sustainable forestry.

Beginning in 1910, when an outbreak of spruce budworm ravaged the Acadian forest, industrial foresters discovered that manipulating venal legislators was an easier task than controlling natural forces un-leashed by a century of profligate cutting. By 1919, 27.5 million cords of softwood had been killed in Maine, and another 200 million cords had succumbed in eastern Canada. The budworm outbreak killed an esti-mated 75 percent of Maine's fir and 40 percent of its spruce.[13]

The inch-long budworm (*Choristoneura fumiferana*) is a natural predator of the spruce-fir forest. Budworm caterpillars initially attack the buds and cones of fir, spruce, and hemlock, with fir the clear favorite. As an outbreak persists, they devour enough foliage to kill trees and eventually seedlings and saplings. Surveyors in the Maine woods in the eighteenth century recorded observations of budworm outbreaks, but these generally localized, patchy events of short duration inflicted relatively little damage to mature, all-aged, mixed-species forests.

Forest ecologists believe that the budworm plays an important role in regulating the composition of spruce and balsam fir stands. Fir, a short-lived, sunlight-loving species, is much more aggressive in colonizing disturbed areas. In time, budworms feast on the fir and help to release the spruce understory.

Intensive logging in the nineteenth century had transformed the old growth Acadian forest into a very young, often even-aged forest. Balsam fir had become much more abundant, and the budworm responded as would any species when natural controls on its population are relaxed. Twentieth-century budworm outbreaks afflicted much greater areas, much more intensively, for much longer periods of time.[14]

Budworm predators—insectivorous birds, reptiles, and small animals—along with a decreasing supply of fir and spruce brought the outbreak to an end by 1919. Maine's forest commissioner Forrest Colby wrote: "With poison sprays and sticky paper we may account for a few bugs and flies; but we would soon be overcome without the aid of our many vigilant little allies—the insect hunting birds and many of the smaller animals and reptiles. So we may well give every protection and support to these busy little helpers that render such great assistance in keeping this insect peril in check." The sort of help the busy helpers would most appreciate is protection of their favored habitat—relatively undisturbed, older, all-aged forests.[15]

In August 1920, Percival Baxter, who became governor of Maine a few months later, climbed Mount Katahdin for the first time. It was "the hardest thing I ever undertook," he wrote a decade later. "While I was there that day, I said to myself, 'This shall belong to Maine if I live.' I have never lost sight of it."[16]

The timber and paper industry lobby stymied Governor Baxter's efforts to acquire Mount Katahdin with state funds. On October 8, 1927, the *Portland Press Herald* opined, "The silliest proposal ever made to a Legislature was that of Governor Baxter who advocated the State's buying Mount Katahdin and creating a state park."[17]

After Baxter left office in 1925, he devoted his life to buying timberland with his personal fortune. Late in 1930, Great Northern agreed to sell its interest in T3R9, Katahdin's township. Baxter paid $25,000 for 5,760 acres. However, he could not clear his title to Katahdin until September 1931 because of the complex ownership patterns developed by the nineteenth-century barons to minimize investment risks.

Baxter donated Katahdin to the state, stipulating that the land "shall forever be used for public park and recreational purposes, shall forever be left in the natural wild state, shall forever be kept as a sanctuary for wild beasts and birds, and that no roads or ways for motor vehicles shall hereafter ever be constructed thereon or therein."[18]

In November 1937 Baxter acquired Traveler Mountain, two townships north of Katahdin. During the next three years he consummated fifteen highly complex transactions with a variety of owners, so by the end of 1940 he had acquired well over one hundred thousand acres in part or in full. He resumed his land purchases in 1944, and by 1955 he had bought nearly two hundred thousand acres. One last purchase from Great Northern in 1962 rounded out his bequest to the state.

When Percival Baxter died in 1969 at age ninety-three, the *Portland Press Herald* saluted the former governor's vision, persistence, and generosity: "His action in acquiring the vast unspoiled area has been called an example of conservationist foresight not duplicated anywhere else in this country by one man." Governor Baxter's private wildlands philanthropy ensures his name will be remembered long after all other Maine governors are forgotten.[19]

The paper industry sank into the doldrums during the Depression, affording Maine's battered forests a brief hiatus from intensive logging. Even at reduced production levels, however, the paper mills discharged millions of gallons of toxic sludge and wastewater into rivers, transforming them into lifeless zones. The state permitted the mills to externalize the costs of protecting river water quality onto the public.

Low river flows on the Androscoggin and massive pollution discharges by paper mills in Jay and Rumford, Maine, and Berlin, New
Hampshire, produced a nauseating stench that assailed citizens of Lewiston and Auburn, Maine, during the summer of 1941. Hydrogen sulfide
fumes rising from the river tarnished metal and turned paint black half a
mile from the river. The three mills flushed as much waste into the river
as a city with 2.5 million residents. The dissolved oxygen content of the
Androscoggin dropped to zero. Aquatic and marine organisms, including trout, clams, lobsters, and the invertebrates they prey upon, could
not survive in this toxic soup. The river had become a public sewer.

The state filed a suit in the Supreme Judicial Court to require a reduction in mill discharges. The mills responded by forming a "Technical
Committee" of industry employees. After six years of inaction, the court
appointed a Bates College chemist, Walter Lawrence, to the post of River
Master to oversee a court-ordered cleanup. The Technical Committee
steered Lawrence in an industry-friendly direction and deftly controlled
the cleanup process for the next twenty-five years.

Lawrence and his industry helpers opted not to require a dramatic
reduction in mill effluent; instead, they dumped six thousand tons of
sodium nitrate into the river to add oxygen. When the scheme failed,
they installed aerators in the river to beat oxygen into the water. The
Maine Department of Environmental Protection persisted with this
failed strategy into the early 1990s.[20]

According to orthodox economics, it is rational for a paper mill to
discharge pollutants into the air and water because this is the least expensive method to dispose of the dirty by-products of papermaking—a
free solution to an expensive problem. It allows the manufacturer to *externalize* costs of production onto the environment and society, instead
of investing in methods of containment and prevention.

By condoning externalities, the government subsidizes polluters
and places profit-taking above ecological and public health. A century
ago, English economist A. C. Pigou proposed taxing externalities that
degrade the public commons and harm natural and human communities. Critics alleged this would lower productivity, pass costs on to consumers, slow economic growth, and increase governmental intrusion
into the free market.[21]

The market ignores evidence that there are limits to growth on a finite planet. It is concerned with reducing direct costs such as labor, raw materials, and transportation. It provides no information about the approaching scarcity of fish, timber, or clean water. Our accounting system ignores indirect costs such as water and air pollution, deforestation, erosion, illness, crime, unemployment, and poverty, often permitting the perpetrators of these harmful practices to externalize those costs onto the land and the public.

As America made the transition from the Depression to a war economy in 1940, prosperity returned to northern New England's paper industry. Over the next twenty-seven years, the number of logging and paper mill jobs in Maine increased from eighteen thousand to thirty-two thousand. Wage gains doubled labor's purchasing power, and benefits such as health care, vacation time, and pensions increased dramatically. The mills paid higher wages to their most skilled workers whose experience and knowledge were essential to the success of the mills. They invested in research, product development, and marketing, and they underwrote numerous community projects.

Beginning in the mid-1950s, several Fortune 500 companies bought Maine mills and their timberland holdings. Scott Paper acquired the Hollingsworth & Whitney Company mill in Winslow. Georgia Pacific purchased St. Croix's mill in Woodland in 1963. Four years later, Scott acquired S. D. Warren in Westbrook; Diamond International bought Penobscot Fiber in Old Town and Eastern Fine Papers in Brewer; and the Ethyl Corporation purchased Oxford Paper in Rumford. Ethyl sold to Boise Cascade in 1976.

The new owners reduced investment in research and development, took a more aggressive stance on union negotiations, and exhibited little interest in the welfare of mill communities. A former employee of the S. D. Warren mill mourned the change: "I felt it wasn't *family* anymore. That it was from out of town. . . . I felt that we'd been sold down the river. I wasn't too happy. . . . They *used us.* . . . They just milked us, I thought."[22]

After World War II, the paper industry began to build bigger, more modern mills in the South to take advantage of faster growing trees, lax environmental regulations, and docile labor. Scott's mill in Hinckley, Maine, is the only new paper mill built in the Northeast since 1970.[23] In the 1970s, the large paper companies began redirecting investment capital to mills far from northern New England. Deprived of adequate investment, the region's mills entered a period of irreversible decline.

In the quarter century following World War II, paper companies forced most loggers to become "independent contractors." They compelled workers to assume the costs for social security, unemployment taxes, workers' compensation insurance, and health-care coverage. Loggers did not receive New Deal–era benefits such as overtime, paid holidays, and vacations. The large landowners paid loggers by the piece rate—the more one cut, the more one made.

Contractors became responsible for the capital investment for skidders and other equipment. Before the advent of chainsaws in 1945, Yankee farmers and French-Canadian loggers still relied upon axes and handsaws, the same tools their grandfathers had used. Chainsaws, along with the skidder and the hydraulic loader, eliminated three-quarters of the labor time formerly required to cut and transport wood. Logger productivity doubled to about four or five cords per day. Fewer loggers cut more wood.

A former horse logger in Maine complained that his productivity increased with skidders and chainsaws, but his income did not: "you probably doubled or tripled your output, but you didn't have much more money when you were done than when you were cutting with the axe." To make payments on their expensive skidders, these "independent" loggers had to keep them running as much as possible: "The skidder didn't get tired. . . . A horse had to have his wind like you did. That's when things started going backwards. A man had to compete with a machine. That's where your injuries came in."[24]

The paper companies pitted loggers against each other bidding for jobs, which helped depress the price they paid for wood. Loggers had almost no bargaining power. John Sinclair, a longtime executive of Seven Islands, the company that manages a million acres owned by heirs of the nineteenth-century timber baron David Pingree, remarked in the 1970s, "You'll find that they do what we tell them." A 1974 study of Maine's paper industry observed: "If the woodsman, in getting low prices for his wood, and suffering all the consequences, is subsidizing the low cost of paper for the consumer, then this is an unfair subsidy and should be stopped."[25]

In the early 1970s, twenty-five hundred "bonded" Canadian loggers were working in the Maine woods. United States labor policy allowed employers to import "bonded" labor when domestic labor was unavailable to perform a job. Maine's large landowners abused this policy by offering wages too low for Maine loggers to support a family. The Canadian loggers enjoyed socialized medicine and other governmental benefits not available to US labor. The Maine Department of Labor listened to the large landowners, not the struggling Maine loggers who gladly would have taken these jobs if they had been paid a fair wage.[26]

By the mid-1970s, a quarter of Maine's loggers had fallen below the poverty line, and they were ineligible for most protections provided by labor laws. In 1975, with the price of wood about the same as it had been in the late 1940s, and their wages averaging about $4,000 to $5,000 per year, disgruntled loggers organized the Maine Woodsmen Association (MWA). The MWA believed that the companies colluded on wood prices and gave Canadian bonds superior stands of wood to cut as a means of discouraging Maine loggers from applying for these jobs. The MWA exposed how the large landowners were not, as the 1952 Immigration and Naturalization Act required, making a sincere effort to recruit US workers.

The MWA called for a strike in October 1975, and for two weeks, woodsmen picketed paper mills around the state. The companies refused to negotiate and secured an injunction against the MWA. The United Paperworkers International Union, representing millworkers, opposed the MWA strike because its militant stance clashed with the union's more compliant relations with the mill owners.[27]

Bill Butler, a burly contractor from Aurora and a leader in the MWA, later recalled that the group's response was "spontaneous and ill-prepared." They had little money and no organized support or experience in labor struggles, and strike leaders had not clearly identified what they hoped to accomplish.[28] The MWA opposed clear-cuts, herbicide spraying, and mechanized harvesting. Some grassroots activists, but no mainstream conservation group, supported the MWA. The paper companies, ultraconservative Maine governor James Longley, and a sympathetic judge broke the strike.

Afterwards, US senator William Hathaway convened a hearing on "Canadian Labor in the Maine Woods." The president of Great Northern claimed that loggers received $9.03 per hour at a time when paper mill workers' pay averaged $5.52 an hour. Loggers in the audience burst into laughter. When a large landowner claimed that Americans didn't want to work in the woods, Hathaway asked him, "But don't you agree that if you just paid them enough you could get all the Americans you needed?" He responded, "I presume that to be true."[29]

The landowners continued to squeeze local loggers; poor timber-dependent communities in the heart of the Maine woods continued to decline, and in the 1980s and 1990s schools began to close, the young moved away, and some small towns chose to disincorporate and turn local government over to the state.

The Budworm Made Me Do It

The entire watershed was clear-cut right to the very trickle of its headwaters.

MARTIN LEIGHTON, MAINE LOGGER

Red spruce can live four hundred years or longer. By 1980, four-fifths of the trees growing in Maine's forest were fewer than seventy years of age; trees growing at the time of the Civil War covered only about 1 percent of northern Maine.[1] After old growth spruce and pine disappeared, fir populations in the early 1970s increased substantially from presettlement forest levels.

Balsam fir is the preferred food of the spruce budworm. United States Forest Service researcher Marinus Westveld advised timberland owners in 1944 to remove fir at ten- to twenty-year intervals. Regular thinning of a stand's fir would reduce the forest's vulnerability to budworm and create openings for the more valuable, shade-tolerant spruce to exploit. However, his admonition "good forest management is good business" fell on deaf ears.[2]

The largest spruce budworm outbreak, affecting about 120 million acres in eastern Canada, Maine, and a portion of northern New Hampshire, began in 1972. The infestation reached epidemic status throughout Maine by 1975 and peaked in 1980–1981. The Maine state entomologist warned of "the grave and extensive holocaust posed to Maine forests by the budworm for 1975." He proposed a $3.6 million spray program with costs to be shared by the large landowners, supplemented by significant state and federal government subsidies.[3]

The state's choice to combat the smaller budworm outbreaks from 1954 to 1967, DDT, had by then been banned. In the 1970s new organo-phosphate and carbamate pesticides replaced DDT. Carbaryl was the active ingredient in Sevin-4-Oil, the pesticide favored by the budworm program. It is highly toxic to solitary bees, beetles, wasps, and spiders — the major budworm parasites or predators. It also caused significant de-clines in the fruit and seeds of a number of plant species important to birds and mammals. Pond and stream invertebrates, including mayflies, damselflies, dragonflies, caddis flies, and stoneflies, as well as amphi-pods (small crustaceans), disappeared after the spraying of Sevin-4-Oil. Low levels of carbaryl affected trout brain chemistry and behavior, lowering survival rates. A study conducted in Baxter State Park in 1982 determined that bird populations in unsprayed areas exceeded those inhabiting areas outside the park that had been "protected" from the budworm by spraying. Important budworm predators, such as Black-burnian, Cape May, and Bay-breasted warblers, declined.[4]

The spruce budworm program sprayed an average of 1.22 million acres annually from 1972 to 1985. At its peak, in 1976, Maine sprayed 3.5 million acres, including fifty acres belonging to a young organic farmer, Mitch Lansky. A few years earlier, Lansky had bought land abutting some industrial forestlands in Wytopitlock, a town about two hours north of Bangor. On a chilly June morning in 1976, a converted World War II bomber sprayed his crops, his spring, and his log cabin with Sevin-4-Oil. Thinking this was a hell of a birthday present, he con-tacted the Maine Forest Service, whose entomologist discovered dead insects and white spray droplets on Lansky's vehicles. The entomologist agreed he had a legitimate grievance.

"I responded as would any red-blooded American," Lansky later wrote. "I sued." He hired a lawyer and entered the Alice-in-Wonderland world of industrial forestry. Few opposed the spray program, and the state government's literature on the effects of spraying betrayed a heavy-handed bias for the interests of the pesticide manufacturers and absen-tee corporate landowners. He was flabbergasted when the Maine Audu-bon Society, the state's oldest conservation organization, testified at a legislative committee hearing in support of continued state funding of the spray program. An Audubon staff member justified the policy as a "realistic" trade-off to secure adequate monitoring of the impacts of the spraying. Lansky answered that more subsidies meant more spraying, not more monitoring.[5]

He settled his lawsuit out of court rather than play delaying games with corporate lawyers and used his small award to establish a grassroots organization, Protect Our Environment from Sprayed Toxins (PEST). Its members ("PESTs") conducted research, published articles and pamphlets, provided information to concerned citizens, attended hearings and conferences, and behaved as resistant pests by staging protests and confronting spray pilots at airports.

One PEST, the wife of a logger, spearheaded a petition drive to ban spraying in the towns of Wytopitlock, Drew, and Bancroft. These poor, rural, eastern Maine towns depended upon the timber industry for employment, yet 96 percent of their residents signed the petition. The leader of the Sportsman's Alliance of Maine opposed both herbicide and budworm spraying out of concerns for the impacts on wildlife. Trout Unlimited supported PEST. The state offered Lansky and other protesters half-mile buffers around their properties if they would drop their lawsuit challenging the Department of Conservation's inadequate buffer requirements. The PESTs laughed off the bribery attempt and persisted.

Accidents and illegal practices plagued the controversial spray program. A four-engine plane crashed into Eagle Lake in the Allagash Wilderness Waterway after dumping eleven hundred gallons of Sevin. Pilots routinely paid fines for dumping pesticides because of human error, mechanical failure, forced landings, and crashes.[6]

In the early 1980s the Reagan Administration ended federal subsidies to the spray program, and the widespread spraying diminished. It finally ceased when the budworm outbreak ended in 1986.

The timber industry views large natural disturbances, such as the spruce budworm outbreak, as economic catastrophes. Scott Paper, owner of nine hundred thousand acres in Maine in the upper reaches of the Kennebec River watershed and Moosehead Lake region, had introduced extensive clear-cutting in the 1960s. In the 1970s all the paper companies adopted the practice allegedly to *salvage* the economic value of budworm-infested stands; some landowners clear-cut entire town-ships. They also clear-cut stands and species unaffected by budworm. In the next three decades, Maine's large landowners built twenty-five thou-sand miles of logging roads—equivalent to the circumference of Earth at the equator—in the process of clear-cutting more than two thousand square miles of forest, an area the size of Delaware.

Clear-cutting removes most of the trees and leaves behind an in-adequately stocked forest stand. Owners of remote tracts justify clear-cutting as necessary to cover the costs of roads, camps, and transpor-tation of wood. But if lands cannot be managed *profitably and sustain ecosystem integrity,* they ought not to be logged at all.

To conceal the visual impacts of clear-cuts from a furious public, foresters left behind thin strips of trees along roads, rivers, and lake-shores. Loggers dubbed them "beauty strips." The industrial forester views clear-cuts as a public relations headache and beauty strips as a convenient aesthetic cover-up of the problem. They reassured the pub-lic speeding along Maine's roadways or paddling its rivers and lakes that all was well beyond the beauty strips.

The fabled Allagash River, protected since 1966 as the ninety-two-mile-long string-bean Allagash Wilderness Waterway, fell victim to the orgy of budworm-era clear-cutting. When the waterway was designated in 1970, Maine had promised to acquire 240,000 acres for it, but to date, it has purchased only about 24,000 acres.

The Allagash Wilderness Waterway nominally extends one mile from the water's edge into the surrounding forests, but the State of Maine owns only five hundred feet in from the shoreline. The state has jurisdiction over timber management plans within a mile of the wa-terway. On a trip down the Allagash in the fall of 1999, we camped at the breached Long Lake Dam. I walked east through the beauty strip precisely five hundred feet where I encountered a large clear-cut. Skid-der trails ran through wetlands, leaving ruts three-and-a-half feet deep. Moose tracks and scat abounded. Despite a heavy rain the previous night, the warm sun and wind had already parched the exposed soil. I observed patches of small, regenerating firs, but few spruce seedlings and saplings. I found a clump of eight-inch-diameter cedar and some scrawny poplar and birch. Occasionally, a white pine, approximately ten inches in diameter, survived. To the east, I spied a patchwork of recent and older clear-cuts. Goldenrod, purple aster, pearly everlasting, and other sun-loving vegetation grew along the roadside. There were no mature trees, nor anything resembling a forest stand.

Downstream of Round Pond, the Allagash turns sharply to the north where Musquacook Stream enters. Intensive logging several miles upstream had turned its waters brown. The contrast between the clear Allagash and the chocolate-soup feeder stream shocked us. The Bureau of Parks and Lands had ignored repeated reports of major siltation problems, preferring not to confront the large landowners.[7] Logging roads, the primary cause of erosion, may cover as much as 10 to 20 percent of an industrial forest operation.

The great conservationist David Brower often quipped, "Trees were invented by the soil so it wouldn't have to move." Soils of a mature forest stand absorb large volumes of water. Networks of fungal hyphae are sticky and hold soils together, increasing the volume of water soils can absorb. Clear-cuts and whole-tree harvests cause mycorrhizal networks to unravel, reducing the amount of water soils can retain.[8]

The ability of soils to intercept, hold, and filter water is compromised when logging removes much of the stand's vegetative cover. Snow melts faster; rainwater runs off more rapidly. Greater surface runoff increases soil erosion and the delivery of sediment into streams. The silt settling in slower water prevents fish eggs from hatching. Reduced runoff in summertime causes streams, stripped of their forest cover, to run too low and too hot to sustain trout populations. The heavy machinery used in intensive forest management operations compacts soils. Removal of most of the overstory and the loss of older tree age classes diminishes the accumulation of litter and coarse woody debris. Soil chemistry changes, and the loss of canopy closure increases soil temperatures and reduces its moisture content. Warmer soils accelerate the decomposition of downed, coarse, woody debris.[9] Large clear-cuts release carbon stored in aboveground trees, on the forest floor, and in soils. Cutting more than growth converts a forest from a carbon sink to a source.

A study authored by three University of Maine scientists states, "Amphibians form a large part of the vertebrate biomass in forested ecosystems in north-eastern North America and play an important role in ecosystem processes." The researchers determined that juveniles of the species under study were more abundant in unmanaged and partially cut stands than in clear-cuts. They warned that "if juvenile amphibians avoid settling in clear-cuts following dispersal [from the pools where they hatched], the available habitat is reduced, along with the population abundance."[10]

Logging during the past two centuries has radically diminished the vertical diversity of the all-aged, presettlement forest. Simplified forests support fewer species than vertically complex forests. Intensive, short-rotation logging disrupts the recovery of vertical diversity.[11] Habitat diversity in a post-clear-cut, even-aged forest remains low for decades. Recovery of mature and old growth forest conditions requires centuries.

Paper company foresters claim that if forests can recover from major natural disturbance events such as hurricanes and ice storms, they can recover from large clear-cuts. This is a deceptive analogy. The largest natural disturbance events have return times of one to several centuries, but industrial clear-cuts became the norm during the budworm era. University of Maine at Orono researchers determined that the mean gap size of small natural disturbance events ranges from less than 2 percent of an acre to about one-third of an acre, with return intervals of fifty to two hundred years. Clear-cuts of only a couple of acres are many times greater than most naturally caused gaps in the forest canopy. Natural disturbances in the Acadian forest leave all the organic material in the forest and diversify the landscape; clear-cuts homogenize it. Moreover, human-caused openings are an addition to, not a substitute for, naturally occurring disturbances.[12] Ice will still form; wind will still blow.

The university researchers criticized intensive industrial forest management: "If the goal is to emulate most northeastern natural disturbance regimes faithfully, then the majority of the landscape must be under some type of continuous-canopy, multi-aged silviculture that maintains ecologically mature structures at a finely patterned scale."[13] Paper industry foresters claimed that the clear-cuts were necessary to "salvage" the budworm-infested forest. They persuaded the general public that nature needs human intervention to recover from natural disturbances.

Harvard Forest researchers David Foster and David Orwig wrote in 2006 that many decisions to salvage "are based on the incorrect notion that forest ecosystems are damaged, destroyed, or impaired following a major disturbance and that this situation should be avoided or remediated." Areas affected by large natural disturbances, they reported, "exhibit low to modest disruptions of nutrient cycling and little nutrient loss because of rapid regeneration, recovery of leaf area and vegetation cover, and effective biotic control of microenvironmental conditions. In contrast, salvage and preemptive harvesting generate more rapid and extreme changes in microenvironment, forest cover, and soil litter and organic layer depth." Foster and Orwig concluded: "In many situations good evidence from true experiments and 'natural experiments' suggests that the best management approach is to do nothing."[14]

When the budworm threat ended in the mid-1980s, the massive industrial clear-cuts continued. If "the budworm made me do it" in the 1970s, economic expediency drove the post-budworm clear-cutting. In the 1980s and early 1990s, industrial foresters overcut cedar, yellow birch, paper birch, and sugar maple—species the budworm had ignored. In 1988 the State of Maine admitted that the industrial forest faced an acute shortfall of spruce and fir.[15]

Industry apologists dismissed the growing public outcry as a question of "aesthetics" raised by urban dwellers who failed to understand that ugly clear-cuts benefit forest health. Ron Lovaglio, a forester with International Paper and Maine's commissioner of conservation from 1995 to 2003, offered a novel take on the aesthetics issue. "[Clear-cutting] is like chemotherapy on cancer patients," he informed the authors of a 1986 *Maine Sunday Telegram* series on the crisis in Maine's paper industry. "It's not very pretty, your hair falls out. But when you're done, you're going to be proud."[16]

The massive clear-cuts failed to reverse the declining fortunes of Great Northern Nekoosa. Its president, Robert Bartlett, blamed the company's woes on foreign imports, depressed prices for newsprint, an oversupply of paper, and a strong US dollar. He brushed aside concerns of the looming shortfall: "There are more urgent problems than the resource question. . . . If we don't solve some of these other problems, we won't be around for the spruce-fir shortage."[17]

In 1986, after nearly two decades of controversy, unrestrained budworm-era forest practices provoked a rebellion in Maine. The Maine Audubon Society convened a working group to develop regulations to restrict the most extreme practices. Even before the group assembled, the society had expressed a willingness to accommodate clear-cuts as large as two hundred acres.[18]

Maine Audubon promoted incremental change. Between 1983 and 1986, its budget doubled. Scott Paper underwrote the society's wood chip boiler. International Paper helped fund a membership poster. Seven Islands and Boise Cascade signed on as corporate sponsors. Maine Audubon's board included the plant manager of the S. D. Warren paper mill in Westbrook. Its executive director said Maine Audubon was not primarily an advocacy group. It directed its efforts toward the most populous areas, and prior to 1986 industrial forestry issues to the north had been a low priority.[19]

In January 1987, neither Maine Audubon nor the Natural Resources Council of Maine opposed the nomination of Scott Paper's Robert LaBonta to become Maine's new commissioner of conservation. LaBonta had pioneered industrial-scale clear-cutting and herbicide spraying decades earlier. The Maine Audubon working group excluded Mitch Lansky, who had opposed the LaBonta nomination.

For the next three years, forest ecologists, industry leaders, and mainstream conservationists worked to develop consensus forest practices regulations. In the spring of 1989, the legislature passed the Maine Forest Practices Act (FPA). Subsequently, the Department of Conservation's industry-friendly definition of clear-cuts reclassified many large clear-cut areas as "selection" or "partial" cuts allowable under the new regulations. Industry lobbyists made certain the FPA did not address high-grading—"cut the best and leave the rest"—or loss of older age classes, forest structure, and dead standing and downed trees. The act overlooked degradation of water quality and soils. It ignored stand conversion that occurs when a clear-cut converts a softwood stand to low-quality hardwood. The FPA allowed industry to cut more than annual

High altitude photo of a massive clear-cut in Townships T4R14 and T4R15 in 1991. The clear-cut is about 4.5 miles long and 2.5 miles wide. The photo was taken by the National Aerial Photography Program. It appeared in Mitch Lansky's *Beyond the Beauty Strip* and in the inaugural issue of the *Northern Forest Forum* in Fall 1992.

growth. It reduced the share of taxes paid by large landowners for fire control from 50 to 25 percent, a friendly tax cut financed by the general public.[20] In a moment of candor, Ted Johnston, executive director of the Maine Forest Products Council, told me that the FPA was "what *we* told them [Maine conservationists] *they* could have."

Martin Leighton began working in the north Maine woods at age five, picking spruce gum and fiddleheads. Over the course of six decades, he trapped, guided, and worked as a horse logger and a scaler. Leighton described the consequences of the mechanized clearing of almost all of Great Northern's township T4R14 (approximately twenty-seven-thousand acres in size) during the budworm era:

> Ragmuff Stream runs into the West Branch of the Penobscot River below Hannibal Crossing. Its entire watershed is flat land and had a great growth of softwood. This area was made to order for the harvester. Here is where it went to work. The entire watershed was clear-cut right to the very trickle of its headwaters. Prior to this, people canoeing the West Branch paddled or poled up this beautiful stream. Now in the spring runoff, it runs bank full, as long as the melting snow is feeding it. It quickly diminishes after that. Now in the summer, you can leave your canoe where the stream meets the river and walk the streambed. You will see, except for the meaningless little strip of trees on each bank, stumps and herbicided clear-cuts everywhere. It's a good candidate for the worst example of clear-cutting on Earth. [21]

The Sum of the Parts

*If this deal is indicative of the future of conservation efforts, then forest land
and wilderness are in serious trouble.*

LEWISTON (MAINE) *Sun Journal,* 1989

Recreational use of northern New England's industrial forest
had intensified in the 1970s and 1980s following the completion of the interstate highway system and the construction
of tens of thousands of miles of logging roads. Land along
lakeshores, riverbanks, or scenic views fetched prices far in excess of the
timber value. Conservationists and timber industry leaders worried that
developers might begin to outbid timber investors for lands the paper
industry increasingly viewed as nonstrategic.

In 1977, the Carter Administration had ordered the US Forest
Service to assess roadless areas in eastern national forests to determine
whether they qualified for wilderness designation. When the Forest Service recommended no new wilderness additions to the Green Mountain
National Forest, grassroots activists in Vermont secured protection for
forty thousand acres of designated wilderness.

The White Mountain National Forest (WMNF) contained 350,000
acres of roadless lands. The Forest Service nominated 163,000 of those
acres for wilderness consideration. The Forest Society's Paul Bofinger
and the state's timber industry wished to retain high-value timber stands
as managed forest. The Appalachian Mountain Club opposed wilderness designation where it required removing one of the club's lucrative
huts. A coalition of the state's conservation and timber industry leaders

countered with a proposal to designate only 77,000 acres—generally land with low economic value—as wilderness.[1]

After a protracted lobbying fight with national environmental organizations, the New Hampshire Wilderness Act of 1984 codified the coalition's proposal. The WMNF was one of the few national forests where Congress designated fewer acres of wilderness than the Forest Service had recommended during the planning process.[2] Following the announcement of the Diamond land sale, New Hampshire conservationists were in no mood for a resumption of the utilitarian-preservationist debate.

Jim Wemyss Sr. had bought the rat-infested Groveton, New Hampshire, paper mill in 1940, revived it, and diversified its product line.[3] In the 1960s, his son doubled the size of the mill. Young Jim, weary of battling his irascible father over how to finance the investments necessary to compete in rapidly globalizing paper markets, engineered a merger of the family operations with Diamond International in 1968. Following the merger, the younger Wemyss joined Diamond's board of directors and became vice president in charge of its paper division.

Sir James Goldsmith, an Anglo-French financier with no prior experience in the paper industry, launched a four-year hostile takeover bid of Diamond in 1978. "Diamond was a fantastic company until Jimmy Goldsmith came along," Jim Wemyss Jr. told me. "You know what was wrong with Diamond? We were too rich. We had no debt. We had four million acres of land on our books for $25 an acre. We were a very, very successful company. Any company like that was a target for these people. You couldn't stop them." I asked why Diamond valued its timberland at a fraction of its market value. "The trees are growing every day, and so their value is increasing every day," Wemyss explained. "You don't have to report it as income on your company and pay taxes on it." When the company sold timber or land, it paid taxes at lower capital gains rates rather than as income. Large paper companies abused the capital gains provision, and some, such as Diamond, paid the price.

Goldsmith and his merchant-banker colleague, Ronald Franklin, exploited this industry accounting practice. They understood they could acquire Diamond's stock at a premium price, spin off its nontimberland assets, and retire their debt. A subsequent sale of the forestlands would earn them a massive profit. Franklin later explained: "Diamond interested us because of our philosophy which pervaded everything we did in America: that the sum of the parts of most conglomerates was worth a great deal more than the whole. The attraction of Diamond was that it was a conglomerate and because it was particularly safe because of the timber."[4] In economics, as Goldsmith and Franklin pointed out, the sum of the parts is greater than the whole. But in wild nature the whole is greater than the sum of its parts. Managing forest ecosystems by Wall Street values has consequences.

As Diamond fought for survival, mill employees in remote Groveton worked on, barely aware that their community was a pawn in the game of global finance. Ted Caouette, a paper machine operator, recalled: "The guys on the machine knew there was something going on, and you'd hear rumors here and there, but no, we just did our job, and waited to see what was going to happen; just do your job and that was it."

Young Jim Wemyss, born and bred a papermaker, led the Diamond board's resistance to Goldsmith. He urged his fellow members, who were intent on maximizing their return on investment, to consider the rights of current and retired employees: "I couldn't get rid of Jimmy Goldsmith. I tried, but nobody would support me. I knew what he was trying to do. The board's position was: let the stockholders vote. If you don't allow that to happen, you're depriving the stockholders. They just, 'I'll take the money,' and the people that are working there—'The hell with them. They lose their job, but I've got my money.' And I don't like that." Thirty years later, Jim Wemyss Jr. was still furious: "Jimmy Goldsmith didn't even know where Groveton was. Never did know to the day he died."

Goldsmith moved quickly to pay off his high-interest debt. Soon after completing the takeover, he sold Diamond's paper division to James River Corporation of Richmond, Virginia, a young, fast-growing conglomerate that generally eschewed owning timberlands. He retained Diamond's lands, valued at more than $700 million. Goldsmith briefly contemplated developing the land but concluded it was too great a risk. He sold the lands to Cie (Compagnie Générale d'Electricité, CGE), a

French communications corporation, late in 1987, realizing a profit of close to half a billion dollars. CGE soon announced the Diamond lands were for sale.

Following Goldsmith's takeover of Diamond International, the region's traumatized paper industry understood it faced an existential crisis. Along with their pulp and paper mills, huge, out-of-state corporations owned 7.7 million acres in Maine in 1988, 500,000 acres in northern New Hampshire, and 300,000 acres in Vermont's Northeast Kingdom.

Wall Street analysts criticized paper companies for poor profitability and advised them to convert undervalued forestland into cash. Between 1982 and 1987, the American pulp and paper industry sold one-third of its productive capacity to avoid the threat of takeover. International Paper created a landholding subsidiary that paid lower taxes than the parent company. Many paper companies sold off "nonstrategic" lands. Others liquidated their standing timber, thereby devaluing their land and stock and diminishing the threat of takeover.[5] Economists view such behavior as "rational," but others wonder: Is it rational to degrade wild nature to create wealth?

Early in 1987, Paul Bofinger heard unsettling rumblings from the paper industry up north. He helped secure funding for forest economist Perry Hagenstein to study the new pressures facing the region's largest landowners. Hagenstein's report predicted a flood of major land sales in northern New England over the next twenty years.[6] He did not mention the sharp decline in investments in the region's aging paper mills beginning in the 1970s.

When Claude Rancourt, an unknown French-Canadian construction worker turned developer from Nashua, New Hampshire, acquired the New Hampshire and Vermont Diamond lands for the asking price of $19 million, New Hampshire's political and conservation elites were flabbergasted. Paul Bofinger later told me, "I just couldn't believe that someone would pay that kind of money."

One of the Rancourt partners wished to develop twenty-eight hundred acres of Diamond lands in Bethlehem, New Hampshire. A day after the sale, Rancourt informed Bofinger he had no interest in retaining the other eighty-seven thousand acres. Within days, New Hampshire senator Warren Rudman submitted a $9 million request to the Senate Interior Committee. State leaders and conservationists met with Rancourt on June 9 to explore the possibility of public acquisition.

Rancourt demanded $500 an acre. Years later Bofinger called the negotiations brutal. He had always respected hard bargainers, except on this occasion. He and Rudman knew they could not secure enough funding to acquire all Diamond lands, so they concentrated on the Nash Stream watershed because they could protect an entire mountain valley.[7] Rudman managed to modify the WMNF purchase boundary to include the Nash Stream, and he threatened to ask the Forest Service to invoke eminent domain if Rancourt refused to drop his asking price.

Pending an independent appraisal of the land's value, Rancourt agreed to sell the Nash Stream, some in-holdings in the WMNF, and several smaller parcels identified by The Nature Conservancy as habitat for rare, threatened, or endangered species and natural communities. The appraisal came to $12.75 million, or $283 an acre. Early in July, the parties signed a legal agreement. Rancourt Associates turned a profit of $3.1 million on lands it had owned for only a couple of months. The public unnecessarily paid an extra $72 an acre because the state's conservation and political elites had dismissed calls to buy the Diamond lands three months earlier.

Even though the US Forest Service provided a third of the funds for the acquisition, New Hampshire would own the Nash Stream. To resolve the delicate matter of joint state-federal ownership, Governor John Sununu arranged for the state to sell the Forest Service a conservation easement on the entire Nash Stream tract. New Hampshire eventually paid $7.65 million from the Land Conservation Investment Program, and the additional $5.1 million came from the Forest Service budget. The WMNF purchased 4,496 acres for $1.175 million. Initially, the Forest Society and The Nature Conservancy loaned the state $3.925 million to complete the purchase of the Nash Stream watershed. In 1989, the state repaid the loan with interest.[8]

Easements had been devised to halt development in areas where suburban sprawl threatened to eliminate a town's last remaining farmlands and forestlands. Most easements covered 100 to 200 acres; in 2000 the Forest Society held about five hundred easements, with an average size of 156 acres.[9] Easements were untested on tracts of tens of thousands of acres.

For the price of $3.95 million, approximately $100 per acre, the US Forest Service acquired a conservation easement from the State of New Hampshire in August 1989. The easement assured perpetual protection of the Nash Stream Forest ecosystem and a variety of public uses, specifically, "forest products consistent with the traditional uses of the land, including public access, and the conservation of other resource values."[10]

The primary purpose of a conservation easement is to thwart development. More than one hundred camps already ringed the shores of the tract's ponds and the Nash Stream Bog, created by a nineteenth-century dam to provide water for log drives to the Groveton sawmills. The dam had been breached by a flood in May 1969 and never rebuilt. The state notified the camp owners that all Nash Stream camps would be removed by 2039.

Several members of Congress criticized the easement, believing that Sununu's deal circumvented the will of Congress. It had appropriated federal funds to help expand the WMNF, not extinguish development rights.[11] Southern New Hampshire residents complained they had received too little of the Trust for New Hampshire Lands funding. Many observers believed that the state had bought the lands to prevent development and the Forest Service easement was unnecessary.

The Lewiston (Maine) *Sun Journal* editorial writer called the deal a "farce," writing: "With such a hefty profit in a short period of time, you'd think that a better deal could have been struck to save Nash Stream. Contrary to what Sununu says, the deal is more a model for how not to protect wilderness. . . . If this deal is indicative of the future of conservation efforts, then forest land and wilderness are in serious trouble."[12] Few observers realized that large easements had just become the major conservation tool in northern New England for years to come.

In the summer 1988 issue of *Forest Notes*, a quarterly publication of the Forest Society, Martha Carlson wrote that "many North Country observers" feared additional large timberland sales in the coming years:

"There are more questions than answers now, but one thing is certain: Saving the North Country will require an effort of the magnitude of the Weeks Act. At least." Paul Bofinger subsequently described a culture he viewed as endangered: "The character I'm speaking of is a way of life— the people in their checkered shirts and their boots and their pickup trucks. You know what I mean. We have to preserve that. We don't want to bring in a lot of conventional tourist facilities and put those people to work as chambermaids for minimum wage."[13]

Conservationists worried that development pressures in southern Maine and New Hampshire in the 1980s could soon expand to the north. Perry Hagenstein reported that the large landowners were contemplating new opportunities for selling lands to developers, adding, "It is in New England's long-term interest to help maintain the integrity of the large forest holdings." He meant economic, not ecological, integrity. To maintain the status quo, Hagenstein advised New England's conservation community to take the lead in developing "support for the present kinds of ownership, although not necessarily for all present management practices." He added: "The continued ownership and management of these lands for timber, wildlife, and related resources should be encouraged by public and private initiatives. Such efforts should not be aimed at preserving areas in their natural state. Rather, they should encourage current and subsequent landowners to continue to hold forest lands in large tracts in order that their existing uses can be continued." He dismissed federal land acquisition as controversial and suggested that easements might induce large landowners to surrender their development rights. He urged the states to seek *federal* funding for landowner incentives.[14]

During the intense negotiations with Rancourt and the Forest Service, Bofinger and Fred Kocher, Senator Rudman's chief of staff in New Hampshire, discussed additional measures the conservation community and Congress could undertake. "Why don't we create a task force to take a look at this sort of thing to see what would happen?" Kocher suggested.[15] They agreed upon the need to involve the governors of Maine, New Hampshire, and Vermont, and after some discussion, they included 7.6 million acres in New York's public-private Adirondack

Park and the Tug Hill region in the proposed Northern Forest Lands Study (NFLS).

The Adirondacks are ecologically similar to northern New England's spruce-fir forests, and paper companies collectively owned more than a million acres within the park. In other respects, the contrasts between Maine and New York were striking. Only 5.3 percent of Maine's fifteen million acres in the study area belonged to the public, and logging continued on most of the state's forestlands, albeit not as intensively as lands owned by paper companies and large nonindustrial owners. Designated wilderness covered only 1 percent of Maine, whereas more than one-third of New York's NFLS lands belonged to the public and was designated as "forever wild."

Congress established the NFLS on September 27, 1988. It appropriated $250,000 to the US Forest Service "for a study of the timberland resources in New York, Vermont, New Hampshire, and Maine." Congress expected the four states to "spend an equal amount." The congressional directive to the NFLS cited fears of change in forestland ownership, threats of subdivision and development, and the "loss of traditional economic and recreational uses of these lands."[16]

The NFLS was an unprecedented collaboration between the federal government and the four Acadian forest states. Steve Harper, its director, had overseen the development of the progressive ten-year management plan for the Green Mountain National Forest. He brought along two talented young Forest Service staffers, Laura Falk and Ted Rankin.

Congress required the NFLS to work with a twelve-member Governors' Task Force on Northern Forest Lands (GTF) "to assure that the region's interests were well represented." Each governor would appoint three members to the GTF: a large landowner, a conservationist, and an employee of state government. Congress expected task force members to represent the interests and concerns of their governors; convene public input sessions; share information on state forest programs, forest economics, and conservation; and assist in analyzing and interpreting information gathered for the NFLS.

The northern forest region stretches 450 miles from eastern Maine to New York's Adirondack Park and Tug Hill region. The twenty-six-

(Copyright © Rachel O'Meara)

million-acre NFLS area was home to fewer than one million people, and it included no cities. Paper mill jobs paid the highest wages in the region.

Congress directed the NFLS to assess the natural and human forces that had shaped the region and the trends then threatening the status quo. Thanks to lobbying by The Wilderness Society, the study was directed to identify "alternative strategies to protect the long-term integrity of traditional uses of such lands. Specifically, the alternative conservation and management strategies shall consider a sustained flow of renewable resources in a combination which will meet the present and future needs of society, permanent public access for recreation, protection of fish and wildlife habitat, preservation of biological diversity and critical natural areas, and new State or Federal designations."[17]

The congressional directive called upon the NFLS to inventory and assess the current status of the ecological and economic diversity of the study region. It challenged the NFLS to answer a series of questions: How did a score of large landowners, including eight Fortune 500 corporations, come to own 9.7 million acres of forestland in the region? How have the owners managed these lands? What are the likely changes in the ownership and conditions of these lands? How will anticipated changes in landownership affect the land health, regional economy, and distinctive culture of remote, timber-dependent communities?

Maine covered 60 percent of the NFLS area. The state's political and timber elites initially expressed skepticism. For nearly a century, the paper industry had fended off efforts to regulate its pollution, forest degradation, and biocide spraying with the claim that such efforts would destroy jobs.

In spring 1987, International Paper, the second largest landowner in Maine, provoked a strike at its Jay mill. The company had bestowed a 38 percent pay raise upon management prior to proposing a 13 percent cut in wages. The company demanded the unions accept the elimination of five hundred jobs by outsourcing maintenance work and increasing productivity. It insisted the unions surrender the Christmas holiday and keep the mill running 365 days a year.[18]

International Paper knew the unions would reject its demands. Before contract negotiations, it constructed a fence around the mill and installed temporary housing inside the fence for nonunion replacement workers. The company also beefed up its security forces and hired a southern company to supply replacement workers. Members of Local 14 of the United Paperworkers International Union and Local 246 of the International Brotherhood of Firemen and Oilers rejected the company's offer in a near-unanimous vote. The strike began on June 16, 1987.

International Paper imported inexperienced labor to replace some of the strikers, eventually employing 970 nonunion workers. Strikers, some with forty years of service, bitterly complained that the company "stole" their jobs and gave them to scabs. One asked, "How heartless, how cruel can a company be?"

The company also pressured the town of Jay to reduce its property tax rate, and it lobbied the state of Maine to weaken environmental regulations and reduce workers' compensation rates. These actions shredded the bonds between mill owners and the community but united the citizens of Jay. The union held Wednesday evening meetings to keep spirits up, pass along information, organize, resist, and establish a food bank. Sympathetic unions from around the country sent contributions to the strike fund. Representatives of Locals 14 and 246 traveled around the state and the nation to share their story with other communities. The strikers adopted the motto "Stop Corporate Greed."

When the wife of a shop steward for Local 14 suffered a brain aneurysm two months into the strike, the union sponsored a benefit for the family. One striker gave them his strike pay. A supporter from Mobile, Alabama, made their house payment.

During the strike, several serious environmental accidents occurred, including a 16.6-million-gallon wastewater spill into the Androscoggin River—the largest spill in Maine's history. A broken valve released 121,000 gallons of chlorine dioxide from a storage tank and forced four thousand people to evacuate. Fortunately, the accident occurred in winter. If temperatures had been above 50 degrees, lethal chlorine dioxide gas would have formed. International Paper treated these episodes as public relations headaches and blamed the messengers. "It's not just the media," Joe Bean, the company's safety supervisor, responded. "It's the whole goddamn town." He added, "I can guarantee this is a far safer place than it was [prestrike]."[19]

The strikers voted in a new board of selectmen. It passed a strong environmental ordinance, hired an environmental enforcement officer, subjected the mill to its first reassessment in a dozen years, and raised the mill's property tax bill by 15 percent. Maine's governor, John R. "Jock" McKernan, whose brother lobbied for the paper industry, sided with International Paper.

The establishment of the NFLS coincided with attempts by Maine's commissioner of conservation, Robert LaBonta, to defang the looming

Maine Forest Practices Act. He was in no mood to tolerate Washington bureaucrats meddling in the state's industrial forest. LaBonta and his former industry colleagues opposed federal regulation of forest practices in Maine or federal acquisition of any lands currently owned by the large landowners. The week the NFLS authorizing legislation passed, Maine indicated it would refuse to participate.

On October 4, 1988, senators Patrick Leahy and Warren Rudman sent a letter to the chief of the Forest Service, purportedly to clarify the mission and operation of the NFLS but in reality to reassure LaBonta and secure Maine's participation. The key passage in this letter read: "The current land ownership and management patterns have served the people and forests of the region well. We are seeking reinforcement rather than replacement of the patterns of ownership and use that have characterized these lands."[20] LaBonta relented, and Maine joined the NFLS. This Faustian bargain effectively bestowed veto power over the work of the Governors' Task Force to the executive director of the Maine Forest Products Council.

For the next six years, conservationists and engaged citizens demanded that the NFLS, and its successor the Northern Forest Lands Council, carefully examine the assumption that these large landowners had served the region well. Agents of the industry vetoed any such inquiry.

On October 10, 1988, six days after the Leahy-Rudman letter appeased Maine, International Paper crushed the sixteen-month Jay strike. The national leadership of the United Paperworkers International Union voted, without consulting the two locals, to call off the strike. One angry striker asserted: "*Our local won the strike.* It was the bastards at headquarters that did us in. In my opinion, the top union leaders were in cahoots with International Paper." The company rehired less than 10 percent of the strikers.

Ignoring the Problem Will
Not Make It Go Away

The public's inability to respond to the sale of land that might be suitable for
public ownership in a timely fashion . . . means that an important potential
owner of the Northern Forest is largely excluded from the market.

Northern Forest Lands Study, 1990

With Maine's agreement to participate in the Northern
Forest Lands Study, Steve Harper and his Forest Service staffers Laura Falk and Ted Rankin adopted an
ambitious work plan. They soon circulated a most
helpful map of the landownership patterns in each of the four northern
forest states. About two score absentee owners of large tracts—paper
companies, heirs of timber barons, and timberland investors—owned
13.3 million acres. Smaller landowners, a preponderance of whom lived
on their lands, held title to 8.4 million acres, usually in blocks of fewer
than 100 acres to a few thousand acres. New York State owned 2.8 million acres of "Forever Wild" forestlands in the Adirondack Park. In
northern Maine, New Hampshire, and Vermont only 1.2 million acres
were in public ownership within the study area. Less than one-third of
these lands was designated as wilderness.[1]

Early in the process Harper's team collaborated with the Governors' Task Force to develop a vision for the region's future: "The
forests—including the air, water, soil, plants, and animals—must
be healthy and available for all to enjoy." Maintaining a forest-based

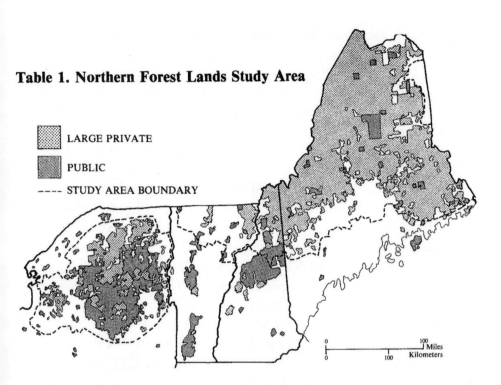

Table 1. Northern Forest Lands Study Area

LARGE PRIVATE

PUBLIC

---- STUDY AREA BOUNDARY

Figure 1. Land Ownership in the Study Area (Thousands of Acres)					
	Maine	New Hampshire	New York	Vermont	Total
PRIVATE LAND					
Industrial	7,700	500	1,200	300	9,700
Large Non-Industrial	3,100	50	500	50	3,600
Other Private	3,400	350	3,100	1,550	8,400
Total Private Land	14,200	900	4,800	1,900	21,800
PUBLIC LAND					
State	700	50	2,800	90	3,700
Federal	80	200	0	6	300
Total Public Land	800	300	2,800	100	4,000
TOTAL AREA	15,000	1,200	7,600	2,000	25,800

Data from 1987 and 1988

Map produced by the Northern Forest Lands Study, October 1988. (Published
in Stephen C. Harper, Laura L. Falk, and Edward W. Rankin, *The Northern
Forest Lands Study of New England and New York* [Rutland, VT: Forest Service,
US Department of Agriculture, 1990], x)

economy, the vision warned, requires the improvement of "certain of the economic, social, and environmental factors which affects peoples' lives. . . . Achieving this vision will demand new imaginative and perhaps radically different thinking and doing. People . . . will have to adopt a common will and work for a common cause. . . . If land is to be maintained in essentially private ownership, private companies will have to become partners with residents and governments in an unprecedented commitment to conservation."[2]

Carl Reidel, who represented Vermont's conservation interests on the GTF, hailed the optimism of the early days of the NFLS: "This may well be the most cooperation we've seen in New England since the Revolutionary War."[3] A meeting in Maine, however, soon dashed those hopes.

When Reidel and his fellow task force conservationists, New Hampshire's Paul Bofinger and New York's George Davis, urged the GTF to develop recommendations for public acquisition and land-use planning, Ted Johnston of the Maine Forest Products Council labeled the idea a threat to his constituency's "property rights," and the Maine delegation threatened to pull out of the study. The GTF capitulated and abandoned efforts to assess the status of biological diversity in favor of just holding the group together. Reidel later wrote that the GTF coalesced around a work plan "to limit discussions to economic assistance for private owners, limited state purchases of easements on critical lands, and other government incentives to maintain traditional patterns of private ownership and land use without major public acquisitions."[4]

The conservationists called for drawing a green line around the northern forest to enable the federal government to restrict the costs of the timber industry's coveted tax cuts to a four-state region, rather than all fifty states. Johnston, backed by Maine's new commissioner of conservation, Ed Meadows, quickly vetoed discussion of the idea. Johnston, who claimed that federal land managers "don't manage well," once told Reidel, "My principal task on this task force is to be damn sure that neither a green line or any new federal reserves are recommended."[5] The GTF acquiesced.

The New Hampshire delegation to the GTF convened a public information session in Lancaster late in January 1989. Only a handful of citizens, most with ties to the timber industry, turned out to testify. Champion International was then cutting its New Hampshire lands at twice the rate of annual growth. From 1988 until 1992, it cut an average of 115,000 cord equivalents a year, more than double the average annual growth. It cut 140,000 cord equivalents in 1991 and 150,000 in 1992, nearly triple the average annual growth. A Champion forester urged the NFLS to uphold the status quo: "The system works, so why fool with it?"[6]

The president of a small wood products firm in Gorham warned, "wilderness is bad." Active forest management, he claimed, "improves the beauty and health of the forest while providing an improved habitat for a more diverse wildlife habitat." He did concede we need better forest management. His recommendation to the study was that "better support and tax incentives to the timber industry" would encourage landowners to retain timberlands.

A leading Coös County politician proclaimed, "We have done an excellent job of managing forestlands in the past." He opposed calls to buy the land with federal dollars, citing Reagan-era federal deficits, but he coveted federal tax breaks for large landowners to prevent future land sales.

My colleague Jeff Elliott challenged the NFLS to assess the ecological consequences of cutting more wood than was currently growing. He rejected the claim that prevailing, unrestrained clear-cuts represent the ecological status quo, asserting that the status quo is not clear-cuts, but "natural succession, which is slowly expressing itself toward more biodiversity, more species."

A heckler shouted, "What are your thoughts on landownership patterns?" Jeff responded: "My concern is the mismanagement, whether private or public ownership. Private ownership doesn't give you the right to abuse the land. You have no right to destroy streams to downstream use. You have no right to dispose of toxic waste in the watershed. I am not against jobs, but if you don't take care of this land, you are going to lose the diversity and the trees, and then where are you going to work?"

My former colleague at the *Democrat*, Peter Riviere, asked the task force members whether the NFLS would require large landowners to practice sound forestry or guarantee that they not develop the timberlands in return for tax breaks, incentives, and other public subsidies.

He summed up the industry strategy for the NFLS: subsidies without strings; representation without taxation.

At Lyndonville the following week, some landowners expressed fears of a federal land grab. Vermont's director of the Agency of Natural Resources, Mollie Beattie, reassured them that the NFLS had no authority to buy land from unwilling sellers. A landowner had recently said to her, "My land is not for sale . . . how much are you offering?"

I was unaware of the Maine delegation's veto powers when I organized a protest against clear-cutting to greet GTF members arriving for their April 1989 meeting at the Forest Society's headquarters in Concord. Several protesters remained for the meeting. A New York timber industry lobbyist complained that the public had a poor understanding of the paper industry. "The image thing," he fretted, "is slipping." A paper industry forester denied that his employer was "denuding" the forest and suggested that industry deserved more "recognition for doing a good job." Both industry spokesmen called for additional incentives for industry, especially more tax cuts.

I reminded the GTF of the wording of the congressional authorization for the NFLS and insisted it address clear-cutting, protection of biodiversity, and public lands acquisition. "That is not our mandate," Johnston asserted, and the discussion returned to tax breaks.

From the outside looking in, I believed the federal government's representatives had acquiesced to the Maine delegation's list of taboo subjects. Unbeknownst to me, the Forest Service staff quietly ignored many of Meadows's and Johnston's efforts to control the NFLS agenda.

In August, Mitch Lansky and I spent a couple of nights in Baxter State Park's recovering wilderness. When we exited the west gate, we entered the surreal landscape of the industrial working forest. Great Northern had transformed Thoreau's "mossy and moosey" forest into clearings covered by brown, parched soils. The landscape was virtually free of trees, except for a lonely white birch here and there, leafless in the late summer sun, a victim of post-clear-cutting herbicide spraying. Few members of the public—or the GTF—had ever traveled into these remote regions.

Eventually, Mitch and I arrived at the five-thousand-acre Big Reed Forest Reserve, the largest old growth stand in New England. The contrast from the no-growth to old-growth chastened us. Here, we discovered a "damp and shaggy wilderness."[7] Moss-covered snags and dead logs, ideal for cavity nesting birds and mammals, abounded. The wild beauty of Big Reed affirmed that aesthetics matter.

Softwood stands, dominated by red spruce, cover one-third of the forest. Sugar maple, yellow birch, and beech are the most prevalent species in hardwood stands that cover 10 percent of the reserve. Six percent of the territory is classified as cedar swamp, where northern white cedar is plentiful. Half of the forest is a mix of hardwoods and softwoods. Other species of note include balsam fir, white spruce, red maple, white pine, and hop hornbeam. Researchers have recorded few sun-loving, shade-intolerant species such as aspen or paper birch.[8]

On the north shore of Big Reed Pond white cedar and red spruce predominated. Spruce, fir, and a modicum of cedar formed the understory. We encountered a recent, extensive blowdown of fir. It was nearly impossible to hike in and around this chaos of uprooted trees. Green vegetation covered the ground. Raspberries flourished. Seedlings, suppressed by the larger trees, shot upward. Soils had not been compacted, exposed, desiccated, blown away, or poisoned. Albeit a hiker's nightmare, the tangled mess provided food and cover for wildlife.

I returned to Maine early in September to join Mitch and his wife, Sue Szwed, on a flight with aerial photographer Alex MacLean over the industrial forest. We flew over eastern Maine and then up beyond Baxter State Park into the heart of the industrial forest as far as Churchill Dam on the Allagash. Alex's pictures documented the extent of the industrial clear-cuts. One weird opening resembled the state of Texas. Eerie "beauty strips," perhaps fifty feet wide, along the banks of rivers and shores of lakes, hid clear-cuts extending hundreds of acres. Alex later shared many of his slides with Jeff Elliott and me.

Georgia Pacific, the world's third largest timber company, announced late in October 1989 it had commenced a hostile takeover of Great Northern Nekoosa, the once-proud symbol of Maine's paper industry. Georgia Pacific coveted Great Northern's holdings in the southeastern United States, not its troubled Maine operations. The two Millinocket-area mills ranked seventh and eighth in profitability of Great Northern's ten mills. From 1979 to 1988, their contribution to the company's profits had declined from 45 to 5 percent.

During the 1980s, Great Northern had withheld needed investments to upgrade the ninety-year-old Millinocket mill. Corporate headquarters had closed six of its eleven paper machines between 1985 and 1989 and laid off 30 percent of its workforce. Great Northern had spent $200 million in 1987 to refurbish the newer East Millinocket mill, but it subsequently shut down two of its five machines. The company redirected investment capital to its newer, faster, and more competitive southern mills to exploit the region's low wages and lax environmental regulations.

Georgia Pacific completed its takeover of Great Northern in February 1990. The NFLS could not have stopped it, but observers understood that easements and tax cuts were unlikely to thwart future takeover attempts.

A leaked copy of a preliminary draft of the NFLS appeared in my mailbox one day in August 1989. It contained troubling statements about timber-dominated communities:

> For many years the general economy has been weaker compared to the counties and states to the south. . . . Economic and social problems are often worse in the study area than elsewhere in the Northeast. Unemployment, low wages, domestic abuse, alcoholism and lack of opportunities for young people are some of the concerns.
>
> Preliminary studies suggest high incidence of alcohol and drug abuse, above average suicide rates and a very serious "brain drain" of young people leaving the region. Many families live in cycles of poverty that are very difficult to break.[9]

When the NFLS released the official draft two months later, these passages had vanished. The October draft reported that per capita income in all but one county in the study region was below the national average, and Maine's highest rates of unemployment occurred in counties most dependent upon the timber industry. The draft asserted the woods products industry was "viable." It did not assess the condition of the region's industrial forests and associated biodiversity issues. It dismissed the notion that the public could acquire large tracts of land, claiming, without examining probable costs, it was too expensive. Ted Johnston eschewed calls for acquisition, assuring a reporter it would cost $200 *billion*—$9,174 per acre! This price tag was greater by a factor of 43 than the $211 per acre Rancourt had paid for the Diamond lands a year earlier.[10]

The Forest Service staff and the GTF scheduled a series of public hearings for the October draft throughout New England and New York. A week before the first hearing, GTF member Mason Morfit, of the Maine chapter of The Nature Conservancy, advised the region's environmental leaders that the forest industry has "veto power" over Maine's government. He warned us to be careful not to ask the NFLS for too much.[11]

The first hearing on the draft report convened in Boston the day after Georgia Pacific announced its takeover bid for Great Northern. Most of the attendees loved visiting the mountains, lakes, and rivers to the north. Several people called for large-scale public land acquisition and wilderness protection. Others recommended strict regulation of industrial forest practices. Lobbyists representing absentee paper corporations insisted that people from away had no business commenting on matters they did not understand. These unwelcome flatlanders, who contributed to the region's tourism economy, would be compelled to pay for the billions of dollars of federal tax breaks demanded by the large, clear-cutting landowner class.

A week later in Concord, I was delighted when the Forest Society urged the NFLS to recommend the establishment of an emergency acquisition fund to deal with future large land sales. I testified that the public could acquire ten million acres of northern New England forestland for $3 billion, the price at the time of six Stealth bombers. The following January, the Forest Society's *Forest Notes* characterized wilderness advocates as extremists "who view land as something with which human beings cannot be trusted, it is purely hands-off: Lock as much as possible away so we won't muck it all up. That's alienating and self-defeating." Six months later, *Forest Notes* described calls for big wilderness as "militant demands that the federal government forego a few weapons systems and buy all the land by eminent domain."[12] I had never mentioned eminent domain.

Public clamor for regulations to stop forest liquidation on managed industrial forests had inspired the timber industry to adopt a seductive euphemism: *the working forest.* This intentionally ambiguous branding term conveyed an image of managed forests working hard for our economy.[13] It implied that large industrial clear-cuts are working as faithfully as forests managed by low-impact methods. All working forests are presumed to be good, even those stripped of merchantable timber for decades to come. Wilderness and older, unmanaged forests fail to qualify as working forests, even though they assure optimal wildlife habitat and clean air and water, sequester and store the most carbon, and support recreation and tourism. Wilderness, an idle slacker, was the enemy of managed forests.

In January 1990, Jeff and I attended all seven NFLS public comment sessions, crisscrossing the north country in bitterly cold weather. We distributed our sixteen-page critique of the draft study, "The Working Forest Is Not Working," and introduced a slide show of Alex MacLean's aerial photographs of rolling clear-cuts.[14] Many people attending the hearings felt they were flying with MacLean but had forgotten to take Dramamine. We had radically altered the conversation about working forests.

Steve Harper, Laura Falk, and Ted Rankin had listened to public testimony with open minds. When they released the *Northern Forest Lands Study* in April 1990, they acknowledged: "At public meetings throughout New England and New York, and in letters written to the [NFLS], people expressed their concern that human activity is affecting the health of the forest. They asked: how can we plan for the future of the Northern Forest region if we don't know the status of the forest's health?"[15]

The study warned against strategies designed to salvage the status quo: "The forces and conditions that have given us the Northern Forest of today can no longer insure its perpetuation." The study acknowledged: "One of the most important challenges will be to convince those within the region that some kind of change is inevitable. Without intervention a series of incremental actions is likely to permanently alter the landscape and lifestyle of this region. Ignoring the problem will not make it go away."[16]

The study wondered whether second home development posed the greatest threat to the northern forests: "Not all forest land is vulnerable to recreational development." Harper, Falk, and Rankin suggested that Existing Use Zoning offered a cost-effective means to thwart undesirable development; they wrote that it "is a simple form of zoning" that "works best in areas where people want uses of the land to remain what they have [traditionally] been, where existing land uses provide public benefits, and where the tendency is for that land to remain in its current use anyway." A landowner wishing to develop farmland or forestland assumed the burden of proof to justify rezoning the land. Under current use taxation programs, a landowner can withdraw at any time and pay a modest penalty.[17]

Harper, Falk, and Rankin linked protection of biodiversity with public land acquisition: "Full-fee acquisition of land could also provide the opportunity to set aside natural areas that would not be managed. Looking to the future, 50 or more years from now, large unmanaged tracts could create a mix of natural landscapes alongside the working landscape. . . . Publicly owned land would be a logical way to provide for large undisturbed and unmanaged tracts. In addition to the benefits for the land and its ecosystems, large unmanaged tracts would provide a type of recreation few are able to experience in the urbanized Northeast." Full-fee acquisition of paper company lands, the study concluded, was relatively inexpensive. Tracts greater than a thousand acres ranged from $175 to $350 per acre, with the average cost at $250.[18]

The study rejected Maine's effort to block federal land acquisition: "The public's inability to respond to the sale of land that might be suitable for public ownership in a timely fashion, however, means that an important potential owner of the Northern Forest is largely excluded from the market." The authors cited the results of an opinion survey of NFLS counties in Vermont and New Hampshire conducted that winter: 85 percent of respondents supported public land acquisition by the states for wilderness protection.[19] In a separate report, the GTF lauded conservation easements: "In all cases, consideration should be given to the benefits of conservation easements over fee purchases where appropriate."[20] The GTF, by treating public land acquisition as the enemy of easements, sought to discredit calls for full-fee land acquisition. It intimated, without evidence, that mega-easements would thwart development, assure sustainable forestry, and preserve biodiversity.

I responded that large easements are a weak, untested tool for preserving biodiversity since they often permit clear-cutting and biocides. Where development is a threat, they cost 60–90 percent of the price of full-fee acquisition. I objected to easements on land with negligible allure to developers. If we are committed to preserving biodiversity, I argued, "easements must be viewed as a minor tool, not as the most important strategy."[21]

During the memorably hot summer of 1988, climate scientist James Hanson had testified before Congress that burning fossil fuels released carbon dioxide, methane, and other gases into the atmosphere, where they trapped and held heat, causing global warming. In the previous three decades, atmospheric carbon dioxide levels had increased from about 315 to 350 parts per million.

In the fall of 1989, Bill McKibben's *The End of Nature* awakened the general public to the growing threat of climate change. Responses to the climate crisis, McKibben noted, had thus far been ineffectual, "in part because the solutions are neither obvious nor easy."[22] He advised against placing faith in seductive, but undiscovered, technological fixes to the unintended consequences of technology.

Replacing coal and oil with natural gas, McKibben warned, might reduce carbon dioxide emissions, but it would dangerously increase emissions of methane, a greenhouse gas eighty times as efficient at trapping heat as carbon dioxide. Methane currently stored in the tundra will be released as the planet warms.

McKibben predicted that a warming planet could drive spruce-fir forests out of northern New England. Iconic species such as red spruce, balsam fir, moose, and loons, might be unable to reproduce successfully as their once-cool, damp habitats warmed.[23]

Six months after the publication of *The End of Nature,* the authors of the *Northern Forest Lands Study* cautioned that global warming might pose a threat to the health of the region's forests. "It is unclear," Harper, Falk, and Rankin wrote, "whether global warming will mean a shift in forest species, replacing the spruce-fir forest with deciduous hardwoods." They advised that "changes must be monitored and people must be prepared to take steps to mitigate global changes to the extent possible." Forest protection, they intimated, was crucial: "Strong evidence exists that global warming, triggered by the 'greenhouse effect,' is partly offset by healthy forests" that "play a significant role in the global carbon cycle."[24]

Intellectually Valid but Not Very Useful

Equal Rights for All Species

Earth First! bumper sticker, mid-1980s

I encountered Earth First! (exclamation point obligatory), a wilderness advocacy group, in the Bitterroot Valley of Montana in the mid-1980s. Fed up with the political compromises of mainstream conservation groups, four professional environmentalists and a former Yippie had formed this wild and woolly grassroots dis-organization with the motto "No Compromise in the Defense of Mother Earth." Earth First! bluntly asserted that industrial civilization cannot evade or compromise natural laws and limits.

Earth First! The Radical Environmental Journal was published eight times a year to coincide with pagan holidays. To support its activities, it sold EF! T-shirts and bumper stickers with provocative messages: "American Wilderness: Love It or Leave It Alone"; "Back to the Pleistocene"; "Equal Rights for All Species"; "Nature Bats Last"; "Neanderthal and Proud"; and "Subvert the Dominant Paradigm."

Edward Abbey's 1975 novel *The Monkey Wrench Gang* about four desperados intent on demolishing the Glen Canyon Dam on the Colorado River inspired many EF!ers. They preached nonviolence toward humans and other life forms. Dave Foreman, the charismatic leader of EF! in the 1980s, assembled the 1985 handbook *Ecodefense: A Field Guide to Monkeywrenching.* Monkeywrenching — or ecotage — targeted inanimate objects serving wildlands exploiters. It was far more effective as psychological warfare than disabling wilderness-devouring machinery. Ecotage, coupled with EF!'s aggressive Big Wilderness agenda, brought the group international notoriety. Horrified mainstream environmentalists, along with the timber industry, oil drillers, and the FBI, branded EF!ers as terrorists.

The media, bedazzled by EF!'s flamboyant actions, largely ignored the pioneering role EF! played in aligning activism with the emerging science of conservation biology. Reed Noss, later the editor of *Conservation Biology;* George Wuerthner, another conservation biologist; and Foreman introduced key concepts of conservation science and thereby transformed the conversation about wilderness and public lands management. Wilderness was not mere scenery; it was the life support for millions of wild species.

Earth First! rejected anthropocentrism, the prevailing philosophy of the Gifford Pinchot school. Channeling John Muir, Thoreau, David Brower, and poet Gary Snyder, EF! espoused biocentrism: earth and all its life forms have inherent value.

In 1989 the FBI arrested Dave Foreman and charged him with funding three northern Arizona activists who had been egged on by undercover agent Michael A. Fain to attempt to topple power lines. Eventually, the case against Foreman fell apart when his defense team came upon Fain's accidental tape recording during a debriefing with his superiors: "I don't really look for them to be doing a lot of hurting people . . . [Dave Foreman] isn't really the guy we need to pop—I mean in terms of an actual perpetrator. This is the guy we need to pop to send a message. And that's all we're really doing . . . Uh-oh! We don't need that on tape! Hoo boy!"[1]

Not long after Foreman's arrest, conservation biology–oriented activists, weary of arguments about political correctness with anarchists, turned their energies to *Wild Earth Journal* (1991–2004), the Wildlands Network, and myriad regional campaigns, including Yellowstone to Yukon (Y2Y) and the Northern Appalachian Restoration Project, a project I helped establish.

In August 1989, I learned that the New Hampshire Fish and Game Department planned to conduct a "pond reclamation" on Little

Diamond Pond in Colebrook around Labor Day. It intended to dump the nerve agent rotenone into the pond to kill off yellow perch so it could stock nonnative, hatchery-raised trout the following spring to appease perch-hating anglers. I called the Fish and Game biologist and urged him to stop the project, but he refused.

Jeff Elliott had spent the summer hiking in old growth forests in British Columbia. When he returned, we visited Little Diamond Pond on a hot day a week after it had been poisoned. The stench of death surrounded the pond: rotting perch, dead amphibians, and legions of aquatic insect corpses. Jeff, a passionate fisherman trained in aquatic biology, was outraged. Two days later, he returned to Little Diamond and then drove south to the Fish and Game office in Lancaster. He informed the receptionist that he had a delivery for the fisheries biologist. After she pointed out the office, Jeff returned to his car and fetched a large cardboard box. He dumped a disgusting slurry of decomposing perch and other victims of the reclamation project on the biologist's desk and exited the premises. The startled receptionist radioed the Fish and Game staff for help.

A few days later, I received a phone call from reporter Gene Ehlert, who had preceded and succeeded me at the *Coös County Democrat*. He asked whether I had been involved in the fish dumping. I said, "No." If, perchance, I encountered the perpetrator, Ehlert requested I inform him that the media sought an interview. Jeff later explained to the savvy reporter that killing much of the aquatic life in a small pond triggers an ecological disaster.

The *Democrat's* headline read "Dead Diamond Denizens Dumped on Department Desk." The article quoted the anonymous fish dumper's explanation for his unorthodox protest. Ehlert and John Harrigan also concocted a map of the crime: "fish died here," "fish dumped here." For aficionados of *Winnie the Pooh*, they labeled the approximate location of my cabin as "Eeyore's House" and marked a spot in Nash Stream as "Heffalump Trap."[2] When the paper hit the newsstands, the Fish and Game biologist called Harrigan and asked whether the perpetrators had provided the newspaper with "that map."

Several weeks passed before the law caught up with Jeff. He qualified for a public defender who appreciated both the weirdness and the seriousness of the case. At the trial, Jeff's lawyer requested that the frozen "evidence" be brought into court. He called Jeff to the stand and asked why he opposed pond reclamation. For the next half hour, Jeff explained pond ecology and the consequences of killing off all fish and a great many amphibians and aquatic insects. The judge, accustomed to motor vehicle and deer jacking cases, appeared bewildered. At length, the defense rested. The fish kept thawing.

The Fish and Game officer who arrested Jeff served as prosecutor. He asked but one question on cross-examination: "Do you now, or have you ever [*pause for dramatic effect*] referred to yourself as Heffalump?" The packed court roared with laughter. As the odor of the thawing fish permeated the room, the prosecution rested its case. Jeff was convicted of a misdemeanor and ordered to pay a modest fine.

The fish dumping escapade earned us a measure of local notoriety. Charlie Jordan, publisher of the monthly *Coös Magazine,* and the ubiquitous Gene Ehlert wrote a feature about us. They highlighted our follies and offered us a platform to explain our unorthodox behavior. They also interviewed some of our critics.

Dave Harrigan, vice president for policy at the Forest Society, credited us with helping to define the issues and added: "Their positions are highly theoretical, intellectually valid, but, as a practical matter, not very useful. They fail to acknowledge political and economic reality." He characterized our stunts as "symbolic, like pouring blood onto draft records" but worried that we might attract "other more dangerous malcontents."[3]

Early in 1990, Jeff and I launched a crudely produced tabloid, the *Glacial Erratic.* In its first issue, I responded to Harrigan's comments: "Dave and I have been quite critical of each other in public, yet Dave has shown no personal animosity toward me, and I thank him for distinguishing between an attack on his ideas and a personal attack. I think he's dead wrong on many issues, but I like and respect him personally."

I thanked Harrigan for praising our intellectually valid ideas but questioned who actually was politically naïve: "[We] believe that we must be pragmatic in an ecological and evolutionary sense. We believe society must be realistic about the carrying capacity of our environment. . . . So, we call upon Dave Harrigan, SPNHF [the Forest Society],

Jamie Sayen (*left*) and Jeff Elliott (*right*). *Coös Magazine,* January 1990.
(Photo by Charles J. Jordan/Coos Magazine. Used by permission)

and the timber industry to join pragmatic, realistic Earth First! to Preserve Appalachian Wilderness. Let's devise a culture [that] can live on a sustainable basis with all native species and ecosystems."[4]

New Hampshire governor Judd Gregg appointed a Nash Stream Advisory Committee (NSAC) to devise a management plan for the new forty-thousand-acre state forest on former Diamond lands. Steve Blackmer, director of conservation at the Appalachian Mountain Club, served as chairman. At its initial meeting in December 1989, Gregg, whose family owned considerable forestland, expressed hope the timber industry would not "lose acreage they depend on for their business."[5]

Jeff and I appeared at the NSAC's second meeting in January 1990, convened at a Concord warehouse. We sat down with the startled committee and acted as if we were members. A few days later, I sent Chairman Blackmer a formal request for an appointment to the NSAC. Steve Rice, the commissioner of the New Hampshire Department of Resources and Economic Development, denied my request.

At the February meeting, Jeff and I aggressively pressed for wilderness and no logging. Arguments became heated. At the conclusion of the meeting, Chairman Blackmer took me aside and told me that if we disrupted the NSAC's meetings, we would be completely ineffectual. If Jeff and I respected his responsibility to conduct a thorough and fair process, he promised to give us every opportunity to make our case. I happily agreed.

For the next few months, three subcommittees performed most of the important work. Jeff and I attended every meeting. We urged the Natural Areas Subcommittee to adopt the principles of conservation biology. We recommended that the Nash Stream Forest Management Plan designate as reserves substantial portions of more productive, lower elevation habitats—the places most coveted by timber interests. Our views did not always prevail, but chairwoman Krista Helmbolt of The Nature Conservancy and the subcommittee members treated the issues we raised with respect. On occasion, Dave Harrigan or Kirk Stone of the Audubon Society of New Hampshire expressed support for one or another of our ideas. Gradually, the core elements of conservation science entered mainstream New Hampshire conservation policy discussions.

The Timber Subcommittee's chairman, Charlie Niebling, executive director of the New Hampshire Timberland Owners Association, and Hank Swan of Wagner Woodlands resisted our ideas. That spring the Division of Forests and Lands released a sobering inventory of the Nash Stream forest: 87 percent of its stands were fewer than fifty years old, and 84 percent of the forest was either pure hardwoods (56 percent) or mixed stands dominated by hardwoods (28 percent). Almost 90 percent of the hardwoods were less than four inches in diameter at breast height, and roughly one-third of those skinny trees were low-economic-value species such as pin cherry and striped maple. The inventory calculated that fewer than four trees per acre exceeded sixteen inches in diameter at breast height.[6]

The Nash Stream Forest Management Plan would ruefully note, "This diameter distribution does not represent the natural cycling of a forest." In the fall of 1990 I wrote in the *Glacial Erratic:* "Whether you are an advocate of the timber industry or wilderness, it is clear that the . . . Nash Stream purchase will do nothing to protect jobs in the

North Country woods for several decades."[7] Lack of regulations, not tree-huggers, had been the problem.

At the May meeting, foresters with the Division of Forests and Lands informed Advisory Committee members that the easement between the state and the US Forest Service prohibited logging at elevations above twenty-seven hundred feet and on steep or shallow soils at lower elevations. A map of the Nash Stream confirmed that roughly half of the forty-thousand-acre watershed was off-limits to logging.

As spring turned to summer, the Advisory Committee committed to producing an ecologically responsible management plan. The Natural Areas Committee adopted the ecological reserve design guidelines favored by conservation biologists: unmanaged core natural areas, buffered from timber management and connected by terrestrial and riparian corridors. The low productivity sites above and below twenty-seven hundred feet were, by default, part of the reserves. Jeff and I proposed designating all of the high-production, lower elevation forest stands as natural areas. Representatives of the timber industry and the state natural resource agencies wanted all of them reserved for the timber program. We lost.

The Timber Management Committee, hamstrung by the sorry condition of the forest, opted to develop a plan for reestablishing a much older forest to supply high-quality sawlogs. It endorsed uneven-aged management and recommended against clear-cutting.

The Recreation Committee's members loved wild places and thought Nash Stream could serve as a model for other public lands. State Forester Jack Sargent, an avid fly fisherman, shared Jeff's aversion to fish stocking; they called for the restoration of native fish populations to Nash Stream. The committee agreed the plan ought to promote traditional, low-impact recreation that, for political reasons, included snowmobiling.

Diamond International had refused access to all-terrain vehicles (ATVs), and the state maintained the ban. The Management Plan prohibited ATVs in the Nash Stream Forest: "The use of all-terrain vehicles (ATVs) and trail bikes is prohibited." The ban on ATVs, one of the NSAC's least controversial decisions, was the first provision of the plan the state repealed.[8]

Wildlife biologists view clear-cuts as an essential tool for artificially elevating populations of white-tailed deer. More deer means more revenue from the sale of hunting licenses for the chronically underfunded department. Jeff routinely reminded the committee that managing *for* common, economically desirable species means managing *against* other less common, ecologically important native species and communities. At the July 12, 1990, meeting of the full Advisory Committee, a biologist from New Hampshire Fish and Game objected to the plan's strong preference for uneven-aged timber management.

In August, Commissioner Rice, four Fish and Game biologists, and a paper company representative attempted to gut the forest and wildlife sections of the proposed plan.[9] The committee stood its ground. A month later, Rice, along with agency biologists and foresters, revised the "vision statement" to permit clear-cuts in core areas for "wildlife management." The entire committee refused to compromise, and Rice withdrew the document.

Despite its failure to designate any productive timberland as unmanaged natural areas, the Nash Stream Management Plan, crafted in 1990, but for technical reasons not released until 1995, represented a dramatic departure from traditional natural resource planning. It proclaimed in its vision that "the management of Nash Stream Forest will be a model of environmentally sound public land stewardship." It pledged to "continue to offer public access to traditional low-impact, dispersed recreation including hunting, fishing, and snowmobiling in designated areas. . . . Management decisions will be consistent with the guiding philosophy of protecting the environmental integrity of the land. . . . Protection of the natural resources and environmental quality will be of primary concern in recreation management."[10]

In 1993, Hank Swan, a timber industry representative on the Governors' Task Force and a member of the NSAC, told me that the process of writing the management plan had educated several members of the NSAC as to the importance of maintaining ecosystem integrity.[11]

I cherish a thank-you letter addressed to "members" of the NSAC, signed by Steve Rice's successor as commissioner of the Department of Resources and Economic Development: "You contributed hundreds of hours of your time . . . to help the Division of Forests and Lands create one of the finest land use plans possible."[12] Showing up pays off.

At the end of October 1990, Jeff and I headed to the Adirondacks to protest a pond reclamation project on remote Tract Pond. I portaged a canoe into the pond, donned a large fish hat, and paddled dreamily around the pond.

On shore, Jeff badgered the Department of Environmental Conservation biologist with questions. How do you justify killing nontarget fish, amphibians, and aquatic insects? How can you leave the dead, rotting fish in the water to deprive the pond of oxygen and jeopardize the survival of aquatic organisms? Why are you reducing the diversity and stability of an ecosystem already under stress from acid rain and climate change? Why utilize a procedure that requires a new round of poisoning every few years?

When they hauled the department boat to the shore, I paddled over to observe, and a conservation officer grabbed the canoe and informed me I was under arrest for obstruction. Jeff, standing on sphagnum moss about two feet from me, protested, and a second officer barked "You're under arrest" and lunged at Jeff. They fell into the cold water. Two news photographers documented the mayhem. After two officers dragged Jeff ashore for handcuffing, two others pushed me toward the trail leading to the road. No one else followed because the treatment of Jeff was the big story.

A couple of minutes later, the lead officer shoved me against a large tree and ordered me to put my hands on it. I hugged the tree. He shouted a series of confusing demands, and when I hesitated because I could not understand what he wanted, he reached down, grabbed my ankles, and ripped them out from under me. My chin slid down the trunk, where a stick at its base impaled it. He jumped on top of me, pinning one of my arms under my torso. He yelled, "Give me your other arm, or I'll hurt you." I informed him his body mass prevented me from complying. When we reached the road, I said to the other officer, "You saw he assaulted me." "I saw nothing," he replied. The two arresting officers handed me off to a pair of state troopers and returned to the woods.

They charged Jeff and me with obstructing governmental administration, resisting arrest, and second-degree felony assault of a conservation officer. My arresting officer had written "under penalty of perjury," "[Sayen] started to flail his arms and kick at me and resisted handcuffing. During the handcuffing he fell to the ground with my arm under his body pain in the shoulder joint of the complainants right shoulder, and the left hip [sic]." The arresting officers charged Jeff with pushing an officer and resisting arrest. "Under penalty of perjury," his arresting officer wrote: "Resisting arrest he did push the complainant in the chest, drag the complainant into the water of Track [sic] Pond" and "the complainants face was scraped and he has severe back pain." He complained of a dislocated shoulder. The officer who arrested me claimed he had suffered an "aggravated gall bladder condition."[13] The following day they checked themselves into a hospital.

The judge set our bail at $5,000 cash each. Off we went to the jail in Malone, New York. On our third night there, guards awakened us around midnight and escorted us to the receiving room. Our Earth First! buddy the late Gary Bennett was counting out five hundred $20 bills he had collected from ATM machines in Rochester.

In February 1991, a grand jury convened. Normally, defense attorneys urge clients to avoid testifying in front of grand juries because defendants have to sign a waiver of immunity acknowledging that anything they say can be used against them. A defendant must answer all questions, and there is no recourse to the Fifth Amendment. Our lawyer, Jack Delehanty, could observe, but he could not communicate or offer advice during our testimony. He advised us to tell our story to the grand jury.

The grand jury subsequently dropped the felony charges, but it levied new misdemeanor charges: Jeff for criminal mischief and me for trespassing on public, "Forever Wild" lands. We were each fined several hundred dollars. Testimony from Bill McKibben, who had attended the protest; photos taken by a local journalist, Larry Maxwell; and an honorable district attorney saved us from prison.

Even though the grand jury clearly believed the conservation officers had lied under oath, it did not indict them for perjury or assault. My arresting officer spent six days in the hospital at taxpayers' expense.

The doctors could not detect anything wrong with him. The Department of Environmental Conservation never admitted to wrongdoing, but in a tacit acknowledgment that something had gone badly awry at Tract Pond, the department moved to train its officers to deal with non-violent civil disobedience. It also quietly "retired" its wounded warrior.

A week after our arrests Jeff and I attended a meeting in Concord. Jeff was still sporting a foam collar, and I had six stitches in my chin. Dave Harrigan of the Forest Society approached us and inquired about our welfare. He had worked in the district attorney's office in Brooklyn, New York, where he had learned that officers guilty of brutality often charged their victims with obstruction, resisting arrest, and assault. When he read the charges against us, he said, he knew we were innocent. We became friends on the spot.

Following the March 10, 1988, emergency summit on the Diamond lands, Jeff and I had felt we had to engage in theatrics to draw attention to important issues the insiders ignored or suppressed. Our adventure in the Adirondacks challenged our thinking, and the experience with the NSAC suggested we could promote conservation science and ecosystem integrity with a less flamboyant, less risky style.

In December 1990, Steve Blackmer convened representatives from about twenty state, regional, and national conservation groups. He proposed we establish an alliance to present a united front to the recently launched Northern Forest Lands Council. The Northern Forest Alliance membership included state, regional, national, and grassroots organizations.[14] Bad blood still lingered from the early 1980s fight between the Forest Society and national groups such as The Wilderness Society and Sierra Club over wilderness additions to the White Mountain National Forest. Few of the well-heeled, mainstream groups were comfortable working with unscripted grassroots activists. The Forest Society, the Maine Audubon Society, and the Vermont Natural Resources Council cultivated close working relations with their states' timber interests, and they frequently opposed grassroots efforts to discuss forest practices regulations, wilderness, and additional federal land acquisition.

Despite these differences, all of the Alliance groups agreed, Carl Reidel later wrote, that "the Northern Forest debate must be elevated to the national level if there is to be any hope of breaking the regional grid-lock and wrestling power from the forest products industry."[15] For a few years, the Alliance often found ways to reconcile the tension between utilitarians and preservationists—the ancient Muir-Pinchot divide.

In its first year, the Alliance struggled to discover how such a diverse assemblage of groups and viewpoints could work together. We were fortunate that the staffers who represented the various organizations were wonderful people. Our bimonthly meetings helped us develop respect for each other when we disagreed over sensitive issues.

As 1990 came to an end, Jeff and I, after years of combative conservation, suffered activist burnout. We continued to work for similar goals, but we never again collaborated. Jeff, who resumed teaching high school earth science, never stopped defending aquatic ecosystem integrity.

In the spring 1991 issue of the *Glacial Erratic* I wrote: "When the Northern Forest Lands Study was created, Paul Bofinger, President-Forester of the [Forest Society] was appointed as NH's enviro representative. He would have been a good choice to represent the timber industry, but he was an embarrassment as an 'enviro.'"[16] At this point, Dave Harrigan interceded. "Why don't you sit down with Paul?" he asked me. I told him I'd be happy to meet with Paul if he could arrange it. A few days later, Harrigan ushered me into Bofinger's office and lingered just long enough to break the ice.

After enumerating our problems with each other, we agreed: let's work together; let's continue to disagree and debate and discuss the issues, but no more personal attacks. We honored our pledge, and I learned to appreciate Paul Bofinger's legacy as the most significant New Hampshire conservationist of the second half of the twentieth century. We could still exasperate each other, but we could also laugh about it.

Government-Financed
Lobbyist Group

Politics: n. The conduct of public affairs for private advantage.

AMBROSE BIERCE, *The Devil's Dictionary*

O n the penultimate page of the *Northern Forest Lands Study*, Steve Harper, Laura Falk, and Ted Rankin wrote, "The Governors' Task Force on Northern Forest Lands has had a difficult time agreeing on the significant issues and potential solutions."[1] The GTF hired a facilitator to help write an eleven-page report that endorsed a "nonregulatory" response to development threats, such as further tax cuts for acutely undertaxed paper companies and other large landowners.

Most GTF members supported the creation of a strong, permanent, four-state council with authority to direct future studies, to oversee land acquisition, and to allocate federal funds. The Maine delegation vetoed this plan and agreed to only a defanged, four-year Northern Forest Lands Council (NFLC), designed along the lines of the GTF, which had written: "States shall retain all existing authorities. That is: there will be no new level of regulatory power. Responsibility for land use planning and regulations remains with state and local governments." At Maine's insistence, the GTF restricted the council's mission to furthering recommendations of the task force's report.

"The continuing pattern of political manipulation of the [study] process by some forest industry leaders was all too obvious," Carl Reidel wrote. "Their early support of the NFLS and the GTF appeared to have been little more than a ploy to thwart park advocates, overzealous land planners, and potential takeover schemes for a few years. . . . In the end they were able to permanently cripple any effective institutionalization of the NFLS report strategies or GTF policy recommendations. . . . The conservation groups and moderate state officials were no match for the forest industry's political infighting skills." Because of "complex property rights and land valuation problems necessary for the effective implementation of a public-private cooperative model" and the requirement of corporate landownership to show a profit, Reidel concluded that "some form of aggressive land acquisition may be the only viable option left open to regional leaders."[2]

Four members of the GTF returned to serve on the NFLC. Vermonter Peter Meyer of E. B. Hyde, a family timberland company, was especially interested in reducing property taxes on timberlands. Paul Bofinger of the Forest Society preferred large conservation easements, not public land acquisition. Ed Meadows, Maine's commissioner of conservation, and Ted Johnston, executive director of the Maine Forest Products Council, insisted that the council not discuss issues that might cast doubt upon the served-the-region-well myth.

Jerry Bley, Maine's conservation representative, told Robert Beattie, author of a Ph.D. dissertation on the NFLC: "There was, at least if you listen to industry, a specific agreement in their willingness to go along with the establishment of the Council, that it would not focus on forest practices, that it would focus on this fragmentation/development issue. . . . [I was] asked if I would abide by that understanding, and I said yes. It became clear as we went through the process, particularly with regard to public input, that that [approach] just wasn't going to fly."[3]

In November 1990, Vermont senator Patrick Leahy, chairman of the Senate Committee on Agriculture, Nutrition, and Forestry, secured $1 million to fund the four-year NFLC. The new council hired Charlie Levesque as its executive director, a position he formerly had held with the New Hampshire Timberland Owners Association.

Senator Leahy's staff also drafted a Northern Forest Lands Act of 1991 intended to provide congressional authorization to the council and offer policy directives, including a role in public land acquisition. Ted Johnston accused Senator Leahy of attempting "to create unwarranted federal intrusion into private forest land management" that could undermine the ability of the states to control forest policy. Ed Meadows, Levesque, and Johnston rewrote several sections of the act. Veteran environmental reporter Phyllis Austin observed in the *Maine Times:* "Johnston's hand is seen clearly in the Council's rewriting of the Northern Forest Lands draft. . . . The Council's version is significantly skewed toward preserving the status quo rather than finding new options for keeping the Northern Forest intact." Leahy staffer Tom Tuchman objected that the NFLC, by rewriting federal legislation to suit itself, was guilty of a "conflict of interest."[4]

At hearings on the Leahy bill in Lyndonville, Vermont, and Bangor, Maine, in July 1991, property rights extremists ambushed the council. A John Birch Society member warned the Lyndonville gathering: "All across the country, we see false pretenses—endangered species, endangered forests . . . being used to justify the federal government coming in and taking control." The NFLC was just another federal "land grab" and was "a major step toward full implementation of Marx's program for domination of a nation by its central government." In Bangor, citizens affiliated with the Maine Conservation Rights Institute hung banners and placards containing messages such as "Northern Forest Puke." Johnston reported that the negativism expressed against the act worried Maine's two senators. The following February, Maine senator George Mitchell, the Senate Majority Leader, fearing the wrath of ideologues and landowners, abandoned the act.[5]

In Ray Brook, New York, in August 1991, more than fifty anti–Adirondack Park locals shouted down efforts to conduct the NFLC's first formal meeting. The frustrated council adjourned, only to discover someone had slashed the tires of two council staffers' vehicles in the parking lot. The following day, the council conducted its business without incident. During the public comment period, Dale French of the Adirondack Solidarity Alliance warned: "We know what your game is. We'll fight you in the Courts! We'll fight you in the hills! We'll fight you in the valleys." Keith Van Buskirk, characterized by Phyllis Austin as a "revival preacher," prophesized, "By the grace of God, the number of constitutionalists here will multiply by the thousands and outnumber the preservationists!" Robert Stegemann, a vice president of International Paper representing New York landowner interests on the NFLC, told Austin that paranoia motivated the property rights activists, "and some of these groups have every right to be paranoid." Stegemann warned: "What landowner rights groups are saying are some of the things industry has said for years . . . respect my property rights."[6]

Shortly after the donnybrook in the Adirondacks, Charlie Levesque urged council members to keep the focus on large landowners: "Although the threat of conversion to nonforest use is important for all ownerships in the northern forests," he wrote, "the *focus ought to be on the large landownerships,* where the threats were identified in the charge to the Forest Service for the study" (emphasis added).[7] Thereafter, the NFLC operated as if the interests of the largest landowners and the needs of smaller, local owners were the same. It enabled the property rights lobby to exploit legitimate grievances of struggling northern forest communities *without offering constructive suggestions for addressing these problems.*

In October, Georgia Pacific sold Great Northern's two paper mills, the hydroelectric rights to the West Branch of the Penobscot, and 2.1 million acres of forestland to Bowater for approximately $380 million—about $180 an acre if the aging mills and lucrative dams were included at no extra cost. Bowater soon complained about Maine's "bad business climate."[8] A good business climate meant fewer regulations, lower taxes, and more subsidies.

A visibly nervous NFLC, chaperoned by security guards, met in Bangor on October 23, 1991, for the first time since the Ray Brook nightmare. In an effort to appease the property rights interests, the council adopted a proposal offered by a Ray Brook protester who had urged the council to include local officials: "Things are stacked against the small landowner (not the large landowner). . . . Unemployment is very high and people live below the poverty level."[9] The governors added two timber industry representatives and two town officials who were hostile to public lands.

Steve Harper's solid work and good faith approach to the *North-ern Forest Lands Study* could have helped the NFLC navigate the fed-eral, state, and regional issues it confronted. He retired after the Bangor meeting, worn out, no doubt, by nonstop wrangling with the represen-tatives of Maine's large landowners. His replacement, an employee of the US Forest Service in Washington, D.C., failed to attend a single pub-lic meeting of the NFLC after February 1992. This abdication of respon-sibility to represent the citizens of all fifty states left the council without a voice to respond to the antifederalism of several council members, the timber industry lobby, and property rights activists.

At the Bangor meeting, three weeks into its second year, the NFLC established four committees: Local Forest Based Economy, Property Taxes, State and Federal Taxes, and Land Conversion. The latter sought to understand the causes for the large land sales and determine how much land developers had removed from the timber base during the previous decade. In the months after the Bangor meeting, the coun-cil created three additional subcommittees: Recreation and Tourism; Conservation; and, under intense pressure from the Northern Forest Alliance, Biological Resources Diversity. Two days after the Bangor meeting, Levesque wrote in the NFLC *NEWS:* "I believe I speak for all Council members when I say that everyone left the meeting happy, and excited about the prospects of moving ahead."[10]

The full council met for a public session every two months, ro-tating the meetings among each of the four states. The sessions lasted three or four hours and were usually well-attended by the sixteen coun-cil members. Attendance by the public, the mainstream conservation community, and the media generally was poor. Ten of the council mem-bers were foresters or had worked in the timber industry. No loggers, biologists, millworkers, wilderness advocates, teachers, nurses, farmers, or labor union representatives served on the council.

For the next two years, the NFLC conducted most of its work in subcommittees, which, for logistical reasons, met by conference call. This was an understandable consequence of a four-state initiative, but it became very difficult for the public to monitor the activities of seven subcommittees meeting outside of the public domain. The bimonthly council meetings routinely ratified decisions made on these nonpublic calls.

The council fielded public comments after each agenda item and at the conclusion of meetings, but, as Levesque wrote in the *NEWS*: "While we obviously should continue giving every opportunity to have the public provide input into the Council process by allowing members of the public to speak at the meetings, I believe it is not proper for us to have dialogues with those people during the meeting. We should take their testimony and leave it at that. Discussions with members of the public . . . should be avoided because it could (among other things) lead to a confrontation."[11] Month after month, citizens formally complained about the NFLC's refusal to address forest practices. Council members received this testimony without comment.

In February 1992, Levesque reported: "the consensus was that the Council would use consensus method on all major decisions." Consensus is antithetical to democratic principles. It pressures a group to evade divisive issues, and it pressures participants to accept some lowest common denominator for the sake of the group. One person or interest group can veto a proposal everyone else supports.[12] The timber lobby's veto over the NFLC's agenda denied the council and the public adequate information about forest practices, biodiversity issues, and the cost of tax cuts desired by large landowners.

Early in 1992, I urged the Northern Forest Alliance to establish a publication to address issues the NFLC refused to address. Initially, the Alliance responded favorably, but as discussion led only to further discussion, I grew antsy. Dan Plumley of the Adirondack Council persuaded me to launch the project on my own.

I named it the *Northern Forest Forum* and adopted for its motto, "Working for Sustainable Natural and Human Communities." The first issue went to press early in September 1992. Gulf of Maine poet Gary Lawless wrote: "I hope that it will be a forum of voices for the bioregions through which the northern forests move. I hope that we can try to speak for the great diversity of life within these regions. . . . [I hope] that we will hear the local cultures, the local wisdom, the deep sense of place and connectedness expressed through many forms of language, from the scientific article to poetry, from interviews to artwork, all of it being part of the deep song of place."[13]

For fun, I challenged readers with several quizzes. The "Land Acquisition Quiz" asked what percentage of the Reagan-Bush–era savings and loan scandal bailout would be necessary to acquire ten million acres of northern forestlands. Answer: "0.5 percent. Yes, the cost . . . would be less than one half of one percent of the current estimate of the cost of the S&L bailout—$500 billion! . . . Maybe land acquisition is a steal (certainly the S&L debacle was)." Other quizzes asked, "Who Got the Tax Breaks?" Answer: Fortune 500 paper companies that were clamoring for additional tax breaks. "Who paid the biggest pollution fine?" Hint: a paper company. A "Local Control Quiz" challenged readers to locate the corporate headquarters of each of the paper companies that owned large tracts of land in the northern forests: Toronto; Darien and Stamford, Connecticut; Atlanta; Boise; Purchase, New York; Philadelphia; and Richmond.

I invited the Alliance to take over the *Forum*, stipulating I wished to be part of the editorial team. But the Alliance leadership never responded, so I published the *Forum* under the aegis of a small grassroots group I coordinated: the Northern Appalachian Restoration Project. Northern Forest Alliance members contributed numerous articles to the *Forum* during its ten-year run.

Tilbury House published Mitch Lansky's *Beyond the Beauty Strip: Saving What's Left of Our Forests* the same month the *Forum* debuted. Lansky offered the first comprehensive examination of industrial forestry in northern New England. Three decades later, *Beyond the Beauty Strip* remains a valuable reference tool for loggers, foresters, and engaged citizens.

In the *Forum*'s inaugural issue, Lansky challenged the "served-the-region-well" myth.[14] Rather than address controversies over current industrial forest practices, he wrote, the NFLC had taken aim on onerous forest management regulations, excessive taxes, and the threat of development throughout the study area. "These assumptions," he argued, "are an assertion of a myth of the 'happy coincidence' that what the industrial landowners of Maine have done in pursuit of cheap fiber and higher revenues has been universally beneficial to the forest, forest wildlife, local communities, and the state's economy."

The NFLC had ignored *traditions* such as industrial clear-cuts and whole-tree harvests, herbicide spraying, and mistreatment of loggers as independent contractors who received no benefits. The council had wildly overblown the threat of development: "Who would want to build a condo in an industrial clear-cut?" Lansky asked. The undesirable ecological harms of recent developments have "been minor over the last decade compared to the impact of industrial management on the millions of acres that lie beyond the beauty strips."

Lansky suggested that the council's pro-industry slant made it "a government financed lobbyist group." He continued: "To the extent that the NFLC focuses primarily in protecting the status quo, as if this protected the forest or local communities, *it is using public funds to lobby for the benefit of private forest owners.*" He offered an alternative approach: "The criteria for appropriate forest policy should be that practices qualify as ecologically sound, socially responsible, economically viable, and sustainable."

At a workshop sponsored by the NFLC's Land Conversion Committee in September 1992, a Wall Street analyst warned that the future of the region's paper industry was "clouded" by mill overcapacity, competition from more modern mills in the south, and the degraded condition of northern New England's industrial forests. A pension fund analyst pointed out that overpriced forestland growing mostly low-grade wood was an unattractive investment.[15]

Later in the workshop, the committee released its preliminary findings, including the fact that approximately thirty-nine thousand acres (sixty-one square miles) in lots larger than five hundred acres had been developed in the northern forest region in the 1980s. During this period, the large landowners had clear-cut 1.3 million acres of Maine forestland (two thousand square miles). Clear-cuts converted thirty times more acreage of industrial forestland than had second home development.[16]

The draft Land Conversion Committee report listed the most common reasons for these land sales: a desire to sell the land to raise cash for other non-forestland uses, estate tax considerations and/or age of the owner, and lack of suitable return on investment. A few sellers, primarily in New York and Vermont, blamed increased property taxes. Only 2 percent of those queried cited "concern about federal income tax policies," such as capital gains. Only 3 percent of the sellers initially expressed concerns about regulations, but when the researchers raised the issue, almost every interviewee became apoplectic. The interviewers surmised that regulations may be despised, but they did not drive the large land sales.[17]

The Land Conversion Committee report debunked the NFLC's fundamental assumptions. Development posed less of a threat in remote northern New England than clear-cutting. Timber regulations, property taxes, and changes in federal capital gains taxes for timber and timberlands had not caused the large land sales.

Unfortunately, the report changed few minds on the NFLC. Robert Beattie wrote in his 1996 dissertation: "Some members, when faced with information about land conversion that conflicted with their own personal observations simply believed that the data on land conversion were so sketchy that the crisis of conversion was simply hidden in the data gaps. The evidence of their own eyes and inferences based on their beliefs were so compelling that conflicting data from the Council's own research was insufficient to sway their belief in the need for new solutions."[18]

Andrew Whittaker wrote in the *Northern Forest Forum* in the summer of 1993: "Beginning from recognition of what is necessary to ensure ecosystem survival, we should learn to live off what such natural ecosystems yield. The most for the cheapest is not productive, unless we decide that 'most' means the highest quality sustenance, physical and spiritual, and that 'cheapest' implies minimal impact on the integrity of the forest, hydrology, and all linking biological systems. Under these terms, we must admit that today's system of production and retailing is expensive indeed."[19]

For decades, raw log exports from the three northern New England states to Canadian sawmills had cost the region's struggling timber-dependent communities thousands of relatively high-paying, value-added manufacturing jobs. In 1992, council member John Harrigan had editorialized: "For too long, we have watched trailer truck after trailer truck headed north with everything from spruce and fir logs for dimension stock to high-quality pine logs for the specialty market, all destined for federally subsidized sawmills north of the Canadian line." Champion International in 1989 exported to Quebec sawmills 85 percent of the softwood sawlogs cut on its 330,000 acres in northern New Hampshire and northeastern Vermont. An estimated 75–80 percent returned to the United States as manufactured lumber.[20]

I asked the Local Forest Based Economy Committee to examine the negative economic impacts of raw log exports and to develop a strategy for adding value to sawlogs locally. Committee chairman Richard Carbonetti, a Vermont forester who worked with Champion, refused, saying, "If we banned log exports, I'd be out of business." Citing "subcommittee investigations," the committee later asserted, "To date, there is no published data documenting negative impact [of raw log exports on jobs or forest health]."[21]

The committee justified the use of bonded Canadian loggers with the standard industry line: "Certain traditional woods jobs are unappealing to local residents and are being filled by imported labor." There is no record that the committee asked any locals whether they would work these jobs if they were paid a living wage.[22] The committee repeated the standard complaint about subsidies to Canadian mills. It did not acknowledge that these alleged subsidies included health care and other social safety net programs, benefits paper companies had avoided paying for when they forced loggers off the company payrolls. Nor did the committee question the massive subsidies the mills and large landowners received from state and federal governments, especially low taxation rates and tolerance of externalities.

When the Local Forest Based Economy Committee endorsed efforts to increase the reach of the global economy into the northern forest region, Mitch Lansky responded with a series of questions: Who benefits from globalism, and who pays the costs? What are the impacts of globalism on local economies, environment, labor force, and land ownership patterns? How can northern forest communities buffer themselves from these impacts? What are the potential ecological and economic impacts of global climate change on the region?

The committee ignored these questions and called for increased international trade in commodities and reform of the regulatory process—a euphemism for weaker environmental and labor protections. Wagner Woodland's Hank Swan dismissed the committee work as "extremely weak," adding, "It is deplorable that [the northern forest states] do not have domestic primary and secondary manufacturing facilities."[23]

In fall 1993, the NFLC released its *Findings and Options*. More than 60 percent of the 406 letters critiquing these findings urged the council to do a much better job of preserving biodiversity through the establishment of ecological reserves and/or the regulation of forest practices. Only one letter in five reflected the view of the timber industry or property rights zealots. A natural resource policy specialist in Vermont's Northeast Kingdom reported that all but one of the towns he worked with had requested assistance in regulating large clear-cuts and poor logging practices.

One citizen wondered how you can manage what you can't understand. Another advised that economic goals ought to respect the constraints of ecosystems. A soils scientist, noting that land conversion accounted for only 0.2 percent of the region during the boom years of the 1980s, wondered why the council had failed to address management practices on the other 99.8 percent of the region.

Jerry Bley, the NFLC member most sympathetic to the views of the Northern Forest Alliance, told Robert Beattie that the council had sought a balance between public and private interests in the forest. It rejected the property rights assertions that the government "had absolutely no right to do anything when it came to private land in the Northern Forest. . . . Then there were those on the other end that felt there was no legitimate private interest in the forest, that the values of the forest were primarily public values that had been diminished through private ownership, particularly industrial ownership, and that the time was ripe to get rid of the 'wrong-doers' and to return those values of the forest to the proper owner, which is the public."[24]

The NFLC played off property rights ideologues and preservationists as equally extreme troublemakers. Nevertheless, I regret that we missed an opportunity to attempt to forge bonds with the more thoughtful property rights voices. In October 1993, the leader of an Adirondack group aligned with the property rights position submitted an articulate and troubling letter accusing the council's *Findings and Options* document of patronizing residents of northern forest communities. The writer felt that the region's poor economy and low-paying jobs had not served the region well. She rejected the council's tax cut policies whose benefits would go to wealthy landowners but whose costs would be shifted onto communities and beleaguered local citizens. The *Northern Forest Forum* printed numerous articles expressing similar sentiments.

When the NFLC released its *Draft Recommendations* in March 1994, it acknowledged that citizens had expressed "considerable concern" over destructive forest practices, but it complained that few commenters had "suggested specific strategies for the Council to recommend." Mitch Lansky called these comments "a particularly insulting bit of rhetoric—not only because some people did make recommendations that got ignored, but because the Council did not request such strategies."[25]

The council scheduled a series of twenty public listening sessions from late March to early May 1994 throughout the four-state region, along with stops in Boston, New Haven, and New York City. In March and April, we produced three issues of the *Forum* for distribution at the listening sessions that provided in-depth critiques of every aspect of the flawed *Draft Recommendations.*

Charlie Levesque feared property rights demonstrations and disruptions, and he worried that calls by the environmental community for regulating forest practices and establishing parks would undermine the council's solution to the region's problems.[26] The council hired professional facilitators and allowed speakers two minutes to comment on the 150-page document.

Three hundred citizens attended the opening session in Bethel, Maine. The first speaker, a college student, listed her concerns about the impact of industrial forestry on the health of future forests. Next, a forester for Idaho-based Boise Cascade, owner of more than seven hundred thousand acres in the northern forest, called for local control and strongly opposed a role for the federal government in the region. A carpenter spoke against raw log exports, saying, "We are exporting our livelihood." An Adirondack property rights activist warned that federal intervention would lead to the establishment of ecological reserves that would expel residents to some "cesspool of a city" because there would be no jobs in the northern forest.

Cathy Johnson of the Natural Resources Council of Maine introduced a six-by-four-foot map of the region, commissioned by the Northern Forest Alliance and crafted by *Forum* artist Jon Luoma, as a prop for her testimony. When we hung a clear plastic overlay highlighting millions of acres of paper company land sales since 1980, audience members gasped. By the end of the evening, thirty-five of the fifty speakers had endorsed measures to protect the health of the forests, not more tax breaks for large clear-cutters.

Three-quarters of the 741 people who testified at listening sessions urged the NFLC to strengthen the conservation provisions in its final report. Less than 9 percent opposed stronger conservation measures. Nearly half of the 178 citizens who testified at Maine sessions criticized the council for ignoring destructive forest practices.[27] Two-thirds of the written comments submitted to the council supported one or more elements of the environmental position. Most called for strengthening recommendations pertaining to biodiversity protection, forest practices, and public land acquisition.

Robert Matthews from Houlton, Maine, offered a logger's perspective: "I have been a professional logger for the past twenty years. In this relatively short span of time, about one-fifth of a stand's rotation, I have been witness to a devastating transformation. Without regard for future cost, we have condoned the exploitation of not only the forests but also of the communities dependent on these forests. . . . I am privileged to witness, almost daily, the intricacies of a diverse system that revolves around this mass of trees we call a forest. I have also witnessed industry's complacency towards these same intricacies."[28]

Council members grew weary reading the public comment letters blasting the NFLC's refusal to discuss forest practices. One former member told Robert Beattie: "It gets to a certain point where somebody gets up, and you read the first three sentences of their letter or you hear the first three sentences of their speech and you know exactly what the rest of it's going to be because they're all speaking from the same play sheet . . . [and] you just tune it out." Beattie concluded that "the Council members actively worked to hide [industry veto power] so they could preserve the perceived legitimacy of their process."[29]

How did the NFLC react to public feedback? "The council was heartened that so many commenters agreed with [our] approach," it wrote in its final report, *Finding Common Ground*. It lectured taxpayers from outside the region who would foot the bill for subsidies to large landowners: "Those living outside and perhaps unfamiliar with the way of life here must understand that it is entirely possible to conserve the forest and sustain towns and villages within its boundaries in ways that neither damage its human nor its plant and animal communities."[30]

In the spring 1993 issue of the *Forum*, I had saluted the vital role of the council in promoting a regional dialogue: "the Council deserves our gratitude for providing the warring elements a forum to state their various platforms—and, most significantly—an opportunity to get to know each other as real human beings who belong to real communities with real problems."[31] It was wishful thinking on my part.

After nearly six years, the large landowner class moved to block further public scrutiny. Landowners wanted to exclude the federal government and leave all future deliberations on the future of the region to state and local governments. Of course, the federal treasury would still pay for coveted capital gains and estate tax cuts, if they passed. The environmental community strongly supported an ongoing regional collaborative with the US government because the ecology and economics of the region are interrelated, and we ought to address them at the regional level. The NFLC disbanded on September 30, 1994.

On September 19, 1994, the NFLC released *Finding Common Ground*. Its final recommendations differed from the March draft only cosmetically. A prominent Adirondack resident noted that the word "Adirondack" did not appear in the report. He asked why the council feared investigating the park and its nearly three million acres of "Forever Wild" forests.[32]

The Northern Forest Forum

Working for Sustainable Natural & Human Communities

Mid-Summer 1993

Volume 1 No. 6

Can We Control Development?

Yes!
Existing Use Zoning

See: "North Woods Conservation Area" Proposal Page 12–14

Finding Common Ground

AN INTERVIEW WITH
Hank Swan of Wagner Woodlands
Pages 7-9
Can the Environmental Community and the Timber Industry Work Together for Sustainable Natural & Human Communities in the Northern Forests?

Also in this issue

New York Appropriates Money for Land Protection

The Northern Forest Lands Council & Forest Management Practices

Natural Disturbance & the Logging History of the Spruce-Fir Forest

The Economics of Place

The Origins of the Adirondack Park

The Ecological Restoration of the Northern Forests

& More

Printed on Chlorine-Free Paper

Cover of the *Northern Forest Forum* 1, no. 6, 1993.

Finding Common Ground advised its readers, "The Council's recommendations are neither quick solutions, nor a response to an immi-
nent crisis." At the time, the US paper industry was in crisis. Bowater,
Boise Cascade, Champion International, and James River suffered first-
quarter losses in 1994. That spring, Bowater's CEO, Anthony Gammie,
told a paper industry audience at the University of Maine: "there are
major changes reverberating throughout the structure of corporate
America. . . . They include such unpleasant subjects as downsizing via
job elimination and disposal of underperforming business units. As unpleasant as it may be, today's competitive global environment rightly
deems such steps necessary."[33]

Soon after the release of *Finding Common Ground,* South African Pulp and Paper Industries (Sappi), relying on junk bonds, bought
Scott Paper's mills and nine hundred thousand acres in the Moosehead
Lake and upper Kennebec River region. Scott Paper, led by "Chainsaw
Al" Dunlap, a former assistant to Sir James Goldsmith, had run afoul
of the shareholder movement. Shareholders seeking maximum short-
term profits rather than steady, long-term dividends and community
welfare viewed traditional longer term investments such as research
and development, fair wages, and community support as a violation of
their rights. Corporations responded to these demands by speeding up
production, battering unions, slashing jobs, and reducing mill capacity.
Mill managers came and went. Managerial decisions, under pressure
from corporate headquarters and without input from host communities, frequently exacerbated the crisis.

Scott Paper cut nearly ten thousand jobs (out of twenty-five thousand) and sold off the S. D. Warren Division to Sappi in 1994 and the
remainder of Scott Paper to Kimberly-Clark in 1995. Kimberly-Clark
closed Scott's Winslow mill three years later. Eventually, the Securities
and Exchange Commission banned Al Dunlap for life from running a
public company because of his unethical accounting practices. In business schools, the demolition of Scott Paper has served as a case study in
vulture capitalism.[34]

It is startling that the NFLC could neither acknowledge the signs
of decline of northern New England's paper industry nor offer a strategy
for assuring the long-term economic and ecological health of the region.

I visited New Hampshire senator Judd Gregg's office in Washington, D.C., in the early 1990s. One of his aides told me that Gregg knew the Berlin pulp mill's future was bleak. I asked about his long-term plan for Berlin, and she replied he did not have one because he was entirely focused on saving jobs for his constituents. If those jobs are doomed, I replied, he must have a strategy to help the region recover from the mill closing. The aide assured me he did not.[35]

After four years of refusing to examine the ecological impacts of industrial forest management, the NFLC belatedly acknowledged the conflict between markets and land health. In the chapter "A Way to the Future," the council confessed:

> In our discussions time and again we faced a fundamental conflict—between market-driven efficiency that encourages maximum consumption of resources with the least amount of effort in the shortest time, and society's responsibility to provide future generations with the same benefits we enjoy today.
> We believe that until the roots of this conflict are addressed and the economic rules changed so that markets reward long-term sustainability and recognize the worth of well-functioning natural systems, existing market forces will continue to encourage shorter-term exploitation instead of long-term conservation of the Northern Forest.
> This report does not address all aspects of this conflict.[36]

When it was too late to matter, the NFLC acknowledged the untenable relationship between global markets and exploited ecosystems—and then disbanded. The council squandered its opportunity to require policymaking to honor natural limits.

A Fork in the Road

When you talk about mainstream and grassroots groups, there's this real
inherent goal difference. They're about control [of pollution]; we're about
prevention.

LOIS MARIE GIBBS, 1996

I n June 1994, Michael Kellett and David Carle of RESTORE: The
North Woods, a regional wilderness advocacy group and member of the Northern Forest Alliance, kicked off a campaign for
a 3.2-million-acre Maine Woods National Park, an area greater
than Yellowstone and Yosemite combined. The proposed boundary of
the park ran from the Quebec border just north of Jackman, Maine, in
a northeasterly direction to Umsaskis Lake on the Allagash, then east to
the East Branch of the Penobscot River and south to Sebec Lake, near
Dover-Foxcroft, then westerly toward Jackman. RESTORE excluded
the towns of Millinocket, Greenville, Rockwood, and Jackman from the
proposed park. Two paper companies, Scott and Bowater, owned most
of the land in 1994, and nearly all the proposed parklands lay within the
unorganized territories.

With land sales in the region between 1994 and 2002 averaging about $250 an acre, the public could have acquired the park for
$800 million.

The park, if established, would include most of the great glacial
lakes of northern Maine, the largest assemblage of remote wild trout
ponds in the eastern United States, thousands of miles of rivers and

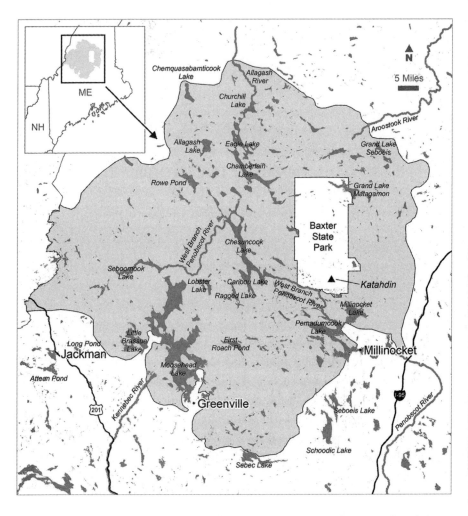

Map of RESTORE's proposed 3.2-million-acre Maine Woods National Park in northern Maine. Note that existing state and federal public lands, including Baxter State Park and the Allagash Wilderness Waterway, would remain under current jurisdictions, and no primary residences are within its proposed boundaries. Map by Brian Hall, adapted from a map produced by Jon Luoma for RESTORE in 1996 that appeared in the *Northern Forest Forum* 8, no. 4 (2000): 16–17. Copyright © RESTORE. (Used by permission from RESTORE)

streams, most of the Moosehead Lake shoreline, and many of Maine's most popular mountains. Baxter State Park, home of Mount Katahdin, would remain under state management, and the Appalachian Trail would remain under jurisdiction of the Appalachian Trail Conference. Maine Woods National Park would buffer Baxter and the Appalachian Trail from the impacts of industrial forestry.

Maine's popular governor Angus King dismissed the park proposal as "the worst idea to come out of Massachusetts since the Red Sox traded Babe Ruth." Members of the Northern Forest Lands Council were furious. Snowmobilers attacked the park proposal. George Smith, head of the Sportsman's Alliance of Maine, the leading lobbying group of hunters and other outdoor sports enthusiasts, used opposition to the park proposal as a fund-raising tool. He complained that a national park would lure too many people to northern Maine and "it would ruin what's so great about the North Woods in the first place: silence and solitude."[1] Smith did not accuse snow machines, ATVs, or feller bunchers of ruining solitude, silence, streams, or forests.

The Maine Audubon Society rushed out a press release the following day, dismissively referring to RESTORE as a group "located in Concord, Massachusetts [that] has a membership of less than 300 people." Audubon staffer Sandy Neily objected to "easy solutions to be imposed on complex territories." She predicted that the "simple and unfortunately seductive plan" was "doomed to failure." The Maine Times offered a more measured response: "How much worse is the administration of a national park likely to be than the absentee mismanagement of the paper companies?"[2]

The fragile coalition of the Northern Forest Alliance had united in its opposition to the NFLC's industry-dictated agenda. The strong public support for the Alliance agenda during the spring listening sessions had demonstrated the power of a unified conservation community. As the NFLC neared its termination date, pressure, especially in Maine, mounted on state conservation groups to play along with local politics, and the old fault lines began to reappear.

A couple of weeks after RESTORE's announcement, Alliance leaders convened a Why Can't We Get Along? meeting. When Neily berated

RESTORE for its failure to consult Audubon and other Maine groups, I tossed a newspaper on the table. Its front-page story announced that Maine Audubon and three other Alliance groups had cut a deal with Kenetech, a wind power developer that planned to construct 630 towers along the ridgeline of the Boundary Mountains in western Maine. The Alliance had just designated this remote, undeveloped region a conservation priority area. I asked why Maine Audubon required RESTORE to seek approval from Maine groups before releasing a proposal to *preserve* land when the four groups had not consulted their colleagues before supporting a proposal to *develop* an area the Alliance wished to preserve. The meeting did not end happily.

The Boundary Mountains wind power project exposed the Alliance's failure to develop a regional energy policy to complement its efforts to protect forests. That fall, the Conservation Law Foundation attempted to organize an energy policy workshop. Few Alliance organizations expressed interest, and the workshop never materialized.

A week after the midterm election in November 1994 gave Republicans control of the House of Representatives for the first time in decades, Jerry Bley sent Alliance groups a memo urging them to support the NFLC's recommendations as the primary vehicle for action. "I think we are approaching a fork in the road," he wrote, "with one road leading toward increased polarization and the other toward more collaborative attempts to resolve issues." Bley warned that the Alliance's credibility would be jeopardized if it failed to support the council's recommendations. Pursuit of other agendas, he warned, "will not be successful and, in fact, will create a divisive climate that will undermine our ability to protect the Northern Forest for years to come."[3]

Early in 1995, New Hampshire senator Judd Gregg introduced the Family Forestland Preservation Tax Act to implement the council's recommendations for reducing capital gains and estate taxes. Most of the benefits of the Gregg bill would accrue to the families of large, absentee landowners, not families of loggers or small woodlot owners. The Gregg bill denied tax breaks to owners who managed their lands for biodiversity and wildlands. Timber liquidators and uncaring land managers could collect the tax breaks.

For years, the NFLC had dodged the question, "How much will the tax cuts cost?" The Congressional Research Service calculated the Gregg bill would deny the US Treasury about $800 million in taxes *every year*.[4] One year of the Gregg tax cuts could have purchased the entire Maine Woods National Park.

Senator Patrick Leahy introduced the Northern Forest Steward-ship Act that summer. The bill attempted to resume some degree of regional dialogue, to make the northern forest states eligible for federal land acquisition funds, and to promote research into cut-less-than-growth forestry. Leahy hailed the bill as "an example of what Congress can achieve when it heeds the public's voice." He declared: "This legislation is guided solely by the Council's recommendations. It goes no further, nor does it fall short." Leahy touted the NFLC's consensus recommendations: "The legislation embodies the conservation ethic of the 1990s—non-regulatory incentives and assistance to realize community-based goals for sustainable economic and environmental prosperity." The Leahy bill appropriated no funds to acquire lands and provided minimal assistance to struggling local economies. It requested a meager $1 million a year budget, explaining, "public funds are scarce; the greatest public benefit must be secured for any additional investment."[5] The Gregg bill expressed no remorse that it would annually reallocate $800 million of scarce public funds to the wealthiest among us.

The Northern Forest Alliance supported the two bills as a package, but the bills ran afoul of the Newt Gingrich revolution in Congress. When the Gregg bill failed, the Maine Forest Products Council demanded—and received—changes to the Leahy bill. In 1998, Steve Schley of the Pingree family, owners of nearly one million acres in northern New England, told the editor of *Evergreen,* a timber industry publication: "As written, it [the Leahy bill] prevents the federal government from intervening in the relationship between private landowners and state governments, unless invited to do so by a governor of one of the states. I don't believe language this strong—describing the relationship between the federal government and the four states—exists anywhere else in federal law."[6] The Senate killed the revised bill.

In May 1994 several citizens warned that if the NFLC disbanded, recommendations requiring federal funding or tax policy changes would not pass in Congress because there would be no regional council to lobby for their adoption. Two-and-a-half years after the council disbanded, Charlie Levesque acknowledged there had been substantial progress on only five of the council's thirty-seven recommendations.[7] The council's work had stalled out.

At another Why Can't We Get Along? meeting in November, I asked when the Alliance would issue a proposal for a regionwide system of ecological reserves. Alliance leaders feared calls for wilderness were "premature" and releasing maps of proposed reserve areas would infuriate the opposition. That winter, the Northern Appalachian Restoration Project withdrew from the Alliance. A few other groups resigned shortly thereafter. The Northern Forest Alliance lingered for another decade, but it never recovered the creative energy of the NFLC years. The Maine Woods National Park proposal served as a catalyst for, but not the cause of, the Alliance breakup.

The pro-industry bias of the NFLC had held the Alliance together. When the council disbanded, the Alliance failed to refocus its energy on the biodiversity and climate crises that compel humankind to align our aspirations with natural laws and limits. Had the Alliance moved from the specific problem of the council to these global challenges, it could have transformed northern New England's conservation politics.

A year after leaving the Alliance, I asked dioxin activist Lois Marie Gibbs how she and her fellow grassroots activists got along with the major environmental groups based in Washington, D.C. She replied, "When you talk about mainstream and grassroots groups, there's this real inherent goal difference. They're about control; we're about prevention."[8] The establishment groups will accept deals to reduce, but not eliminate, the poisoning of a community's air, water, or soils. The mothers and community activists with whom Gibbs worked wanted the poisoning stopped, not endless debate over arcane formulae to legalize corporate poisoning of their families up to certain levels; they demanded protection for the health of their communities. Ecological conservationists, seeking to protect land health, experienced similar frustrations with mainstream organizations.

(Copyright © Jon Luoma)

The Northern Appalachian Restoration Project continued to publish the *Forum* and to work with Alliance members on a variety of state and regional forestry issues. Our budget rarely reached $100,000 a year, yet we managed to support eight activists with meager stipends and publish a feisty journal for nearly a decade.

Andrew Whittaker succeeded me as editor of the *Forum* in the summer of 1997. He had teamed with Barb Alexander, a creative and indefatigable activist, to lead a grassroots campaign in the mid-1990s to prevent aerial herbicide spraying of paper company clear-cuts in Vermont's Northeast Kingdom. Their research, organizing, and lobbying efforts persuaded the Vermont legislature to adopt in 1997 a moratorium on aerial herbicide spraying.

Daisy Goodman and Tom Obomsawin organized a citizens' group to pressure New Hampshire to stop issuing spray permits to paper companies. After the Forest Society opposed a bill modeled on the 1997 Vermont herbicide spray moratorium, the legislature killed it.[9] The spraying only stopped when, a few years later, timber investors, with no interest in expensive, long-term investments, bought the Boise and Champion lands.

Pamela Prodan, a lawyer from western Maine, led the citizens' campaign against the Kenetech wind power project. The state had sided with the wind developers, but Prodan's effective organizing and legal acumen thwarted the speeded-up approach the boosters had expected and forced the state and Kenetech to complete a comprehensive permitting process. When Kenetech failed to provide satisfactory answers to vital questions, the ensuing delays exposed the weakness of its financial support. Eventually, Kenetech's bankruptcy spared the Boundary Mountains. Throughout this protracted campaign, Prodan articulated the need for a lower impact, regional energy policy to complement efforts to preserve, protect, and restore biological diversity.[10]

The Coastal Waters Project of the Northern Appalachian Restoration Project, directed by Ron Huber, played an important role in the campaign against developing a deep-water seaport at Sears Island to facilitate the shipment of biomass chips to other continents. Huber also advanced visionary proposals for establishing large marine reserves designed to preserve oceanic ecosystem integrity.

Bill Butler, a leader in the 1975 Maine Woodsmen Association strike, attended virtually every meeting or conference addressing Maine forest policy. His experience, knowledge, and ability to ask incisive questions infuriated industry insiders. His informative, witty reports in the *Forum* exposed industry myth-making.

Mitch Lansky contributed articles to virtually every issue of the *Forum*. He also organized and led the Maine Low Impact Forestry Project and later edited *Low-Impact Forestry: Forestry as if the Future Mattered.*

T • W • E • L • V • E

No Jobs on a Healthy Planet

When we had that clear-cut referendum, there were a lot of people that were
told that if they voted to ban clear-cutting that they'd lose their jobs. But look
how many have lost their job since then. And all the mills that have closed.

HILTON HAFFORD, Allagash Plantation logger, 1999

On Election Day 1995, the Green Party of Maine secured
more than fifty-two thousand signatures to place a citizen-
initiated Ban Clearcutting in Maine Referendum on the
November 1996 ballot. The initiative sought to stop clear-
cuts greater than one-half acre and limit cutting of a particular stand
to the amount it had grown between cuts. The ban applied only to the
unincorporated, largely undeveloped townships of northern Maine. It
did not affect incorporated towns.

Outdoor sports enthusiasts, snowmobilers, loggers, and foresters
signed the petition. Paper mill towns responded positively. A poll conducted that winter reported that 71 percent of Maine's voters supported
the referendum. Industry leaders reacted with horror. "They see this as
the end of life as they know it," Jerry Bley reported, "and they are correct." Boise Cascade forester Si Balch accused referendum backers of
trying to create "a beautiful landscape but with people who are poverty
stricken . . . where you give a child false teeth for a graduation present
because they all fell out."[1]

On January 11, 1996, the head of the Maine Forest Service, Charles
Gadzik, submitted a memo to Governor Angus King: "The two strategy

options . . . are to pursue an outright defeat or to raise a competing measure." A day later the governor's aide, Susan Bell, advised referendum opponents to "oppose the referendum while not supporting the status quo regarding traditional forest practices; not getting framed as supporters of corporate America, and being [perceived as] environmentally sensitive."[2]

Late in January, Jonathan Carter, leader of the Ban Clearcutting campaign, met with Maine conservationists. Every organization, except the Maine Audubon Society, seemed inclined to support the referendum until a former commissioner of conservation introduced Gadzik's idea of a competing measure. I asked whether conservationists would support something weaker than the reforms proposed by the referendum. He assured me they would only support something as strong or stronger. The competing measure idea stole the show.

The large landowners bankrolled a political action committee with the folksy name Citizens for a Healthy Forest and Economy. "Mills will close and planned investments will be reversed," its director, Bill Vail, wrote to Governor King. "It puts the future of forest ownership in jeopardy. . . . [I]n the final analysis there won't be more jobs, because there won't be any mills. . . . There will be a dramatic shift of focus onto the organized towns in pursuit of timber. . . . High grading of stands will be likely."[3] Industry seemed to be saying if you don't allow us to continue overcutting industry lands, we'll begin high-grading smaller woodlots.

Vail's group hired a nationally recognized consultant on how to defeat citizen-initiated referendums. It preached that the side that frames the debate on its own terms early in the contest wins the election. After the consultant conducted a series of focus groups, it recommended that the large landowners frighten the public with predictions of economic collapse if the referendum passed. Persuade the public that clear-cuts create jobs.[4]

Logging jobs had declined by 40 percent during the previous decade's clear-cutting frenzy. John McNulty of Seven Islands explained, "This is a relatively small number if you look at the number of employees associated with the forest products industry of the state."[5] Real job loss was acceptable if it contributed to industry's quest for increased profits, but hypothetical job loss caused by efforts to protect forest health from further degradation was a scandal.

In the late winter and early spring of 1996, Governor King and the Maine Forest Products Council convened a working group to develop the competing measure. The Maine Audubon Society joined, and the Maine chapter of The Nature Conservancy served as a facilitator. The dealmakers excluded representatives of the fifty-two thousand petition signers.

The Natural Resources Council of Maine (NRCM) called for including referendum supporters. On March 26, 1996, NRCM announced it would endorse the referendum unless the legislature enacted a stronger alternative before July 1. Governor King's administration, recipients of large timber industry campaign contributions, intimated that NRCM's legislative agenda would suffer if it opposed efforts to marginalize referendum supporters. NRCM capitulated.[6]

Early in June, negotiations nearly collapsed. Maine Audubon and NRCM possessed significant political leverage, *if they had been willing to walk away from a bad deal.* When Governor King put a metaphorical gun to their heads, they folded. At the press conference announcing the Forest Compact, Audubon Society executive director Thomas Urquhart called the negotiations "rewarding," adding, "You get more through cooperation than one-size-fits-all regulations." A Maine legislator, sympathetic to the referendum, later wrote in the *Forum*, "More than one source told me that the 'Compact' was essentially what the industry came in with at the start."[7]

The competing measure was not as strong or stronger than the referendum. It permitted clear-cuts smaller than seventy-five acres and weakened parts of the Forest Practices Act. It allowed whole-tree harvests, plantations, herbicide spraying, and short-term rotations. Mitch Lansky warned, "In some circumstances, a clear-cut under the FPA definition would not be a clear-cut under the Compact definition if there is an abundance of small-diameter trees." The compact placed additional burdens upon towns considering adopting local forest practices ordinances to protect their forests from further overcutting. The compact's authors failed to reach agreement on cutting standards and the terms of the Sustainable Forest Management Audit. These issues would not be resolved until after the election. Compact supporters urged voters to trust a mystery document cobbled together in secrecy that failed to address core issues.[8]

Robert Seymour, of the University of Maine at Orono, worried that the compact "institutionalizes and codifies mediocrity instead of setting high standards." Wolves and national parks are not the problem, he added: "The real threat is mediocre forestry."[9]

In July, the State Planning Office and the Maine Forest Service released a taxpayer-funded report claiming that 15,600 jobs would disappear in the first year of the clear-cut ban. The report ignored the many thousands of logging and mill jobs lost during the preceding decade, even as cutting levels had increased dramatically. It failed to ask whether low-impact forestry practices might increase logging jobs and stimulate greater investment in locally owned, value-added manufacture. It assumed that cleaner rivers, better fishing, nicer views, and better hiking opportunities would create no new jobs in tourism and recreation. The cover of the *Forum* featured a Jon Luoma drawing of the grim reaper and the headline, "No Jobs on a Healthy Planet."[10]

Maine's media touted unsubstantiated predictions of massive job loss but ignored data from the US Forest Service's 1995 draft inventory reporting sharp declines in Maine's spruce and other economically important species. Greg Gerritt, one of the leaders of the referendum, later wrote, "I was told that several editors said that their hands were tied by the owners of the papers."[11]

The compact angered industry hardliners who wanted to smash the referendum head-on with their superior financial assets and political clout. As summer waned, a "vote no on everything" campaign emerged under the leadership of Mary Adams, who claimed that the public had no right to regulate private landowners because it's *their* private land.

The Ban Clearcutting campaign was in disarray. Jonathan Carter had opted to raise big bucks for television and radio ads instead of building up a statewide network of activists. By late summer, the campaign

'No Jobs on a Healthy Planet'

The Maine Forest Service & State Planning Office Economic Impact Study of Ban Clearcutting Referendum 'Proves' Maine Economy Will Collapse if Citizens Vote to Ban Clearcutting and Protect Maine Forests

Cover of the *Northern Forest Forum* 4, no. 6, 1996.

had neither money nor an effective grassroots organization. Maine's elites distracted attention from the destruction of the Maine woods with a series of nasty personal attacks against Carter. The referendum trailed the compact by a factor of four to one in opinion polls.

State law stipulates a referendum must receive more than 50 percent of the vote to pass. Following a front-page story in the *New York Times* in late September, the referendum campaign raised enough money to run television ads during the final two weeks of the campaign.[12] The compact received 47.4 percent of the vote; the referendum garnered the support of 29.3 percent; and Mary Adams's "vote no" position captured 23.3 percent. Three-quarters of the voters had repudiated the status quo, but a runoff the following November pitted the compact against the last-place-finishing no-action position. Ordinarily in a democracy, the two top finishers contest runoffs.

Back in March 1996, the paper workers' union had joined with management to oppose the referendum. Despite the loss of many mill jobs, the union believed the remaining jobs were secure. In the months after the 1996 referendum, Georgia Pacific expressed its gratitude to labor for opposing the referendum by laying off four hundred work-ers. S. D. Warren eliminated about seventy-five jobs. From 1996 to 2003 roughly six thousand forest industry jobs disappeared in Maine despite the defeat of the referendum.[13] Maine Audubon and the NRCM lost membership for collaborating with industry.

The extremely odd couple of Mary Adams and Jonathan Carter led two separate campaigns to defeat the still partially written compact again in November 1997. Mitch Lansky summed up the mess: "It ap-pears that as a result of the intense negotiations between environmen-talists and landowners, the landowners agreed to abide by standards they were already following."[14]

The timber industry and political conservation groups soon em-braced green certification as the nonconfrontational, market-based al-ternative to regulating forest management. A landowner that can afford to pay the considerable costs of the certification process submits to an independent, third-party examination of its forest practices, its protec-tion of biological diversity, and various factors such as treatment of loggers and the economic and social impacts of the landowner's practices on local communities.

Early in 1995 the American Forest and Paper Association, long a leader in fending off regulations on intensive forest practices, unveiled its Sustainable Forestry Initiative, the paper industry's version of green certification. The initiative would certify landowners whose clear-cuts *averaged* no more than 120 acres and who obeyed all laws governing pesticide use. The initiative also increased the responsibilities of loggers and reduced their productivity, but it did not oblige certified landowners to compensate them for lost pay. The *Northern Logger* dubbed the initiative as "the Sustainable Forest *Industry* Initiative" and suggested that its goal "is to create a public relations environment free from the threat of crippling legislation and other forms of public backlash in the coming years and decades." The Northern Forest Alliance dismissed the initiative as an "industry-controlled 'no one can fail' exercise" and endorsed the Forest Stewardship Council, an independent nonprofit that certifies the certifiers.[15]

In 1995, Seven Islands, the land managers for the Pingree heirs, became the first company in New England to purchase green certification from Scientific Certification Systems, one of the Stewardship Council–approved certifying groups. After certification, Seven Islands continued to export more raw logs and wood-processing jobs from Maine than any other landowner.

In May 2000 Scientific Certification Systems and the Forest Stewardship Council awarded green certification to J. D. Irving's 569,520 acres in the Allagash-Aroostook region. The council acknowledged that the New Brunswick colossus had long been cutting its spruce and fir at rates in excess of growth. This was acceptable, the certifier declared, as long as Irving practiced "silviculture"—such as replanting followed by herbicide spraying, precommercial thinning, and short rotations. Scientific Certification Systems guidelines require certifiers to award certification for current performance, not for promises that those practices will become ecologically responsible sometime in the future.[16]

In 2014 Robert Seymour and David Sherwood reported that cut exceeded growth on certified private lands, but not on certified public lands. Two years later, Mitch Lansky wrote that counties in Maine with the highest percentage of certified lands grow the highest percentage of seedlings and saplings. Clear-cutting and herbicide spraying are greatest in those counties, and average volume per acre is lowest. There still are no regulations to require cutting less than growth, the bare minimum requirement for allowing forests to serve as carbon sinks. Certification programs do not require landowners to increase carbon storage year after year.[17] Certification promises the wood buyer that the higher prices for certified wood ensure excellent forestry. If consumers think the certification promise is false, they will avoid certified products.

The Natural Resources Council of Maine had been delighted with Irving's certification in 2000 but had been surprised by the New Brunswick conglomerate's high grades for financial and socioeconomic issues. Two years earlier, loggers and truckers in northern Maine had also expressed surprise, but Scientific Certification Systems certifiers, who had been approved by Irving, dismissed logger and trucker complaints. They were unsure "what weight to place on anecdotes." "[F]or every complaint," they reported, "there is 'another side of the story' which is obviously difficult to ascertain without intensive investigations."[18]

Deep in the heart of the north Maine woods, a well-managed forest ought to bring prosperity to its hard-working citizens. But the population of Allagash Plantation in northern Maine had declined from more than 680 in 1950 to 237 in 2020. In 1997 its school, with only thirteen students, had closed. The median age in Allagash in 2017 was 56.8 years. Allagash had no industry, no mills, no value-added processing of logs cut in the area.

In October 1998, Hilton Hafford, a fourth-generation logger from Allagash Plantation, helped organize a loggers' blockade of the Canadian border. The loggers protested the importation of bonded Canadian loggers to cut the Maine woods at wages so low the families of Maine loggers could not survive. The 1952 Immigration and Naturalization Act permitted nonimmigrant aliens to harvest agricultural products (including timber), *provided those jobs could not be filled by domestic labor.* If the free market is operating properly, wages should rise in response to a shortage of local loggers. In 1998, loggers in northern Maine earned around $7.00 per hour. The large landowners used the immigration act to depress the wages of domestic loggers.[19]

I visited Hafford in July 1999. Why had he resorted to civil disobedience? "Because we don't want to move out," he responded. "There was no other option." I asked about his feelings toward the individual Canadians who were coming across the border. "They're just regular people," he replied, "same as me."

Logging trucks rumbling through town hauling heavy loads to sawmills in Quebec frequently interrupted our conversation. "Here's a town right in the heart of the lumber industry," Hafford told me. "Right in the middle of the best of the lumber and there's no mill here. . . . Free trade for us here is a load of round lumber going out and a load of air coming back." A steady stream of overloaded logging trucks headed to Canada. "They're spoiling the road up above here," he said. "We're paying to maintain the roads . . . so that [large landowners] can wreck 'em. . . . That truck that's hauling overweight up that road could haul a smaller load if the rate was there."

We set out on a tour of the forest. He stopped his pickup at an area that had been sprayed by herbicides to kill off the hardwoods and pucker brush so that more economically desirable softwoods might reach economic maturity faster. "Right here there's a little cold spring brook flows out of the valley. Right down here's one of the best fishing spots there was because of the cold spring. Now they cut that, and they sprayed it. That fishing spot has been ruined. . . . They cut it so hard along that brook that the sun beats on that water while it's running down. Now the brook's too warm; there's no fish there. The trout are gone."

We stopped at a black spruce plantation established in 1998. After Irving clear-cut the forest, it sent Central American guest workers to plant nursery-raised black spruce seedlings. It would later spray the plantation with herbicides to kill off grasses and broad-leaf competition. "A tree plantation is not a forest," Hafford asserted. "There's nobody alive today . . . that'll ever see a working forest there. . . . It doesn't seem to me that you can grow a tree that's a better seed than the one that was naturally put there. . . . The companies spray these herbicides in the woods. They say there's no danger at all there. How do we know there's none? We only know what they tell us."

"When we had that clear-cut referendum," he said, "there were a lot of people that were told that if they voted to ban clear-cutting that they'd lose their jobs. But look how many have lost their job since then. And all the mills that have closed. . . . Don't talk to me about the future. There's no present for me."[20]

Alternative to Federal Ownership

We all own [a national park] and we all share it. It's so democratic.

ROXANNE QUIMBY, 2008

S ir James Goldsmith, catalyst for the paper company land sales in northern New England, died at age sixty-four on July 18, 1997. Soon thereafter, northern New England's big sell-off began. Struggling Champion International announced late that year it planned to sell all its New York and Vermont timberland holdings, as well as eighteen thousand acres in New Hampshire. A year later, the Conservation Fund paid $208 an acre for the New Hampshire lands, $200 an acre for the Vermont holdings, and $322 for the Adirondack Park lands. New York requires permits before landowners can conduct clear-cuts larger than twenty acres. The 60 percent higher price Champion fetched for its Adirondack lands suggests that even mild forestry regulations benefit landowners.[1]

In June 1998, South African Pulp and Paper Industries announced it intended to sell 911,000 acres in the Moosehead Lake region. Chuck Gadzik of the Maine Forest Service told the *Bangor Daily News,* "the land in question is some of the most intensively harvested in the state, with the highest proportion of clear-cuts."[2] Bowater was openly shopping the former Great Northern mills and lands.

In July 1998, with more than half of the proposed 3.2-million-acre Maine Woods National Park for sale, the region's conservation community gathered at the Maine Audubon Society's headquarters to craft a united

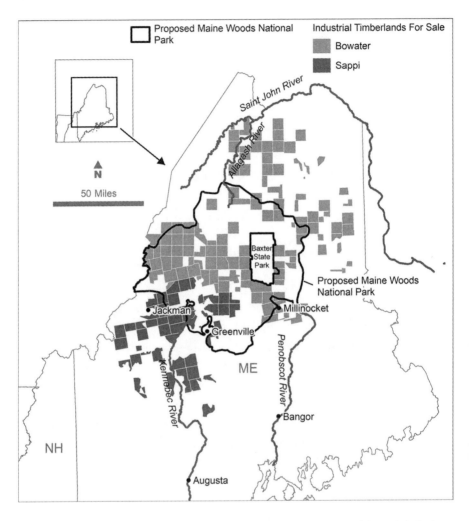

Most of the proposed Maine Woods National Park (outlined by solid dark line) was for sale in 1998–1999. The dark shaded areas were then owned by South African Pulp and Paper Industries (Sappi); light shaded areas were then owned by Bowater but were formerly owned by Great Northern Nekoosa Corporation. Map by Brian Hall. (Adapted from a map copyright © RESTORE and published in the *Northern Forest Forum* 6, no. 6 [1998]: 32. Used by permission from RESTORE)

response to the flurry of land sales. They agreed to support a statement proposing public acquisition of several hundred thousand acres for wilderness and ecological reserves. Before they settled on the wording of a press release, a member of the Audubon Society board was summoned by an Audubon staffer. He immediately attacked the plan. Within a few minutes the meeting degenerated into a shouting match. Maine Audubon opposed wilderness designation for significant portions of the lands then for sale. A decade after the Diamond land sale, New England's conservation community still could not offer a coherent response to large land sales despite strong public support for public acquisition of paper company lands.

On October 8, 1998, Plum Creek Timber Company, headquartered in Washington State, bought the Sappi lands for about $200 an acre. The new owner acknowledged it did not practice sustained yield. Over the next nine months, Bowater sold the former Great Northern lands in three transactions. New Brunswick–based J. D. Irving Corporation purchased 981,000 acres in northern Maine. A shakily financed mystery firm from Quebec, Inexcon, acquired the mills in Millinocket and East Millinocket, along with 380,000 acres. Great Northwoods LLC, owned by the McDonald Investment Company, an Alabama-based family business, acquired 656,000 acres on the West Branch of the Penobscot for $231 an acre. It sold half interest to a mystery client of Wagner Woodlands, called Yankee Forest LLC.[3]

International Paper sold 185,000 acres on the Saint John River to The Nature Conservancy in 1999. Approximately 80,000 acres are classified as wildlands with no timber management. The conservancy manages the remaining 105,000 acres for timber.

After the NASDAQ tech bubble burst in 2000, several large investors turned to large timberland investments. In 2003–2004, International Paper decided to divest its New England holdings. GMO Renewable Resources, a Boston-based investment management firm with timberlands in the South and the Northeast, offered $241 an acre for International Paper's 1,041,000 acres, mostly in Maine, but also including 20,000 acres in New Hampshire. GMO took ownership at the end of 2004 and quickly spun off 75,000 acres with the greatest development potential, earning back $50 million.

In 2007–2008, the timber bubble increased the value of northern New England's undeveloped forests to record heights. GMO correctly bet land prices would never be that high again, and it began looking for a buyer. In 2011, John Malone, then the fourth richest American, paid $375 an acre for nearly one million acres. Malone is now the largest private landowner in the United States. GMO sold the former International Paper lands for nearly twice the price it had paid seven years earlier.

Savvy investors view large timberland as the worst asset class unless underwritten by easements, carbon offset credits, or direct subsidies.

An opinion survey commissioned by the Sierra Club in 2000 reported surprising results: 63 percent of Mainers supported the Maine Woods National Park proposal; only 22 percent opposed the idea, with 15 percent undecided. When the Sierra Club's pollsters asked Maine citizens whether they preferred full-fee public acquisition or mega-easements that permitted logging, 54 percent said, "buy the land for a park"; only 25 percent preferred easements. All demographic classes preferred acquisition.[4] These poll numbers suggest that conservation policymakers have long been out of step with public opinion.

In October 1992, the Northern Forest Lands Council had included in its mission statement, "When acquisition is appropriate . . . consideration should be given to the benefits of conservation easements over fee purchases." Proponents claimed that large easements were an excellent tool for assuring responsible forest practices and protecting biodiversity. David Carle of RESTORE and I responded, "Easements are unproven vehicles of protection for large tracts of land over long periods of time."[5]

In May 1994 Steve Schley of Pingree Associates reminded the NFLC that its research had disproved the assumption that development threatened the industrial forest. Five years later, Schley and his family sold an easement on 762,192 acres in Maine for $28 million, or $37 an acre, to the New England Forestry Foundation. Pingree Associates retained the development rights on 200,000 acres with greater potential for development. Public access to the Pingree easement lands is not guaranteed by the easement.[6]

On behalf of Great Northwoods LLC and Yankee Forest LLC, Wagner Woodlands entered into negotiations for an easement on the

656,000-acre West Branch tract. After two years of tough negotiations, the deal became mired in controversy. Great Northwoods dropped out, reducing the deal to 329,000 acres. A few months after the public learned that Yankee Forest was a subsidiary of the Yale University Endowment, Yankee Forest sold to Merriweather LLC, another mysterious Wagner Woodlands investment group.[7]

According to forest economist Lloyd Irland, the easement lobby views the secrecy of easement negotiations as a virtue.[8] Secrecy simplifies negotiations and allows dealmakers to conceal the assessed value of the land. Jym St. Pierre of RESTORE began asking unwelcome questions about the West Branch deal. Are these lands really threatened by development? Is this the most cost-effective response to a limited threat? What ecological protections will be built into the easement? How is the land being appraised, and who is appraising it? What was its appraised development value?

When the dealmakers ignored his questions, St. Pierre filed a freedom of information request. He learned that the draft easement would *require* logging and permit-heavy industrial clear-cuts, herbicide spraying, monoculture plantations, and toxic sludge spreading. The owners could construct roads, bridges, and logging camps, as well as create up to six subdivisions. The state could view, but not modify, the landowner's forest management plan, provided the state pledged not to make public its terms.

The state would hold the easement, yet the draft required it to sign a confidentiality agreement before it could even review the landowner's timber management plan. The easement denied Maine the right to approve the plan or contest elements such as salvage logging in the event of a major natural disturbance. The draft also sought to exempt the landowner from compliance with the federal Endangered Species Act and any subsequent changes to state landowner liability laws.

St. Pierre also received two memos written by Jeff Pidot, chief of the Natural Resources Division of the Office of the Attorney General. Pidot wrote, "forest management activities of the landowner are given primacy, and the State's rights are deemed subordinate." The draft easement language forbade these lands from becoming part of a future national park. An easement, Pidot argued, ought not restrain who may own it, especially in a case, such as the West Branch, where dealmakers proposed to use federal funds to prevent future federal ownership of those lands. Pidot wrote: "While I recognize the premise of this transaction that forestry-related uses of the Property will be retained by the landowner, *the primary purpose of a Conservation Easement . . . is usually more focused on conservation objectives*" (emphasis added).[9]

Scrutiny of the deal by the office of the attorney general, as well as public criticism, forced negotiators to make revisions. A modified final plan, released in January 2004, reassigned ownership of the easement from the state to the Forest Society of Maine, a private nonprofit industry-oriented group, a change that limited public oversight of Merriweather's forest management.

Maine acquired roughly 47,000 acres outright for $22 million, or $468 an acre—double the price Merriweather had paid half a decade earlier. Maine intended to log all but about 5,500 acres of these lands.[10] The easement cost about $10 million, or $35 an acre on the 282,000 acres Merriweather retained. Merriweather recouped 41 percent of its initial investment. The Forest Legacy Program of the US Forest Service provided $19.7 million—then the largest Forest Legacy deal.

The Forest Legacy Program provided Maine with $74 million (as of 2016) for thirty-four easement projects covering 731,000 acres. During this period, federal ownership in Maine increased only slightly, and the largest addition, the 87,000-acre Katahdin Woods and Waters National Monument, did not receive any Forest Legacy funding.[11] Senator Leahy, the program's sponsor, intended legacy funds to be used for both easements and full-fee acquisition of lands threatened with conversion to nonforest uses. State forestry agencies successfully modified the program to serve their agendas.

Since 1988, Maine has quadrupled its conservation land to 4.3 million acres. More than three-quarters of this land is in conservation easements or managed forestlands Maine owns outright. Only 711,173 acres (3.6 percent of the state) are protected from development *and* timber management.[12] Some large easements do not guarantee public access despite Maine's tradition of more than three centuries of public commons for recreationists.

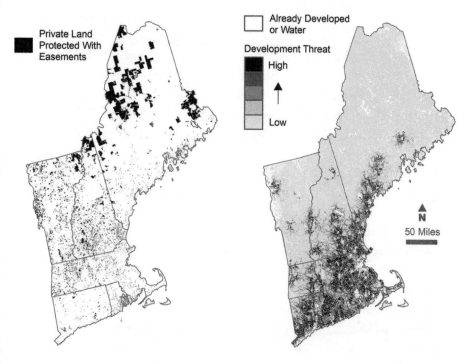

Maps developed by Harvard Forest show private lands protected with easements in New England (*left*) and New England lands most threatened by development (*right*). Note that in northern New England, where the large easements on industrial and large nonindustrial lands are located, the threat of development is very low. (Maps by Brian Hall. Protected lands data from Harvard Forest [2020]. New England Protected Open Space [1.0.0] [Data set]. Zenodo. https://doi.org/10.5281/zenodo.3606763. Data on threats of development from Jonathan R. Thompson, Joshua S. Plisinski, Pontus Olofsson, Christopher E. Holden, and Matthew J. Duveneck [2017], "Forest Loss in New England: A Projection of Recent Trends," PLoS ONE 12[12]: e0189636, https://doi.org/10.1371/journal.pone.0189636)

At a New Hampshire meeting in 2000, I objected to buying large easements on timberlands with scant development potential. The state forester, Phil Bryce, formerly a James River Corporation forester, replied that the legacy program helped deal with the threat of "conversion" to publicly owned wilderness. He worried that well-funded organizations based in New York City wanted to preserve these lands from logging. Bryce had advised the Wyoming state forester that New Hampshire had used Forest Legacy money to prevent federal acquisition: "We look at Legacy as an alternative to federal ownership." When the Forest Legacy board later considered adopting an amendment to prevent the program from acquiring lands with "Forever Wild" covenants attached, a Forest Service representative warned that this action was probably illegal.[13]

In 2002, a congressional committee investigating serious abuses of the legacy program concluded there was inadequate administrative or financial oversight, especially with regard to states' cost shares, appraisals, and easement content. State negotiators often lacked the experience or fortitude to negotiate complex easement deals. The investigators reported that funding for easement monitoring was inadequate.[14] Easements must be conscientiously monitored to assure that the public is receiving full value for its tax dollars. Unfortunately, monitoring is the orphan of land management and conservation. If conducted at all, it is rarely performed thoroughly.

In 2007, the Open Space Institute and the Wildlife Conservation Society acknowledged that no one knows whether large easements are an effective tool for preserving biodiversity and ecosystem integrity: "[We] realized that we simply didn't know whether working forest easements had a beneficial, harmful, or perhaps just neutral effect on the landscape. With land trusts holding six million-acres of conservation easements across the country, simply *believing* that easements were effective was not sufficient."[15] They hired ecologist Jerry Jenkins to evaluate the claim.

Jenkins learned that large easements list few benchmarks for sustainability or age class balance, that biologists rarely participate in preparing management plans, and that easements never require a "stand-alone biodiversity management plan." Large easements often did not require that the easement holder approve the timber management plan. Only two of the six large easements Jenkins examined required monitoring of progress in achieving the goals of the easement. None mentioned climate change. "In most cases," he wrote, "the easement did not provide for the protection of better-than-average examples of common forest communities, and so these forests were unprotected."[16]

Since most of the former northern New England industrial forest continues to be unthreatened by development, Jenkins suggested, "it may be cheaper and more effective to create new late-successional forests in reserves or on nonprofit ownerships than on for-profit ones."[17] If preserving habitat of climate-stressed species and optimizing a forest stand's ability to sequester and store carbon in the long term are conservation goals, large conservation easements are the least beneficial, most expensive option.

The NFLC sought to stabilize the large landownerships, but its preferred tool, large easements, provided timberland investment management organizations (TIMOs) an incentive to speculate in timberland. Lyme Timber sold an easement to New Hampshire when it purchased the Connecticut Lakes tract in 2002 from International Paper a year after that company had swallowed Champion International. Less than a decade later, Lyme sold the lands, by then overrun with ATV traffic, and earned an impressive return for investors.

Rick Weyerhaeuser, of Lyme Timber, wrote in 2005: "By selling off the development rights, a timberland investor in effect gets a return of capital up front without sacrificing income or appreciation from the timber component—which was the original rationale for the investment. This return of capital decreases exposure and risk, increases the return on the remaining investment (same income less principal invested), [and] provides capital for the next investment."[18] Critics viewed these large easements as a huge public subsidy to both seller and buyer that distorts the free market.

If easements lead to improved forestry, then the intensity of cutting on easement lands ought to be noticeably lighter than cutting on adjacent lands not "protected" by an easement. A study conducted in the early 2020s determined that cutting rates in the former industrial forest remain similar on easement and adjacent noneasement lands. This was true of long-term ownerships and short-term speculator-owned lands. Only a third of the large easements require landowners to submit an annual monitoring report, a meager 16 percent of them allow the easement holder to conduct ecological monitoring of the land. Monitoring compliance is difficult and expensive and a reason why large easements generally lack meaningful restrictions on degrading forest practices. The study concluded there is little evidence the massive expenditures on large easements have had a positive conservation impact.[19]

A 2019 study of timber harvesting in northern New England reported that 53 percent of Maine's spruce forests are in a degraded condition, as are 43 percent of the state's northern hardwood forests. Most of the overcutting occurred in the former industrial forest region. The authors blamed "frequency of ownership change" for exacerbating the problem: "As landowners acquire new lands with new debt and additional transaction costs, they are likely to conduct timber harvesting to meet financial objectives related to the acquisition."[20] The lands had not recovered from the intensive cutting of the budworm era, but the TIMOs cut them hard to pay down the debt they incurred when acquiring the land. A decade or so later, a new investor would repeat the process.

Some sales to TIMOs included long-term fiber contracts requiring the new owners to supply a given amount of pulp to the mills that sold the land. Mill owners earn money with the land sale and secure a guaranteed, long-term supply of pulpwood. The new landowners must pay taxes and insurance and bear the costs of storms, disease, and insect outbreaks. Jym St. Pierre rhetorically wondered, "Why put up with the headaches of landownership when you can get all the benefits with none of the risks?"[21]

Landowners with long-term fiber contracts often prematurely cut sawlogs with high value-added potential and sold them to mills at commodity prices. University of Maine emeritus professor of forestry Robert Seymour told me: "Secretly, a lot of foresters were happy when the Bucksport [paper] mill shut down [in 2014]. They were sending nice spruce sawlogs down because they didn't have enough spruce and fir pulp to send them."[22]

In northern New England, large easements have delivered substandard forest practices; little, if any, improvement in the protection of ecosystem integrity; and inadequate monitoring. The hundreds of millions of dollars spent on mega-easements contributed little, if anything, to mitigating climate change, providing unfragmented habitat for climate-stressed species, and revitalizing the depressed economies of timber-dependent communities.

Forest Legacy spent $74 million to acquire 731,000 acres in easements in Maine.[23] The public could have used that sum to acquire roughly 300,000 acres of ecological reserves at the price GMO paid International Paper in 2004.

After 2000, the blockbuster land sales continued. In a series of transactions between 2003 and 2005, Irving sold parts of three townships abutting Baxter State Park's eastern boundary to timber contractor Herb Haynes and developer William T. Gardner for close to $700 per acre. Local leaders and Maine's working forest lobby did not make a fuss when Gardner began to clear away thousands of acres of very old forests surrounding Katahdin Lake.

Roxanne Quimby, a 1970s back-to-the-lander in Monson, Maine, who founded Burt's Bees, paid $12 million for Township 5 Range 8, a twenty-four-thousand-acre parcel abutting the eastern boundary of Baxter State Park. Millinocket town manager Eugene Conlogue became hysterical. "I think it's an appalling sale by Irving because they know full well what her agenda is," he told the *Katahdin Times.* "They should have appreciated that fact and not necessarily sought out the highest bidder." Conlogue claimed he supported "the rights of property owners to control their land and make decisions that are reasonable regarding use."[24] Quimby's protection of wild nature, apparently, was not a reasonable use.

Mary Adams had opposed the 1996 Ban Clearcutting Referendum, claiming that citizens of Maine do not have the right to tell the large landowners what to do with *their* land. In December 2003, Adams asserted Quimby had no right to manage her land as wildlands because "the land belongs to the people [of Maine]."[25]

Inspired by the Maine Woods National Park proposal, Quimby had joined RESTORE's board of directors in 2001. Two years later, with revenues at $60 million a year, she sold 80 percent of Burt's Bees for $141 million. In a series of transactions, Quimby, no longer on RESTORE's board, acquired close to one hundred thousand acres of northern Maine. She told her critics: "Irving didn't give me this land. I didn't inherit it. I didn't win the lottery. I sweated and worked for years and earned the privilege of being the steward." She also noted, "I'm not forcing anybody to sell me anything for less than their asking price."[26]

The *Bangor Daily News* opined: "Except for the fact that she advocates for a national park, she is not much different from the investment companies that now own millions of acres in the Maine woods. They have limited public access to their land, terminated some leases and manage their holdings for the long-term—with minimal public complaint. If Ms. Quimby wore a suit and hired Canadian loggers to cut trees on her land, there would be much less controversy over her purchases."[27]

Quimby intended to hold on to her lands until Congress established a Maine Woods National Park. Then, she said, "turning it over to the National Park Service would be my ultimate satisfaction." She told *Yankee Magazine:* "To me, ownership and private property were the beginning of the end in this country. Once the Europeans came in, drawing lines and dividing things up, things started getting exploited and over-consumed. But a park takes away the whole issue of ownership. It's off the table; we all own it and we all share it. It's so democratic."[28]

Eventually, Quimby and her son Lucas St. Clair, weary of the anti-park demagoguery, began to lobby for the creation of a national monument established by presidential decree. On August 24, 2016, a day before the one-hundredth anniversary of the establishment of the National Park Service, President Barack Obama created the Katahdin Woods and Waters National Monument with Quimby's gift of 87,500 acres. She endowed the monument with an additional $40 million. More than forty thousand people visited the park in 2020, to hike, canoe, ride snowmobiles, bike, fish, hunt, and stargaze. The $2.7 million they spent supported thirty-eight jobs in the area and generated $3.3 million in economic activity.

Quimby's critics have gone silent. Local opposition to public lands proposals invariably turns to support once a new national park or monument begins to contribute to the local economy. In August 2022, Senator Angus King, a former foe of the Maine Woods National Park idea, proposed adding nearly forty-three thousand acres to the new national monument. Four months later, the Trust for Public Land acquired

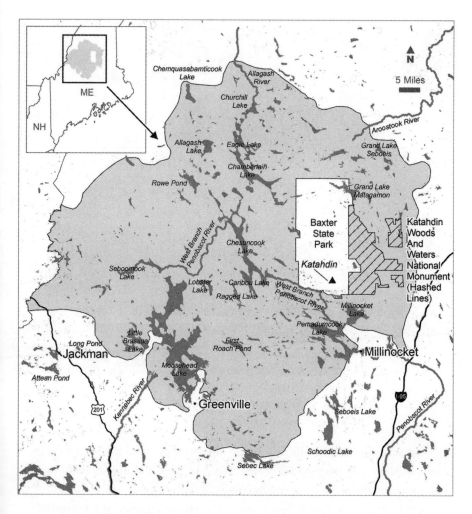

The establishment of the Katahdin Woods and Waters National Monument (hashed area just east of Baxter State Park) in 2016 was made possible by Roxanne Quimby's generous act of wildlands philanthropy. RESTORE's proposed 3.2-million-acre Maine Woods National Park inspired Quimby. The 87,563-acre monument marks a great beginning to a hoped-for Maine Woods National Park. (Map by Brian Hall. Adapted from map produced by Jon Luoma for RESTORE in 1996 that appeared in the *Northern Forest Forum* 8, no. 4 [2000]: 16–17. Copyright © RESTORE. Used by permission from RESTORE)

(Copyright © Jon Luoma)

31,367 acres between Millinocket and the southern end of the national monument. The trust hopes to sell this tract to the National Park Service to provide a southern entrance to Katahdin Woods and Waters.[29]

Quimby's wildlands philanthropy partially rectified the failure of conventional conservation politics to acquire large tracts of land for the public during the paper industry's big sell-off. Must we wait for other generous wildlands philanthropists to follow up on Quimby's generosity? Or is it time for the federal government to spend taxpayer money to acquire wildlands instead of conservation easements on lands with scant development potential?

FOURTEEN spaced as: F • O • U • R • T • E • E • N

Uncontrollables

The woods are gone, and the people who liquidated them are gone.

Now the mills are going.

BILL BUTLER, 2001

The US paper industry was in crisis in the 1990s. Fifty-two pulp mills had shut down or converted to the production of recycled pulp between 1989 and 1999, and 105 North American paper machines ceased to make paper from 1999 to 2002. In 2017, Maine paper mills supported only 4,344 jobs, down from 19,048 in 1985 and 8,425 in 2008.[1] Since 1997, fifteen Maine paper mills have closed, including Great Northern's mills in Millinocket (2008) and East Millinocket (2014) and the former St. Regis–Champion mill in Bucksport (2014). The Burgess pulp mill in Berlin, New Hampshire, suffered shutdowns, fire sales, bankruptcy, and criminal ownership in the decade and a half before its demolition in 2007.

Twenty-five miles west of Berlin, Wausau Papers shut down the Groveton, New Hampshire, paper mill in December 2007, after 116 years of papermaking. Late in 1982, Sir James Goldsmith sold Diamond's paper division, including the Groveton mill, to James River of Richmond, Virginia. Following nearly two decades of rapid expansion, James River had become one of the world's largest paper corporations. In the late 1980s, deep in debt from its many mill acquisitions, the company curtailed investment necessary to upgrade its less competitive mills. In August 1990, James River hung a "For Sale" sign on Groveton and twenty-nine other mills.[2]

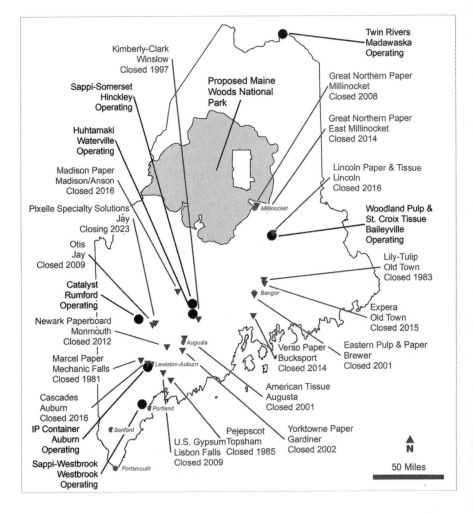

Paper mill closings in Maine since 1981 (gray triangles on map) and mills still in operation as of 2023 (black circles). Since 1997 fifteen paper mills have closed in Maine. (Map by Brian Hart, adapted from a map compiled by Jym St. Pierre, copyright © RESTORE. Used by permission from RESTORE)

Tom Bushey, a young engineer at the Groveton mill, recalled:

That was a really tough time. I was making good money, but you always had that dark cloud over your head, and you had to be careful about personal finances because no one really knew where we were headed. From 1990 to '92 there was this roller-coaster of trying to keep that place running, trying to make it profitable, and James River not giving any money for capital improvements to resolve problems that were causing financial losses month after month after month. They were so crazy about saving money. They would have all these meetings to sit down and talk about ways to improve the plant. If you couldn't figure out how to go out there and do it without any money, you never did it. After two and a half years of this, it was just screaming that we needed money.

Wausau Papers, a small fine and specialty papers company headquartered in Wisconsin, bought the mill and two fine papers machines late in 1992 for $20 million—about one-fifth the cost of a new paper machine. Wausau poured money into Groveton from 1993 to 2000. Joe Berube was a machine tender on Number 3, reputedly the largest paper machine in the world when installed in 1907. He marveled at the quality of paper produced by Wausau's new computerized color system: "These real bright neon colors—what they call 'solar yellow' or 'cosmic orange,' 'reentry red.' I mean, these colors would pull your eyeballs right out of the sockets; they were so bright. They were used in advertising to get people's attention."

Wausau promoted Dave Atkinson, a Groveton native, to the position of superintendent of the mill and vice president of Wausau in 1999, just as it began to curtail investment in the mill. In mid-2002, Atkinson reported that veterans of the paper industry called this period the "worst industry slowdown" in many years. Wausau's earnings began to yo-yo from one quarter to the next.

Depressed markets for premium paper compelled the Groveton mill to make more commodity runs. Profits for specialty papers tend to be about 30 percent; commodity paper earns about 10 percent profit. Groveton was earning a 7.5 percent return on capital, but corporate headquarters demanded a 15 percent return. "We have been in the black," Atkinson wrote, "however, not black enough." For the first time he addressed the growing concern that the paper mill might not survive: "Does this mean we are in trouble and close to shutting the doors?

ABSOLUTELY NOT! However it does mean that if we don't make a change that longer term we would be in trouble."[3] From 2001 to 2005, 150 paper machines in the United States shut down. Wausau lost money in 2005 and again in 2006.

"Uncontrollables," such as skyrocketing natural gas and pulp prices, declining paper prices, shrinking demand for paper, and increasing competition from foreign mills, pushed Groveton's small mill closer to the precipice. Desperate to contain costs, Atkinson and his co-workers focused on "controlling controllables" by reducing broke generation (unusable paper), customer complaints, workplace accidents, and the use of energy and water. "We'd have monthly meetings," Atkinson explained. "I would say, 'We need to stay focused on what we can control. We can't control the market. All we can control is how efficiently, how cost effectively we work. Focus on that, and we'll be okay.'"

Mill engineers and maintenance crews concocted ingenious, inexpensive techniques to reduce the amount of water and energy required to produce a ton of paper. Tom Bushey proudly recalled: "That project was instrumental from us getting from 20,000 gallons a ton of paper down to 5,000 or 6,000 gallons a ton, [and] in getting us [from] 15 and 18 [million] btus per ton down to 8 and 9 [million] btus per ton. Huge, huge."

Groveton produced some of the parent company's best paper and had usually turned a profit, but it was far from corporate headquarters. In August 2007, facing soaring energy prices, shrinking commodity paper markets, and debt from the 1997 acquisition of a mill in Brainerd, Minnesota, Wausau's board and CEO decided, without consulting Dave Atkinson, to shut down the New Hampshire mill at the end of the year.

On October 23, Wausau informed Groveton employees the mill would cease operations at the end of December. Tom Bushey remembered:

> When I walked into that conference room that day, I had the
> sense that there was some bad news coming. Maybe an an-
> nouncement that we need to trim a percentage of the work
> force to stay in the black. Never dreamed it was going to be
> a flat-out, utter, shut-it-down. I don't think anybody saw
> that coming. There was emotion like you wouldn't believe.

There were people in the room that stood up and got argu-
mentative. There were a few people that stormed out of the
room. A lot of people just cried. So many of us were just
shell-shocked.

Adding to the insult, Wausau attached a "covenant" to the mill
deed forbidding the future manufacture of paper on the premises. To
the mill community, closing the mill was a tragedy; the covenant was
a betrayal. "I feel that Wausau did a gross injustice to this community
[saying] that the paper machines couldn't make paper on this facility,"
said Roger Caron, a maintenance foreman who held the dubious honor
of holding the last mill job as caretaker of the shuttered mill until 2012.
"We had an excellent workforce and a can-do attitude. That should have
been illegal. To me it was wrong."

I asked Atkinson whether he shared my outrage with Wausau for
excluding him from discussions that sealed the mill's fate. He told me:
"Do I feel hurt or pissed that I wasn't consulted? Not really. I never felt
that way." But he agreed that it's wrong when decisions are made without consulting those who bear the brunt of those decisions. "That's what
sucks about the corporate world," Atkinson said—having a kind of life
and death control over the community. "What's important is quarterly
earnings, not long-term. That is Wall Street driven." He added, "I look
forward to the day when corporate America doesn't run us."

After the mill closed, CEO Tom Howatt urged Dave Atkinson to
continue working for Wausau as a vice president. Atkinson declined: "I
got called three times. I'm glad I didn't go." The decision to terminate
his career at Wausau and to remain in the area has endeared Atkinson
to the community. Caron spoke for most former millworkers: "No one
on the floor blamed Dave Atkinson or the managers. A good share of us
felt this was a Wall Street decision and not a Main Street decision that
shut this place down. It wasn't the work ethic by any means that caused
this place to go down."

Hadley Platt worked in the mill from the late 1940s into the early
1990s. He expressed a near-universal sentiment: "The mill was the life of
the town. The mill did good for this town, and it's really hurting without
it. I wouldn't have this home if it hadn't been for that mill."

"I tell you, they ruined this town," Lawrence Benoit, an oiler employed at the mill for more than four decades, charged. "I think they just hated this area or something and wanted to bankrupt this town. That's my feelings anyway."

Shirley MacDow, hired as a secretary when she was a seventeen-year-old high school graduate in 1951, retired as a vice president. Groveton, she recalled, "was a busy little town. There was all kinds of stores, restaurants. There was a lot of activity. But nowadays, you could walk up the street naked at night and nobody'd notice you. Sad, sad, sad to see what's happened." In the mill's heyday, thirty storefronts on Main Street and State Street sustained a vibrant downtown. In the early 2020s, only ten active businesses remained.

Joe Berube, approaching retirement when the mill closed, worried about the future: "There's not a lot of opportunities today for any of the younger generation, that's for sure. If they want a job once they graduate [from high school], they're going to have to relocate somewhere." Pam Styles was fortunate to land a job as secretary of Groveton High School after thirty-seven years in the mill's office: "I think it's taken a big effect on the town, especially that tax [not] coming from Wausau, that the town was guaranteed every year. Now the slack has got to be picked up by the taxpayers in town."

The mill "was like another family," Styles said. When there was a death in the family, an illness, or a tragedy, the mill community came together. Dave Atkinson concurred: "There was always an envelope [in the paper testing lab]—a collection for someone who had a fire or chemotherapy. Significant collections. There was a great philanthropic family atmosphere at the mill. It didn't matter—union, salaried, there was an envelope there."

Several years after the mill shut down, Tom Bushey was worried about the weakening of community bonds: "I'm 44 years old, still young. Definitely could move out of this area. I'd like to see my home town come back to life, to have some semblance of a community. Because that's what it always was. Growing up, you pretty much knew the inside of every home in the town because it was like one great big family. Now, with the closing of the mill, people aren't coming together as much as they used to. I just feel like the fabric of the town is unraveling a little bit each day."

Decades after Sir James Goldsmith's takeover of Diamond, Jim Wemyss raged about the impact of financiers on the paper industry: "It's terrible. It's terrible. It's destroyed the industry as far I was concerned. I hate them with such a passion." Following one of his frequent rants against Goldsmith, I challenged him: "I thought you were a capitalist." "*I'm a building capitalist*," he shot back. "I'm not a person who tears things apart for gain. I wouldn't do it. These people in Wall Street have been disgraceful—what they've done in the past fifty years in this country."

To fill the void created by the paper mill closings, northern New England's timber industry, state economic development agencies, and several natural resource–oriented conservation groups turned to industrial bioenergy—huge boilers that burn wood chips to generate electricity. In response to the energy crises of the 1970s, Congress passed in 1978 the Public Utility Regulatory Policy Act (PURPA). The new law obligated utilities to buy power from nonutility power producers whose costs were lower than the cost of additional purchases of energy. When oil prices rose, PURPA was designed to provide a huge boost to small, decentralized producers of hydro power, wind and solar power, and bioenergy power. Instead, corporate giants such as AETNA Insurance, Westinghouse, and General Electric exploited PURPA's generous subsidies and tax incentives.[4]

Vermont promoted energy conservation, or demand reduction, rather than encouraging construction of new energy supplies; New Hampshire passed the Limited Electrical Energy Producers Act to encourage development of diversified energy production. In the mid-1980s, a fifteen-megawatt plant in Bethlehem, New Hampshire, and a sixteen-megawatt plant in Whitefield, New Hampshire, began to generate electricity. PURPA and New Hampshire legislation required Public Service of New Hampshire (PSNH) to pay the Bethlehem biomass plant 9.04 cents per kilowatt hour in off-peak hours and 12.03 cents per kilowatt hour during peak hours at a time it paid 3.5 cents per kilowatt hour for fossil fuel–generated electricity.[5]

Paul Bofinger of the Forest Society hailed bioenergy in 1987: "It's the most exciting thing that has happened since I've been in forestry." The Forest Society believed that caring landowners could conduct timber stand improvement cuts to remove low-value wood and allow higher quality trees to grow with less competition. Whole-tree chipping, the theory held, would reward excellent forestry. The Forest Society conceded that the long-term effects of repeated biomass harvesting were as yet unknown and success depended upon responsible timber harvesting.[6]

Not long after I moved to New Hampshire, a friend described a tour of the Bethlehem plant. He asked whether the plant generated the electricity to power the lights in the room. His guide informed him that the plant sold everything it produced to the grid at the high rates set by PURPA. It repurchased the plant's electrical needs at much lower rates. In the 1990s, as oil and natural gas prices came down, the PURPA-driven contracts with the biomass plants became increasingly onerous to state utilities. Central Maine Power bought out several plants, and PSNH tried to escape its overpriced contracts.

Interest in industrial biomass revived early in the new millennium. Energy policy in the United States encouraged the development of industrial-scale wind, solar, and biomass projects with tax incentives and promises of renewable energy subsidies. By 2020, more than two hundred bioenergy plants were operating in the country, with more on the drawing boards. Some of these plants burn toxic waste as well as wood chips.

The Burgess pulp mill's boiler became the centerpiece of the largest biomass plant in the northeastern United States. President Obama's 2009 stimulus package, the American Recovery and Reinvestment Act, awarded more than a billion dollars to the biomass industry in the form of "Payments for Specified Energy Property in Lieu of Tax Credits." Laidlaw Energy Group, the original developer of Burgess Biopower, received $80.65 million—a hefty chunk of its $274 million construction cost. The plant added another $72.5 million in other grants and loans. In 2013 Laidlaw paid a $3.1 million fine for misleading investors about the financial condition of the company.[7]

Burgess Bioenergy Plant, Berlin, NH.
(Photo by Barbara Tetreault, used by permission)

That year, Laidlaw cut a deal with Eversource (which had swallowed PSNH) for a Purchase Power Agreement in which Eversource would pay $100 million more than market prices for Burgess's electricity. Burgess would pass much of the $100 million on to wood chip suppliers. Meredith Hatfield, the New Hampshire consumer advocate at the time, called it an unfair deal for ratepayers who paid the costs. Republicans later denied her a reappointment as payback for defending ratepayer rights. Laidlaw sold its interest in Burgess to Cate Street Capital shortly thereafter. A Cate Street subsidiary later declared bankruptcy in Maine to evade repaying the state $16 million in loans designed to stimulate biomass production.[8]

The state of New Hampshire viewed the Burgess Biopower plant as a jobs savior and a bailout for large logging contractors. During the groundbreaking ceremony in 2011, then-Governor John Lynch hailed it as a win-win-win deal. Winners included the wealthy biomass investors, the wood chipping contractors, and the state of New Hampshire's obligation to achieve 20 percent "renewable energy" by 2020. The businessman-governor glossed over the rest of the story: taxpayers and utility ratepayers paid for the subsidies; three-quarters of the energy potential in wood chips is wasted; and industrial biomass is a major source of carbon emissions, releasing nearly 50 percent more carbon per unit of energy than coal releases to generate the same amount of energy. Biomass plants also emit nitrous oxides and particulate matter at much higher rates than coal and natural gas, but the Environmental Protection Agency regulations on those emissions are more lax.[9]

The biomass lobby has persuaded politicians that wood chips reduce fossil fuel emissions and deserve to be included in state renewable energy portfolios. In 2016, Congress, led by Maine senators Susan Collins and Angus King, passed a rider proclaiming that biomass is "carbon neutral" and does not increase net greenhouse gas emissions. This sleight of hand legislation claims that carbon emissions today will be gradually resequestered by trees in the future. However, we need a dramatic reduction in emissions *now and for decades to come.* Cutting and burning a forest releases carbon into the atmosphere immediately. The resequestration of that carbon requires 40 to 150 years, depending upon the stand condition, the site, and the intensity of the cutting.[10] Burning wood chips to generate electricity exacerbates the climate crisis. The myth of carbon neutrality allows the bioenergy industry to qualify for favorable tax treatment and clean energy credits.

Industrial bioenergy plants are a terrible investment *unless the public provides massive subsidies to investors.* In 2018 the biomass lobby, led by the New Hampshire Timberland Owners Association and the Forest Society, persuaded the legislature to pass two massive biomass subsidy bills, SB 365 and SB 577. The $100 million ratepayer subsidies granted to Burgess in 2013 were to be doled out over a twenty-year period. After only five or six years they had run dry. Burgess's owners claimed they could not turn a profit without them. SB 577, supported by Eversource, extended the subsidy another three years at a potential cost to ratepayers of $50 million.

Governor Chris Sununu journeyed to Berlin late in June to reap the political benefits of an outdoor bill signing along the banks of the Androscoggin River. The governor told the crowd this bill was all about jobs. He did not mention his veto of SB 365 a few weeks earlier. That bill, nearly identical to SB 577, authorized substantial ratepayer subsidies for the state's older biomass plants. Eversource, eager to shut down those older, smaller plants, lobbied aggressively against SB 365, and Sununu vetoed it, calling it an "unjust burden on ratepayers." No one asked the governor to explain why ratepayer subsidies to an Eversource client was a just burden, or why he didn't care about the jobs at the older bio-mass plants.

Throughout the summer of 2018, the Forest Society spearheaded the successful campaign to override the veto of SB 365. Jane Difley, then-president-forester of the society, conceded that the vetoed bill was a public subsidy, but, she affirmed, it also represented a "worthwhile in-vestment in the backbone of our economy." She warned: "Decapitating existing energy markets for low-grade wood will not advance a century of progress in restoring the resilience of New Hampshire Forests."[11]

In 2018, the Forest Society's website admitted that "over 70% of the standing timber on the Forest Society's 56,000 acres of forestland is 'low grade wood.' Our planned timber harvests involve regenerative cutting (or removing essentially all trees in a specific stand in order to regener-ate new trees), which typically results in a larger percentage of low-grade wood."[12] Why, after a century of forest management by licensed profes-sional foresters, is there such a glut of low-value wood?

Several winters ago, my wife and I watched as large machines gob-bled up a forest tract on a hillside two miles from our cabin. The timber tax forms at our town office confirmed that a high percentage of the wood from that liquidation operation had been chipped and burned at Burgess. The following spring, a friend and I visited the 245-acre whole-tree harvest operation. Except for three forlorn pines on the hillside, virtually nothing grew more than three feet above the ground. New rivulets had washed down deep skidder ruts and carried away topsoil. Six- and eight-inch-diameter hardwood stumps offered evidence that this poorly stocked stand had been cut heavily by a previous owner not that long before.

This operation supplied about twelve thousand green tons of wood chips. Burgess requires eight hundred thousand green tons a year, the

View of the 245-acre whole-tree harvest two miles from our cabin in Stratford,
New Hampshire, 2015. (Photo by Kitty Kerner, used by permission)

equivalent of nearly seventy 250-acre liquidation cuts *each year*. When
I discussed the Stratford whole-tree harvest with retired silviculture
professor Robert Seymour, he sadly commented: "You'll never have a
productive forest with biomass. Just from a management standpoint,
nobody will be able to afford to own it because there's no money in it
for a landowner."[13]

I presented a slide show of my friend's photographs to the June
2015 meeting of the Forest Advisory Board of the New Hampshire Division of Forests and Lands, a collection of forest policy insiders that
had not met since 2013. One member told me, "on average" the annual
statewide cut is less than growth. I responded that averaging cutting in
the nonindustrial forests of southern and central New Hampshire with
the intensive overcutting in Coös County masks decades of unsustainable logging of spruce and fir. A study of forest harvesting in northern
New England published in 2019 conservatively estimated that 57 percent

of the spruce-fir type, the dominant softwood species in northern New Hampshire, is "degraded." In northern New England, 40 percent of private lands are in a degraded condition, compared with only 20 percent of the region's public lands.[14]

Jasen Stack, executive director of the Timberland Owners Association, dismissed my call for effective regulations. He reminded the advisory board that four years earlier the legislature had denied New Hampshire towns the authority to adopt municipal ordinances on forest practices. Only the state could restrict abusive clear-cutting and whole-tree harvesting. Because of decades of effective lobbying by Stack's organization, the state steadfastly refuses to regulate overcutting. In a follow-up letter to the board, I wrote, "Failure to regulate ecologically destructive behavior harms forests, rewards irresponsible actors, and punishes responsible actors." I urged the board to meet on a monthly basis to address this problem.[15] I received no response. The Forest Advisory Board next convened two-and-a-half years later.

In 2020, the Division of Forests and Lands' ten-year *Forest Action Plan* promoted subsidized bioenergy as an essential component of the state's timber economy. Biomass, pulp, and firewood accounted for roughly 75 percent of the volume of New Hampshire harvests. These lower value commodities contribute about 5 percent of the value of state forest products. Sawlogs, only about 25 percent of the state's cut, account for approximately 95 percent of the value of New Hampshire forest products. The plan conceded that biomass "provides little economic return to the landowner."[16]

When bioenergy plants lose their subsidies, investors will abandon the industry. It is long past time to redirect those misguided subsidies to local communities struggling to recover from generations of forest exploitation. With some public assistance, northern New England could transition to a diverse, low-impact, locally controlled, value-adding economy.

Nightmare of the North

Protect the natural qualities and integrity of the land, natural communities,

native species, and ecological processes. . . . Manage the land with as little

interference as possible with natural ecological functions.

"Vision," Nash Stream Forest Management Plan, 1995

After the Nash Stream Advisory Committee completed the work of developing the vision and management guidelines in 1990, the staffs of the New Hampshire Division of Forests and Lands and New Hampshire Fish and Game required several years to complete the plan's more technical aspects. The Division of Forests and Lands released the management plan in 1995, and a substantially reconfigured advisory body, the Nash Stream Citizens Advisory Committee (CAC), convened three times between November 1996 and May 1998. It discussed a variety of subjects, including efforts to accelerate the first timber sale since the state acquired the Nash Stream; a proposal to establish a Cohos Hiking Trail that enters the Nash Stream Forest from the south and runs north along its eastern side, eventually exiting in the northeastern corner; and a proposal by the Stratford School to develop an outdoor classroom and interpretative trail program at the Nash Stream Forest. Few members of the public attended these early meetings.

At the CAC meeting of September 29, 1998, thirty-five members of the Stratford ATV Club overwhelmed the committee, and their leader, Ted Burns, presented a petition calling for the opening of the Nash

Stream to ATV riders. Anti–public lands local politicians strongly supported the club. The chair of the CAC stated that allowing ATVs in the Nash Stream Forest would require a change in the 1995 management plan.[1] The CAC did not meet again until May 2001, and by then, the ATV lobby had taken control of the committee's agenda.

On September 25, 2001, Representative Fred King, the most powerful Coös County politician and an uncompromising opponent of public lands, joined the CAC. He accelerated the work of altering the plan to allow ATVs into the Nash Stream. The committee also voted to make Ted Burns a member.[2]

In October, the CAC convened public comment sessions in Plymouth and Groveton. Of the 114 citizens who testified, 88 supported ATV expansion into the Nash Stream Forest and 26 opposed the proposal. Members of the public also submitted written comments. One ATVer summed up his side's position: "State of New Hampshire has obligation to thousands of registered ATV owners and you must be working towards opening more trails for us." A resident of Lancaster complained that when she went to the Nash Stream in the fall, hunters drove her out; snowmobiles spoiled winter recreation, and if the state allowed ATVs into the Nash Stream, she would be unable to enjoy peaceful recreational opportunities in the summer. She asked, "When do I and people like me, people who don't care to navigate Nash Stream on the back of a machine . . . get OUR turn to use the property?"[3]

The New Hampshire Legislature's ATV Study Committee issued a number of conclusions on December 19, 2001, notably:

- "A successful enforcement program is critical to the long-term success of ATV trail expansion and development."

- "Environmental concerns and potential degradation of an area must always be the paramount consideration."

The legislative committee's report, released on December 28, summed up the conflicts between ATV riders and nonenthusiasts: "Issues for property owners and residents, especially those who live adjacent to trails, typically are: trail erosion, illegal driving on land of others, noise, dust, dominance over other forms of recreation in trails, and operation illegally at night."

The report then changed the subject: "members of the Committee participated by invitation of the Chief of the Trails Bureau . . . in an ATV drive and display day including discussion with professionals of several New England states concerning ATV and Trailbikes issues." Committee members did not visit neighborhoods afflicted with the negative impacts of ATVs.

The legislative committee report agreed to allow the Bureau of Trails to develop a system of ATV trails on public and private lands, but only on the condition that "such trails must be operated such that all applicable state laws can be, and are, appropriately enforced." Recommendation no. 5 stated: "New ATV trails shall be created *only* when . . . [2] DRED [Department of Resources and Economic Development]/Trails Bureau has the resources to monitor and maintain trails for ATV use, and [3] Fish and Game has the resources and made the commitment to *reasonably* monitor ATV use and enforce applicable laws" (emphasis in original). Nine days earlier, this committee had acknowledged that Fish and Game was incapable of enforcing state laws: "NH Fish & Game, admittedly, is understaffed and under equipped to provide the necessary law enforcement component."[4] New Hampshire opened the Nash Stream Forest to ATVs in full knowledge that this violated the committee's conditions.

In the fall of 2001, Phil Bryce, director of the Division of Forests and Lands, requested a legal opinion from the US Forest Service to ascertain whether allowing ATVs into the Nash Stream Forest violated the terms of the 1989 easement between the state and the Forest Service. The White Mountain National Forest bans ATVs because the noise and environmental damage they cause are incompatible with the purposes of the national forest. Tom Wagner, superintendent of the WMNF, approved the proposal as long as the ATV trail remained an internal road and not a connecting (or through) road.[5]

Wagner ignored the wording of Section II-C of the easement that states New Hampshire reserved the right to preserve and manage certain specific uses in the Nash Stream Forest. Section II-C continues: "Uses which are not expressly reserved by the State shall be prohibited by the State." New Hampshire did not expressly reserve ATVs as a permitted use; therefore, the state lacks jurisdiction over ATVs in the Nash Stream.[6]

On November 5, 2001, Phil Bryce had informed George Bald, DRED commissioner, that the CAC was likely to approve opening the Nash Stream to ATVs "since they voted to put Ted Burns on the Committee." Three days later, Bryce established a Citizens Advisory Committee ATV subcommittee to "understand what the potential impacts of ATV use would be." He appointed Fred King as chair and invited Ted Burns to serve as a representative of the local ATV community.[7]

The subcommittee met once for ninety minutes, requested no data or studies, and refused to convene a second meeting. The minutes of the February 13, 2002, CAC meeting reported that the subcommittee "felt it was premature to consider the interior trail and concentrated on the connecting trail."[8] At that meeting, the CAC approved amending the management plan to permit opening the Westside Trail, an existing snowmobile trail that parallels Nash Stream for seven miles, to ATV use. By opening a through-trail connected to the trails network on private lands west of the Nash Stream Forest, the state violated the Forest Service's interpretation of the Nash Stream easement. There is no letter from the US Forest Service approving this change.

Peter Benson of The Nature Conservancy and David Publicover of the Appalachian Mountain Club submitted a minority report challenging the legitimacy of the process: "Such a decision should not be inappropriately legitimized by reference to a Study Committee that collected little information, identified no issues or concerns, and produced no written report that could help inform the Citizens Advisory Committee, DRED, the legislature, or the public. . . . In no way did the Committee's work represent the in-depth analysis called for by Director Bryce."[9]

Bryce's subcommittee ignored concerns about erosion, sedimentation, siltation, and degradation of water quality; impacts on native brook trout; habitat fragmentation; the effects of noise on wildlife and nonmotorized recreationists; and conflicts between ATVs and traditional recreational uses explicitly protected by the Nash Stream Forest management plan. The subcommittee ignored the contribution of ATV emissions to climate change and the impacts of ATVs on climate-stressed species.

Following the CAC's February meeting, DRED amended the Nash Stream Management Plan to allow ATVs on the Westside Trail on a trial basis. The amended plan expressly prohibited the development of any additional ATV trails on the Nash Stream Forest: "Beginning in the summer of 2002, about 7.6 miles of trail are now available for ATV travel utilizing [the Bordeaux Trail, the West Side Road, and the Andritz Trail]. . . . *No other roads or trails are open to ATVs on the property*" (emphasis added).[10]

At that meeting, Fish and Game biologist John Lanier said he needed one season without ATVs to gather baseline data. The politicians had other ideas, however, and in May, the New Hampshire Legislature voted to permit ATVs in the Nash Stream. At the CAC's May 16, 2002, meeting, Chris Gamache, of the Bureau of Trails, reported that the new Westside Trail required forty-four new culverts and two reroutes to avoid a beaver pond and a wet section. Gamache assured the committee, "there are currently no air quality concerns," even though, in the United States, ATVs emit several million tons of carbon annually.[11] DRED commissioner Bald approved the Westside Trail pilot project in June, and it opened to ATV traffic on August 1, 2002. Any baseline studies would have to be performed with ATVs whizzing by.

The CAC ceased operation after May 16, 2002. On March 31, 2006, the Nash Stream Forest Citizens Committee (NSFCC), established by legislation in 2004, convened its first meeting. Fred King served as chair for the next half dozen years. On March 21, 2007, Commissioner Bald informed King he had approved the Westside Trail for another three years, effectively making it a permanent fixture. Bald added: "During this pilot period several studies were conducted to assess the impact of the ATV trail on wildlife, noise levels, and surface water. The final results were presented and discussed at the Nash Stream Forest Citizens Committee on January 25, 2007."[12] The minutes of that meeting, however, contradict Commissioner Bald's claims.

By 2007, with heavy ATV usage, the vegetation that formerly covered the Westside snowmobile trail had disappeared, resulting in serious problems with dust, erosion, and mud. At the January 2007 NSFCC meeting, Bryce reported that results of the three-year mammal study had been "inconclusive," and "there were many problems with the

(Copyright © Jon Luoma)

study."[13] There is no record of an attempt to conduct a conclusive mammal study.

The minutes of that meeting stated that a bird study had concluded, "ATV's seemed to have little effect on birds. This study provided good baseline information for future surveys for monitoring or if conditions change or usage changes." In fact, the report on bird studies along the Westside Trail in 2002 and 2003 had stated, "A number of questions need to be answered before it will be possible to estimate the extent of ATV noise effects on breeding birds in the Nash Stream Forest." It warned, "these questions are of increasing importance to both public and private land managers." The state misrepresented the findings of the bird study and never attempted to answer the questions of increasing importance.[14]

In 2004 New Hampshire Fish and Game and Trout Unlimited launched a decade-long, $2 million nationally acclaimed brook trout habitat restoration project. No state agency has ever conducted water-quality sampling tests. There is no baseline or monitoring information on whether, and to what degree, the dust and sediment from ATV-caused erosion has compromised water quality. From 2002 to 2021 the state never submitted an annual monitoring report on the impacts of the Westside Trail—as required by RSA 215-A42(b).

In 2012, the ATV lobby proposed several additional ATV trails within the Nash Stream Forest to allow riders east-west passage through it. They settled on the Kelsey Notch Trail, a new snowmachine trail across the northern sector of the Nash Stream Forest. When the issue was introduced to the NSFCC on March 7, 2012, the minutes of that meeting stated, "The Nash Stream Plan would need to be revised in order for this project to move forward." There is no record that DRED amended the plan to permit the Kelsey Notch Trail. DRED claimed that the NSFCC approved the proposal, but committee approval occurred in a meeting without a quorum and with no formal minutes.[15]

When WMNF Superintendent Tom Wagner signed off on allowing ATVs in the Nash Stream in 2001, he noted that connector trails, such as the proposed Kelsey Notch Trail, required Forest Service consent and participation. There is no record that such consent was sought or granted.

In December 2012 the State Lands Management Team solicited agency comments on the Kelsey Notch Trail proposal in the northern sector of the forest. Jim Oehler of Fish and Game wrote on January 28, 2013:

> The continued expansion of North Country ATV trail riding opportunities has increased the demand on law enforcement substantially.... This demands that the NHFG [New Hampshire Fish and Game] Law Enforcement Division stretch existing funds and manpower thinner and thinner. Additional enforcement efforts on the Nash Stream SF [state forest] or other new trails in the North Country will be marginal at best. *There doesn't seem to be a clear plan for meeting law enforcement needs on the expanded Nash Stream SF ATV trail system or other proposed North Country ATV trails*.... ATVs were not a part of the original management plan.... [T]he NH Fish & Game Department will concur with the proposed trail expansions at Nash Stream SF only under the condi-

tion that the planned expansions go through an amendment process that effectively gains input from a broad array
of Nash Stream stakeholders. The plan amendment should
adequately address potential impacts to fish, wildlife, and
their habitats, especially wetland and stream connectivity
issues, an assessment of law enforcement and trail maintenance needs and how those needs will be met, and an assessment of alternative routes. [Failure to perform such a plan
amendment] *will likely lead to intense criticism by individuals
and groups who are interested in the State Forest's other uses
for which the property was originally acquired.*[16] (Emphasis
added.)

The state did not amend the management plan; it did not secure
the permission of the Forest Service, and it never conducted a formal
assessment of potential impacts to fish, wildlife, and their habitats, or
conduct a coarse filter–fine filter analysis of the proposed trail route. It
ignored Oehler's warning that Fish and Game was unable to guarantee
it could meet law enforcement needs. In April 2013, Phil Bryce, acting
commissioner of DRED, approved the Kelsey Notch Trail pilot project, even though the 2002 management plan amendment that he helped
write explicitly forbade any new ATV trails in the Nash Stream forest
without an additional plan amendment.

In 2013, the new DRED commissioner, Jeffrey Rose, appointed Ted
Burns, the leader of the Stratford ATV club, to serve as the "Designee
of the Commissioner of DRED" on the NSFCC. The state had committed to transform the Nash Stream Forest into an ATV nightmare of the
north.

On August 2, 2016, Fish and Game biologist John Magee wrote to
Director Glenn Normandeau:

I was disappointed to see [on a visit to the Kelsey Notch Trail
in November 2015] the road erosion problems on this trail
and the resulting truckloads of sediment that were obviously
entering the perennial streams there. This is a direct result of
a lack of suitable erosion control on this OHRV [off-highway

recreational vehicle] trail. . . . The erosion issue may be even worse now because the needed work still has not been done. Therefore, it seems that this trail should be closed until a solid, signed agreement is in place and the erosion problems are fixed. Furthermore, the agreement should include details about how often and when assessments will be done and by when erosion issues will be fixed. Again, the sediment coming off this road and entering perennial streams is TREMENDOUS.[17]

The Bureau of Trails allowed the Kelsey Notch Trail to remain open and unrepaired until the fall of 2017, when it trucked in 105 loads of gravel and fill (12 cubic yards per load) to replace the eroded gravel and soil. The Bureau of Trails annually receives $3 million from ATV registration fees. It paid the $22,000 cost for the gravel from those funds.[18] Where did 1,260 cubic yards of eroding materials end up?

The Council on Resources and Development (CORD), an interagency group, is charged with oversight of lands acquired by the Land Conservation Investment Program. The state, in RSA 162-C:6, acknowledged that this program was partially funded "by citizens of the state who intended that the conservation value of these lands be protected in perpetuity." On May 5, 2016, the Appalachian Mountain Club, the Forest Society, and The Nature Conservancy wrote to CORD: "Existing [ATV] Trails in Nash Stream [are] in Clear Violation of RSA 215-A: 42." The three groups quoted the 2002 amendment to the management plan that opened the Westside Trail: "No other roads or trails are open to ATVs on this property."[19]

Jeffrey Rose, commissioner of DRED, responded to the conservation groups in a letter to CORD in July. He repeated the false claims about ecological assessments: "Baseline information was gathered beginning in 2002, including a bird survey, baseline noise study, surface water study, mammal track study, turtle survey, and the studies continued."[20]

The inconclusive studies had not continued, and there had been no monitoring of the impacts of ATVs on the Westside Road in the fourteen years since it had opened in 2002. Only one noise study had been conducted by the Bureau of Trails back in 2002. The minutes of the January 2007 NSFCC meeting reported that Chris Gamache, then director of the bureau, told the committee: "Overall, if ATVs stay below 25 mph the sound doesn't register on the noise meter. The greater number of ATVs obviously increases the noise." Gamache's bureau never tested the noise of ATVs traveling in packs at speeds in excess of twenty-five miles per hour. On December 8, 2016, four years after the Kelsey Notch Trial began, CORD ruled that the trial could continue, but Nash Stream managers must submit annual monitoring reports on the trail.[21]

The Bureau of Trails scheduled Kelsey Notch monitoring visits *after* annual fall maintenance work had groomed over the sources of erosion from the trail to streams and wetlands. The 2020 monitoring report stated: "water diversion devices (rubber flaps) had been cleaned out. . . . however the rubber flaps were already filled with sedimentation again."[22] Maintaining the pristine water quality required by trout necessitates *preventing* erosion, not *controlling* its impacts after the fact.

The 2020 monitoring team discovered phragmites, a nonnative invasive reed that almost certainly entered the Nash Stream on ATVs or trail maintenance vehicles. The Division of Forests and Lands requires its contractors and logging operations to wash their machines before entering the Nash Stream Forest, but the Bureau of Trails, as of November 2021, did not.

New Hampshire Fish and Game treated the phragmites with glyphosate, a popular herbicide that according to the World Health Organization is a probable carcinogen. In June 2020, Bayer, the maker of Roundup, the most popular commercial glyphosate herbicide, paid $9.6 billion to settle more than one hundred thousand lawsuits brought by people exposed to Roundup before learning they suffered from non-Hodgkin's lymphoma.[23] If the state banned ATVs in the Nash Stream, there would be no need to apply herbicides.

In the 2020 monitoring report, Fish and Game wildlife biologist Jacob DeBow expressed "continued concern" over the impacts of noise pollution on wildlife: "we have concern about potential increases in flight behavior around active trails. . . . We have concern for how this may disrupt the normal cycles of wildlife within ear shot of the trail by interfering with breeding behavior, decreasing time spent foraging, and increasing time spent on alert and on edge as machines constantly pass by."[24]

In 2017, Fish and Game biologist Will Staats had warned, "should traffic become heavier on the trail in the future, it might preclude some animals from crossing or denning near the trail." The Bureau of Trails installed counters on Kelsey Notch for the first time in 2021, and it recorded 12,293 ATVs during the 137-day season. In 2022, Corridor C-North counters recorded 10,167 ATVs. On Saturday, May 28, 2022, there were 427 trips and 629 the following day, for a total of 1,056 trips in a two-day period.

The Kelsey Notch Environmental Compliance report of 2022, reiterating concerns recorded in the previous year's report, stated: "Fish and Game continues to have concern regarding wildlife impact of ATV noise during high volume trail use days. This is of particular concern during spring and early summer months (May/June) when song birds are nesting/ fledging and mammals are in the early days of raising young."[25]

On August 20, 2020, the Appalachian Mountain Club, The Nature Conservancy, and the Forest Society advised CORD that Kelsey Notch is incompatible with existing, low-impact forms of recreation and the trail could cause further fragmentation of Nash Stream Forest wildlife habitat.[26] These are issues that the Nash Stream Forest Technical Team has raised in the past, but political decision-makers from the Department of Natural and Cultural Resources have repeatedly ignored them.

In November, the three conservation groups submitted a legal opinion from attorney Ryan S. Duerring of the Boston legal firm of Ropes & Gray. It stated: "Based on my research of relevant New Hampshire law and regulations applicable to snowmobiles, all-terrain vehicles ('ATVs') and other off-highway recreational vehicles ('OHRVs'), I conclude that the legal opinions set forth in the [2001 Forest Service] Opinion regarding the permitted use of ATVs on the tract of forestland known as the 'Nash Stream Tract' and subject to the Easement Deed are inconsistent with applicable New Hampshire law." In January 2021, eight years into the "trial," CORD extended Kelsey Notch's provisional status for an additional two years, citing inadequate information to make a decision. CORD did not address the Ropes & Gray letter.[27]

In January 2022, the chairman of the NSFCC formally requested that Commissioner Sarah Stewart of the Department of Natural and Cultural Resources seek a legal opinion from the Forest Service regarding the meaning of Section II-C of the 1989 Nash Stream Forest easement. Stewart denied the request. The Appalachian Mountain Club, The Nature Conservancy, and the Forest Society submitted a letter to the commissioner strongly supporting the request for a legal opinion from the Forest Service. Stewart rebuffed them also. She also ignored a letter signed by thirty-five concerned citizens making a similar request. On March 8, 2022, WMNF Superintendent Derek Ibarguen refused to revisit the legality of the 2001 Forest Service decision.[28]

In January and March 2023, CORD, with 80 percent membership turnover in the preceding two years, decided the fate of the Kelsey Notch ATV trail. Fearing the worst, I recorded the March 9 meeting, where Fish and Game staff, behaving as if under political pressure, walked back their criticisms of the trail since 2013. When pressed, they conceded that concerns about inadequate safety and enforcement, and the absence of meaningful studies of the impacts of ATVs on wildlife and water quality, remain unaddressed.

Only the commissioner of agriculture spoke at length prior to the vote. He justified the lack of ecological studies: "We don't have the money." He ignored the offer from The Nature Conservancy in 2016 and again in 2020 to work with CORD to locate funding. Ignoring RSA 162-C:6, he dismissed the "intent" of the state when it acquired the Nash Stream in 1988: "Intent is only guidance. It has no legal standing. . . . What the intent was back when this was done is really irrelevant thirty-five years later."

CORD never discussed the option of closing the Kelsey Notch trail until the completion of independent ecological studies that should be funded by ATV registration fees. Instead, a dozen bureaucrats, with scant knowledge of the impacts of ATVs on the "conservation values" of the Nash Stream Forest, voted unanimously to make the trail permanent.

The Stratford Select Board appointed me to represent the town on the NSFCC in the fall of 2021. Prior to my first meeting, I learned that the number of hours Division of Forests and Lands and the Department of Fish and Game staff had devoted to ATV issues was "substantial" and invariably dealt with demands for more ATV trails in the Nash Stream. Since 1995, state agencies have complained that they cannot perform required monitoring on Nash Stream forestlands because of inadequate agency funding, yet these agencies can afford to divert substantial staff time to respond to the demands of ATVs. This constitutes a huge subsidy to a high-carbon activity.

DRED pitched the Kelsey Notch Trail to CORD in 2013 with the claim that the trail was a "vital part of the economic initiative of the North Country OHRV Coalition."[29] When New Hampshire promoted a massive buildup of the ATV economy in Coös County after the paper mill closures in Berlin and Groveton, it did so without a master plan, and it conducted no studies of possible benefits and drawbacks. To this day, no credible study has examined the role ATVs play in the Coös economy.

The ATV lobby commissioned a study of the economic benefits of OHRVs to the New Hampshire economy in 2021. It ignored adverse costs of OHRVs, and two of its positive findings raised red flags: (1) Roughly half of the "benefits" to the state were from sales of machines and gasoline to operate them. These profits leak out of the state economy to fossil fuel corporations and ATV manufacturers. (2) The study claimed that the ATV economy created eighteen new physician jobs. One can presume many of those new physician jobs are in the emergency room. Serious injuries should not be treated as economic benefits.[30]

Coös County needs a comprehensive economic study that includes the costs and benefits of ATVs but also examines a diverse array of other economic development options. Such a study needs to examine the negative impacts of ATVs on traditional, nonmotorized recreation and businesses that cater to these activities, and the costs to towns for maintenance and law enforcement on town roads open to ATV traffic. It also needs to tally the state and federal subsidies to the ATV lobby and the quantity of carbon emissions due to ATV activity.

The 1989 easement and the original Nash Stream Forest Management Plan pledged to preserve the health of the forests and waters of the Nash Stream. Global climate and biodiversity crises have grown more acute since then. Management of the Nash Stream Forest ought to concentrate on mitigating the effects of climate change and reducing threats to the climate-stressed species of the Acadian forest.

Northern New Hampshire's timber economy has declined markedly since 1988. The Nash Stream's modest timber program is a tiny fraction of the cutting in Coös County. The authors of the easement considered sawlogs and pulpwood the primary forest products of the Nash Stream. But in an era of extreme climate change, Nash Stream's most economically valuable forest product is carbon sequestration and long-term carbon storage. Adoption of passive management of the entire Nash Stream watershed would minimize habitat fragmentation for species seeking more favorable climate conditions and optimize its carbon sequestration and storage potential.

Designating the Nash Stream Forest as wildlands can serve as a model for public lands management—a rewilding landscape that is mitigating climate change and gradually restoring age class diversity. It can become a living natural history education center, with interpretive trails, natural history programs, local school programs, and untrammeled backcountry to be explored and contemplated.

The Nash Stream Forest could become a long-term ecological research project to study how overcut, former industrial Acadian forestlands recover from intensive logging in a climate crisis. How are amphibians, insects, plants, trees, and mosses responding to climate change? What new plant associations are forming? Are various species, ranging from birds and bears to lichens and trees, able to disperse at a rate necessary to keep ahead of the worst impacts of climate change and sustain their prospects for survival?

Bid the Tree Unfix His Earthbound Root

Who can impress the forest, bid the tree
Unfix his earthbound root?

MACBETH, act 4, scene 1, lines 95–96

Strong evidence exists that global warming, triggered
by the "greenhouse effect," is partly offset by healthy forests.

Northern Forest Lands Study, 1990

A t the time of the American Revolution, humans emitted fifteen million tons of carbon dioxide annually. That figure had doubled by 1800, and it reached two billion tons in 1900. Today, humans are emitting close to forty billion tons annually. The United States has released 30 percent of those emissions during the past two centuries. Between 1901 and 2021, average global temperatures increased 2.4°F (1.1°C). Climate scientists warn that the mean annual temperature could increase 7.6°F (4.2°C) by 2100.[1] Since 1895, precipitation across New England has increased 0.56 inches a decade, an increase of 6.6 inches.

Forest ecologists agree that spruce-fir forests will gradually disappear from New Hampshire, Vermont, and most of Maine if humankind fails to act expeditiously to reduce greenhouse gas emissions *and*

White cedar, Big Reed Pond, northern Maine.
(Photo by author)

draw down atmospheric carbon levels. The spruce-fir component
of the Acadian forest is expected to lose much of its southern range.
Red spruce, balsam fir, northern white cedar, black spruce, and eastern hemlock probably will decline under all emission scenarios. Their
chances of long-term survival in northern New England are bleak under the business-as-usual scenario. Paper birch, big-toothed aspen, and
quaking aspen will lose nearly all of their suitable New England habitat. Northern hardwoods, with more southerly ranges, should persist. If
atmospheric carbon dioxide levels exceed nine hundred parts per million, sugar maple, quaking aspen, yellow birch, beech, and white pine
will decline significantly in New England.[2]

Red spruce and dominant northern hardwoods are long-lived species. A warming climate may restrict red spruce to far northern Maine and the highest elevations in the mountains, but they should persist through the twenty-first century, albeit with diminished vigor and reproductive success. A 1996 survey of biodiversity in Maine reported, "Recent research indicates that red spruce has the lowest genetic variability of the spruce species found in the eastern U.S." However, when researchers compared second growth red spruce with surviving patches of old growth, they determined the "old-growth stands had higher genetic variability . . . reflecting the absence of harvest pressure in their development." Loss of genetic variability constrains red spruce's ability to adapt to climate change.[3] As warming conditions drive spruce from the southern portions of its current range, its genetic variability may further diminish.

High-elevation spruce-fir forests in the northeastern United States and eastern Canada provide 90 percent of the breeding habitat for Bicknell's thrush, a globally rare, neotropical migratory species. An additional temperature increase of 1.8°F (1°C) would reduce its habitat by half. If summer temperatures increase 10.8°F (6°C), Bicknell's thrush would be unable to breed even on the summits of Mount Washington and Mount Katahdin.[4] A few alpine plant species, such as the globally rare dwarf mountain cinquefoil (*Potentilla robbinsiana*), face extinction. The future also is bleak for insects confined to rare or narrow habitat types, such as the Katahdin arctic butterfly and the purple lesser fritillary butterfly.

Annual and decadal averages of changes in temperature and precipitation mask considerable seasonal variation. Maximum New England winter temperatures increased 3.5°F (1.9°C) between 1901 and 2011; minimum winter temperatures increased 4.2°F (2.3°C). We can expect snowfall to diminish, with December experiencing the most significant declines. Without the insulation provided by deeper snow cover, ground will freeze to greater depths, and trees will become more susceptible to root damage. Increased floods and ice flows could scour streambeds and kill aquatic insect larvae.[5]

Snowshoe hare may be more vulnerable to predators when there are longer mismatches between the color of their fur and the ground.

With shorter hibernation periods, we can expect increased conflicts between bears and humans. Coyotes, wild turkeys, and woodcock should
benefit from greater winter food availability. Moose rely upon balsam
fir for winter forage and are intolerant of heat. As fir retreat to Canada,
moose populations may decline or disappear. White-tailed deer will expand their northern range as the snow cover diminishes. They carry a
brain worm fatal to moose. Deer browsing will negatively affect northern white cedar and northern hardwoods.[6]

Species at the southern edge of their range, such as the northern
bog lemming, American marten, and Canada lynx, may disappear from
northern New England. Lynx require one hundred inches of snowfall
per year, and marten about seventy-five inches annually. As snowfall
levels decline in warmer winter scenarios, and as spruce and fir disappear, bobcats and fishers will probably displace lynx and marten.[7]

Less snow and more precipitation in the form of rain and sleet will
compromise winter recreation seasons. Logging machinery inflicts less
damage to frozen ground. As winters warm, the potential for greater
soil erosion and compaction increases unless winter logging is curtailed.

Between 1961 and 2010, as winters became milder, springtime last
freeze dates arrived ten days earlier in the Northeast. First freeze dates
are happening somewhat later in the autumn. By 2100, under high emissions scenarios, the growing season in the northeastern states could increase four or more weeks.[8]

Some tree, plant, and animal species have already modified behav-
iors to survive new climate conditions. Many plants now flower earlier
in the spring. North American tree swallows advanced egg laying by
up to nine days in a thirty-two-year period (1959–1991), probably in
response to the earlier emergence and peak abundance of flying insects
responding to warming conditions. Temperature is the most important cue for temperate-region frogs to emerge in the spring and migrate
to breeding sites. Researchers in Ithaca, New York, have heard spring
peepers, wood frogs, gray tree frogs, and bullfrogs calling ten to thirteen
days earlier than a century ago.[9]

Rapid climate change threatens to disrupt the timing between her-
bivorous insects and their food plants. If flowers and their pollinators
respond differently to climate change, who pollinates the flower? What

will sustain the pollinators? Climate change could disrupt timing between predators and their prey.

Generalist bird species will probably adapt to climate change or
successfully disperse to new habitat. Unless current warming trends are
soon reversed, the blackpoll warbler, an insectivore of the spruce-fir
forests, may be extirpated from New Hampshire, Vermont, and much
of Maine by 2080. Boreal chickadees, white-winged crossbills, yellow-
bellied flycatchers, spruce grouse, gray jays, ruby-crowned kinglets,
three-toed woodpeckers, and black-backed woodpeckers rely on mon-
tane spruce-fir forests of the northern Appalachians. Under a business-
as-usual scenario, suitable habitat for most if not all of these species will
disappear from northern New England. Declines in bird reproductive
success may lead to an increase in insects.[10]

The common loon may lose substantially more than 50 percent of
its northeastern US habitat. It faces additional threats to its winter habitat
where warming temperatures and rising sea levels, along with relentless
development pressures, are expected to cause further declines in coastal
wetland quality. Loons will persist in Canada, but New Englanders may
no longer enjoy the wild loon tremolo and its mournful evening wail.[11]

Under higher emissions scenarios, short- and long-term summer
and fall droughts will increase dramatically by 2100. Warmer air temperatures will increase evapotranspiration rates. As wetlands dry out and
shrink under summer drought, species dependent upon them decline.
When streams, rivers, lakes, and ponds warm, dissolved oxygen levels
diminish, threatening the survival of trout and other cold-water species.
Transitory habitats, such as vernal pools, are vulnerable to severe hydrological disruptions, with potentially devastating effects upon amphibian
reproductive success.

Soils will probably store less water in summer when a higher proportion of winter precipitation is rain followed by earlier spring runoffs.
Plants and trees will continue to draw water during droughts, further
diminishing soil moisture content. Droughts cause forest productivity to
decline, and trees become more vulnerable to pests and pathogens. Sugar
maple, birch, and ash species suffer dieback from prolonged drought.[12]

Insect species capable of rapid phenotypic adaptations and oc-
cupying a variety of habitats across a broad range of elevations and

latitudes will expand their ranges, and formerly benign insect species may become significant pests. Nonnative pests, such as hemlock woolly adelgid, beech bark fungus, and white pine blister rust, will benefit from warmer conditions. The hemlock woolly adelgid cannot survive during extended periods of temperatures below −20°F (−29°C). Forest ecologists now expect the adelgid will infest hemlock populations in northern New England once considered to be safe.[13]

The greatest increases in precipitation over the past century have occurred in October, November, and May. We can expect more intense and more frequent windstorms and late summer hurricanes. Autumn foliage could be muted as maples succumb to stress and warming temperatures. Drought conditions and declining forest health could impact bird migrations south.

Vegetation lags behind climate, and today's vegetation communities reflect past, rather than current, climate conditions. In times of mild climate variation, the lags are not as pronounced as they can be in times of rapid change. Scientists believe that for every 1.8°F (1°C) increase in temperature, species need to migrate northward approximately sixty miles across an often-fragmented landscape. During the Holocene, tree migration rates averaged six to thirty miles per century across an *unfragmented* landscape. Plants, mosses, fungi, lichen, most invertebrates, and small vertebrates such as amphibians disperse more slowly, at different rates, and in differing directions. Changing species associations produce new predation, browsing, and pollination challenges, and natural selection may be unable to keep pace.

Visually, the stressed forests of the twenty-second century are unlikely to exhibit significant change in composition or distribution of tree species. Over the next millennium, ecologists expect forests will remain quite disturbed, much younger, and in a state of flux. Today's tree species will persist in their current ranges, and newly arrived tree species from Massachusetts, Connecticut, and New York will be in the seedling and sapling stage.

As climate conditions worsen, expect increased mortality of older trees and decreasing success of seedling germination. Drier soils and increasing competition from more southerly species may prevent stressed species from successfully regenerating in portions of their current range. In the course of time, ghost forests of old trees may reign over an understory of seedlings and saplings of more southerly species. Expect unwelcome surprises.

Species of central and southern New England, especially red, white, black, and chestnut oaks and sweet birch, will be among the earliest species to colonize northern New England two hundred miles to the north, but probably not before 2100. Few if any stands will be dominated by three-hundred-year-old oaks north of the White Mountains before 2500, even if conditions for oak dispersal are favorable.

North Carolina's climate could reach the Acadian forest in another century, but its species will require centuries, perhaps millennia, to disperse seven hundred miles across a highly developed landscape. Not all species driven from the greater North Carolina region will reach northern New England.

If carbon dioxide levels are brought down to 350 parts per million by the year 2050, the ecological impacts of anthropogenic climate change could be relatively mild. If the levels are at or above 550 parts per million by 2100, we can expect irreversible ecological and hydrological changes in northern New England's forests. The northern hardwood forest would cover less than 10 percent of its current area. Mature and old growth forests, composed of a greater diversity of age classes and species, and abundant deadwood, should retain more of their character for longer periods of time than heavily disturbed younger stands. The outlook for maple sugar production is unclear. Sugar maples are shade tolerant and currently are less assailed by insect pests, but they appear to be very sensitive to nutrient loss caused by soil acidification, and this may restrict their ability to reproduce under increasingly hotter climate conditions. Yellow birch and American beech may retain only small amounts of their current ranges. Familiar spring wildflower species would diminish, but dispersing wildflowers from farther south may not yet have arrived.

Climate scientists agree that reducing carbon emissions is essential for preventing temperature increases greater than 2.7°F to 3.6°F (1.5°C to 2°C). Reduced emissions only slow the rate of increase of atmospheric carbon levels. To lower atmospheric carbon dioxide from the 2020 level of 417 parts per million, we need negative emissions—the removal of large amounts of carbon from the atmosphere by trees and other plants via photosynthesis.

More carbon is stored in forests than in Earth's atmosphere. Live northern hardwood trees, including their roots, store 43 percent of a forest's carbon; live spruce-fir trees and roots store 26 percent. Deadwood stores 7 percent in both forest types. Northern hardwood soil organic matter and leaf litter store 50 percent of forest carbon; in spruce-fir stands, soils and litter hold 67 percent of the forest carbon.[14]

Logging in the United States emits more than seven hundred million tons of CO_2-equivalants, roughly one-seventh of annual US emissions. Logging and deforestation account for 88 percent of forest carbon emissions; native insects, wildfires, and other natural disturbances are responsible for the remaining emissions.[15] Intensive cutting also reduces a stand's resilience to climate stress and compromises the quality of forest ecosystem services, such as water quality, nutrient cycling, soil formation, and relatively stable climate conditions.

A 2019 study reports more than half of the climate-stressed spruce-fir stands in New Hampshire and Maine are in a degraded condition after a century and a half of intensive logging; 40 percent of northern hardwoods in New Hampshire and Maine are classified as degraded. Another study, released in 2021, reported that harvesting in New England released twelve times more carbon into the atmosphere than development in New England released.[16] In northern New England's industrial forest, intensive logging, not development, is by far the greatest greenhouse gas emitter.

There is no future for industrial forestry.

The understocked forests of northern New England have the potential to store considerably more carbon if we allow trees to mature in ecological, not economic, terms, and the goal of forest management is maintenance of ecosystem integrity.

Foresters claim that younger forests, dominated by trees four to sixteen inches in diameter in stands roughly thirty to seventy years old, boast the highest carbon sequestration rates. This is misleading.

Following intensive cutting, a forest continues to be a carbon source for another decade or two. Older trees and forests store vastly more carbon than young forests. In a talk delivered late in 2021, forest researcher Charles Canham declared: "There is this myth that young forests are more productive than old forests. . . . In principle, at some point forests have to stop accumulating carbon. . . . It just turns out that there are no forests in the eastern United States . . . that have reached that limit. . . . Even our highest biomass forests are continuing to add carbon at a very respectable rate."[17]

University of Vermont forest researcher William Keeton and co-authors wrote in 2011: "Our results support the hypothesis that biomass has the potential to increase very late into stand development, showing only slight declines as dominant trees pass 300 years of age, and continued additions to 400 years and beyond. . . . Correlations between total aboveground biomass and dominant tree age were related not just to increases in the standing dead tree component but also to substantial biomass accrual in live trees." They suggested young to mature secondary hardwood forests could, if left unmanaged, double and possibly quadruple forest carbon storage.[18]

Unmanaged forests sequester and store much more carbon than managed forests. Keeton and Jared Nunery wrote: "We showed that even with consideration of C[arbon] sequestered in harvested wood products, unmanaged northern hardwood forests will sequester 39 to 118% more C than any of the active management options evaluated." Their recommendation? "This finding suggests that reserve-based approaches will have significant C storage value."[19]

Paul Catanzaro and Tony D'Amato, authors of a 2019 report on forest carbon, conclude that "a passive approach to forest management will likely maximize forest carbon storage through the accumulation of carbon in each pool as the forest grows older." Managed private lands in northern New England boast few stands more than one hundred years of age. The public owns most older forests.[20]

Fierce Green Fire

In those days we had never heard of passing up a chance to kill a wolf. . . .

We reached the old wolf in time to watch a fierce green fire dying in her eyes.

I realized then, and have known ever since, that there was something new to

me in those eyes—something known only to her and to the mountain.

ALDO LEOPOLD, "Thinking Like a Mountain"

In the mid-1990s, two respected conservation scientists, Michael Soulé and Reed Noss, promoted a new strategy they called rewilding. They wrote: "Our principal premise is that rewilding is a critical step in restoring self-regulating land communities." The three characteristics of rewilding are large, strictly protected core reserves; connectivity between cores; and the restoration of large predators: cores, corridors, and carnivores. "Studies are demonstrating that the disappearance of large carnivores often causes these ecosystems to undergo dramatic changes, many of which lead to biotic simplification and species loss."[1]

If we protect the habitat needs of wolves and cougars, we protect most of the native plant and animal species and natural communities of the northern Appalachians, as well as hedging our bets when very large disturbance events, including climate change, occur. Few core areas are large enough to sustain wolves and cougars. We need to connect cores with each other via corridors along rivers, animal migration routes, and other wild pathways. Soulé and Noss asserted that rewilding is "scientific realism, assuming that our goal is to insure the long-term integrity of the land community."[2]

(Copyright © Jon Luoma)

Where human activity is low, and there is adequate prey, wolves will thrive. A University of Maine wildlife ecologist concluded in 1998 that the twelve million acres of northern Maine could support a minimum of 488 wolves. The following year, a deer biologist with Maine's Department of Inland Fisheries and Wildlife reacted to that study with a shocking memo urging the state to permit hunting and trapping of wolves every day of the year.[3]

The designation of a network of large reserves throughout North America, coupled with a dramatic reduction in logging intensity and area harvested, is essential to combat climate change and preserve wild nature. In the undeveloped former industrial forests of northern New England, there is an opportunity to establish climate reserves of several million acres. In 2001, Bill McKibben wrote, "The notion of a rewilded East has moved from the category of hazy hallucination to the category of clear and prophetic vision. . . . It is, in conservation terms, all of a sudden the most rousing spot on the planet."[4]

The Northern Forest Lands Council's original work plan ignored biodiversity preservation, public land acquisition, and the need to establish a regional network of ecological reserves. In December 1991, the Northern Forest Alliance united to force the NFLC to address these issues. When the council released its draft plan in March 1994, Recommendation 13 called for the northern forest states to assess public and private conservation lands and, "where necessary, create ecological reserves as a limited component of their public land acquisition and management programs." New reserves could be established only after "rigorous scientific justification, verified by external peer review."[5]

Middlebury College biology professor Stephen Trombulak responded that protecting representative examples of northern forest ecosystems fails "because it does not address the issue of restoration of biotic integrity of the region. . . . because it explicitly states that ecological reserves should be a limited component of public land acquisition strategies. . . . because it advocates giving sole responsibility for conserving biological diversity to the states. . . . [and] because it is the only recommendation made by the Council that calls for rigorous justification and external peer review." Trombulak wrote that a successful conservation policy aims for the restoration of extirpated native species; the establishment of large, connected, and buffered reserves; and the practice of ecologically responsible forest management.[6]

The NFLC final report, *Finding Common Ground*, ignored these concerns and recommended the work of the Maine Forest Biodiversity Project, where a "preliminary scientific assessment" had concluded "a reserve system would be limited in size, encompassing only a small portion of the landscape."[7] The project, led by NFLC member Roger Milliken, adopted a "consensus" strategy to protect a few scattered, small representative examples of Maine's natural communities. When I challenged the project to adopt the goal of preserving ecosystem integrity, Milliken refused. I turned to University of Maine at Orono biology professor Malcolm Hunter and asked whether a system of representative reserves would protect the state's ecological integrity. He answered, "No."

In January 1996, the Maine Natural Areas Program produced a report for the Forest Biodiversity Project, *Biological Diversity in Maine,* that highlighted a number of troubling findings:

• Little is known of insects, arachnids, and other invertebrate phyla, but populations of most invertebrate species native to Maine are probably shrinking.

• The state of our knowledge of bryophytes (mosses, etc.), lichens, fungi, and protista (algae, protozoa) ranges from "not well known" to "very poorly known."

• There is no long-term monitoring data on amphibians, a class experiencing documented declines in eastern states.

• Reptiles are facing greater threats than amphibians.

• Fish have been more severely affected by human activity perhaps than any other group of organisms.

• Data on nongame mammals are sparse.

• "Good natural examples" of even the most common forest types, such as the spruce-fir forests that dominate the northern half of the state, are "rare."

• "Perhaps the most disturbing finding in terms of biodiversity trends is an apparent elimination, for many years at least, of [invertebrate] species considered to require mature forests."[8]

In 2001, Maine established thirteen ecological reserves covering 68,974 acres on state-owned lands located in the industrial forest region—about 0.3 percent of the area of the entire state. Reserve size averaged 5,300 acres, and 69 percent of the reserved lands could not sustain timber harvesting because of elevation, slope, wetlands, or water. The state allowed ATVs to stir up mud and dust within reserved areas. The remainder of Maine has still not been evaluated for a statewide ecological reserve network. A 2010 assessment of the effectiveness of land conservation in Maine determined that most of the state's high ecological value lands remain outside reserves and easements. Designated reserves are too small, isolated, and fragmented to maintain viable populations of most species and are inadequately buffered from managed lands.[9]

Initially, New Hampshire adopted a more progressive approach to ecological reserves: aim for the preservation of ecological integrity. In 1998, the Scientific Advisory Group to the New Hampshire Ecological Reserves Steering Committee concluded that there was "an urgent and scientifically-established need for concerted conservation" of the state's biodiversity. The advisory group recommended the "establishment of a well-coordinated, comprehensive system of ecological reserves that, in conjunction with good management of commercial timberlands, wildlife populations, and watersheds, will protect the full spectrum of biological diversity in the state over the long term." The group found that almost 60 percent of the rare natural communities and nearly three-quarters of the known rare plants have two or fewer occurrences on conservation lands.[10]

The directors of New Hampshire Forests and Lands and the Department of Fish and Game encouraged the Ecological Reserves Steering Committee to develop a statewide reserve network. However, a few months later, a core group, composed of New Hampshire Fish and Game, the Division of Forests and Lands, The Nature Conservancy, the Audubon Society of New Hampshire, and the Forest Society, dissolved

the Ecological Reserves Steering Committee and quietly buried the Scientific Advisory Group's report. Two decades later, New Hampshire
has no ecological reserves system. The New Hampshire Division of
Forests and Lands' *New Hampshire Forest Action Plan—2020* contains
no mention of ecological reserves.[11]

The politicization of the Maine Forest Biodiversity Project, coupled with the Northern Forest Alliance's unwillingness to propose a reserve strategy for the industrial forest, provoked me to ask, "How large
can reserves be in northern New England?" As a first step, I mapped the
region's absentee-owned lands and drew in all major state roads, such as
Route 201 from Skowhegan to Jackman and Route 16 from Errol, New
Hampshire, to Flagstaff Lake in Maine. This exercise identified sixteen
core reserves that encompass the headwaters of northern New England's
great rivers—the Connecticut, Androscoggin, Kennebec, Penobscot,
Allagash, and Saint John.

In the summer of 1995, I proposed an 8.7-million-acre Headwaters
Wilderness Reserve System covering most of northern Maine and significant chunks of northern New Hampshire and Vermont's Northeast
Kingdom.[12] It included the entirety of the proposed Maine Woods National Park. Imagine a national park surrounded by another five million
acres of unmanaged wildlands.

The Headwaters proposal, more than four times the size of Yellowstone National Park, is large enough to withstand the largest natural
disturbance regimes. When implemented, it would protect habitat for
nearly all rare plant and animal species native to northern New England. It provides optimal conditions for the return of ecologically viable populations of cougar, lynx, wolf, and caribou. The Headwaters
Reserves offer unknown microflora and fauna—soil microbes, fungi,
and invertebrates—a fighting chance to survive, recover, thrive, evolve,
and someday be studied and catalogued by naturalists.

Climate change exacerbates habitat loss. For many climate-stressed
species, dispersal may be the best, or only, option for survival. At more
than two hundred miles along its north-south axis, Headwaters would
provide temperature-sensitive plants and animals with unfragmented
pathways to more climate friendly northern habitats. Even if climate

Map of the Headwaters Wilderness Reserve System proposal. It covers 8,704,147 acres of absentee-owned industrial and large nonindustrial lands in northern Maine, New Hampshire, and Vermont. Research led by the Harvard Forest and Highstead has determined that as of 2022, 797,147 acres within the proposed Headwaters Reserve enjoy high levels of wildlands protection. (Source: David Foster, Emily Johnson, Brian Hall, Elizabeth Thompson, Brian Donahue, Jon Leibowitz, Edward Faison et al., "Wildlands in New England: Past, Present and Future," Harvard Forest Paper 35 [Petersham, MA: Harvard Forest, 2023]. Map by Brian Hall, adapted from map produced by Cartographic Associates, copyright © *Northern Forest Forum*, that appeared in *Northern Forest Forum* 3, no. 5 [1995]): 16–17.)

change drives the Acadian forest out of New England, Headwaters can mitigate the loss of genetic diversity of species near the southern limits of their range and optimize the carbon sequestration and storage capabilities of these lands.

Existing public lands would remain under current state, federal, or nonprofit conservation organization management. The Maine Woods National Park, if established, would be managed by the National Park Service.

The Headwaters network would connect scattered public land holdings from the Allagash Wilderness Waterway, Baxter State Park, and Katahdin Woods and Waters National Monument to Umbagog National Wildlife Refuge, the White Mountain National Forest, and the Silvio O. Conte National Fish and Wildlife Refuge, along with many smaller state units. Headwaters could connect with reserves in eastern Canada, the Green Mountains, and the Adirondacks as part of a continental network of reserves.

Since 1995, a small percentage of the lands included in the Headwaters proposal have been preserved as wildlands. Implementation of the Headwaters vision today would not alter the status of such lands. Lands under conservation easements will, hopefully, become wildlands in the near future.

A 2019 study from the University of New Hampshire concluded that more than half of the forestland in northern New England is in a degraded condition. A Harvard Forest study that year warned that if current industrial-scale timber management practices persist over the next half century, the industrial forests of northern New England will be responsible for 68 percent of all of the greenhouse gases emitted from managed forests in New England.[13] Northern New England's former industrial forests on average are approaching thirty to fifty years of age. They are primed to begin to sequester carbon at an impressive rate and are excellent candidates for passive management.

The highest and best uses of the former industrial timberlands are for wildlife habitat and carbon sequestration and storage. Enacting the Headwaters proposal eliminates the single greatest source of forest carbon emissions in the region and transforms the former industrial forest

from a carbon source to a sink with great potential to pull carbon from
the atmosphere and store it for centuries to come.

In the 2010s, timber investors, such as university endowments and
hedge funds, began to turn away from investing in the northern forests.
The absentee land speculators who acquired much of the former paper
company lands are now eager to unload their degraded lands. Unless attractive new subsidies such as carbon offset credits are in the offing, investors will continue to shy away from overpriced, poorly stocked lands.

As they grow desperate to sell poorly performing timberland investments, landowners may accept offers from the federal government
or wildlands philanthropists that reflect the land's true market value.
A poorly stocked acre ought to fetch considerably less than the $375 an
acre John Malone paid GMO Renewable Resources in 2011. On easement lands, the value of the land is in its standing timber, and the cost
of an easement must be subtracted from the acquisition price.

The transition from industrial forest to Headwaters Reserve will
not happen overnight, but it is time to start the process. In the next
decade, the public could acquire a considerable amount of land from
timberland investment management organizations. Not all large timberland owners are eager to sell out today, particularly the Pingree heirs,
Irving, and Malone. Ending subsidies to speculators, clear-cutters, wood
chippers, and raw log exporters ought to diminish the allure of investing
in New England's former industrial forestlands.

Ambitious public land acquisition initiatives need not raise our
taxes or force the treasury to print money, provided we adopt honest accounting practices to internalize externalities and redirect harmful subsidies toward public land acquisition. *As former northern New England
paper company lands come on the market, the public should acquire them
and enroll them in the Headwaters Wilderness Reserve System.*

E • I • G • H • T • E • E • N

Frugal Prosperity

Measuring the world in monetary units makes us blind to the
ecological constraints on sustainability.

ANDREW WHITTAKER, 1999

I t is unconscionable that the global economy forces rural communities to choose between jobs and ecosystem health. We can never
achieve a viable, low-carbon rural economy until we embrace an
ethos of frugal prosperity that desires little, yet meets our basic
needs.

A flourishing rural economy begins with a healthy landscape.
Headwaters offers hope that northern New England can enjoy land
health *and* jobs. If we can extricate local and regional economies as
much as possible from the clutches of global capital, and minimize
those threats we cannot entirely escape, we may begin the transition
toward a low-carbon economy and a healthier landscape.

Extreme quarantine measures, where applied swiftly and effectively, slowed the spread and lethality of COVID-19 in the spring of
2020. We learned we can transform our lifestyles and economy overnight. There was a dramatic, albeit temporary, 17 percent global reduction of carbon emissions in the first month of the stay-at-home new
world order.[1]

The COVID lockdowns reinforced many of the same lessons at-
tentive citizens have learned from climate change over the past several
decades: we cannot escape natural limits, and ignoring a crisis won't

(Copyright © Jon Luoma)

make it go away. We experience the impacts of pandemics almost immediately; the consequences of climate change, however, are slower to play out and therefore easier to ignore, deny, or delay addressing. Whether the consequences of a global crisis are nearly instantaneous or slow to develop, disaster awaits those who fail to act in a timely, appropriate manner. Lessons learned from the early COVID-19 shutdown include the following:

The simple life is the good life. The abrupt lockdown caused acute economic disruptions and hardships, yet most citizens endured it with grace—at least until right-wing demagogues roused the rabble. Nightly songs from urban balconies, more time with children, and a rediscovery of a simpler lifestyle in a more caring—albeit temporarily fractured and isolated—community have reminded us how resilient we can be, and how we can join together when confronted with existential threats. The lockdown challenged us to reconsider what is truly essential for a fulfilling life. Many of us did not miss the junk our hyper consumerist, throw-away economy produces.

Nature is a solace. Gifts of nature are free, leave low-carbon footprints, and send nothing to the landfill. Those of us fortunate to live near natural places enjoy tracking the return of the spring birds and wildflowers. When we visit green spaces, they reward our alertness, attentiveness, and inquisitiveness. Happiness is a child's delight in trying to catch a frog or a firefly.

As we spend more time in nature, we begin to sense how an ecosystem is so much greater than the sum of its individual species. We perceive how change renews, revitalizes, and enriches natural communities. We absorb the wisdom of Aldo Leopold's land ethic: "A thing is right when it tends to preserve the integrity, stability, and beauty of the biotic community. It is wrong when it tends otherwise."[2]

We can reclaim common lands and our roles as commoners. The simple life of the COVID-19 lockdown greatly increased the use of parks. The Trust for Public Lands wrote in 2020: "Parks are proving to be an essential part of how we cope and recover from this crisis."[3] We need more common lands and more commoners who embrace a Leopoldian land ethic to achieve a lower carbon lifestyle.

Hundreds of millions of American citizens, mostly urban and poor, live without tree cover or easy access to untrammeled green spaces or urban parks. Their communities are much more likely to suffer from air and water pollution and toxic waste. This injustice jeopardizes their physical and mental health. It is everyone's birthright to live within a half mile of one or more green spaces.

Conservationists and environmental justice advocates must collaborate to protect urban green spaces for food production, recreation, and increased forest cover that sequesters carbon, provides shade, and reduces urban temperatures. Green spaces in cities and suburbs can become part of a network of greenways, waterways, and larger wild spaces.[4] Greening cities can help transform our consumerist culture into one that cherishes time spent exploring the outdoors with children, grandchildren, and friends.

Nature is a stern guide. Scientists warned in April 2020: "Rampant deforestation, uncontrolled expansion of agriculture, intensive farming, mining and infrastructure development, as well as the exploitation of wild species have created a 'perfect storm' for the spill over of diseases from wildlife to people. This often occurs in areas where communities live that are most vulnerable to infectious diseases."[5] Treating land with respect and a lighter touch offers hope for fewer human-caused disasters, and greater happiness for all. Continued climate denialism and dithering promise increasingly harsh natural disasters.

Anthropologist Marshall Sahlins wrote that modern humans have "erected a shrine to the Unattainable: *Infinite Needs.*" A nineteenth-century Concord wag concurred: "A man is rich in proportion to the number of things which he can afford to let alone."[6] Today's climate and extinction crises challenge us to reduce our global demand for nonessential consumer products and the energy required to procure raw materials, manufacture goods, and transport them.

We cannot alter laws of physics, chemistry, biology, and climate science. We can transform human behavior. In 2022, atmospheric carbon dioxide levels reached 417 parts per million, a nearly 20 percent increase since the summer of 1988 when James Hanson warned Congress of the intensifying threat of anthropogenic climate change. Erratic, extreme weather events have become routine.

Our current jumble of energy policies reflects a belief, unsupported by any evidence, that we can maintain current levels of production and consumerism *and* rapidly reduce carbon emissions. We are obliged to reject nonsense such as "demand is sacred" and "we can solve the climate crisis without inconveniencing consumers, corporations, and investors." Rather than chase phantom technological fixes, let us reduce demand *and* protect unmanaged, photosynthesizing forests.[7] A reliable carbon accounting system, once adopted, will confirm that "demand reduction"—a combination of energy avoidance, conservation, and efficiency measures—is the cheapest and most effective method for reducing our carbon emissions. The gains from demand reduction will enable us to shut down older, inefficient power plants before we need to consider the construction of new, lower carbon energy sources.

Let us dispense with plastic products, junk mail, junk food, pesticides, and internal combustion machines. Air conditioners and clothes dryers may be convenient, but smart architecture and clothes lines provide similar services with a much smaller carbon footprint. The payback

(Copyright © Jon Luoma)

for demand reduction is immediate, certain, large, and affordable—
provided all sectors of society, from the family unit to the largest corporate and governmental levels, participate.

   A tax on carbon is a proven, but unpopular, incentive to reduce a
corporation's carbon emissions. In the 1990s, market-oriented conservation groups developed an alternative program to allow greenhouse
gas emitters to purchase carbon offset credits from forestland owners as a substitute for actually reducing their own emissions. Smaller
landowners, who are more open to practicing lower impact forestry,
may be unable to participate in the program because the cost of enroll-
ing and monitoring thousands of small landholdings is prohibitively
high. Monitoring complex carbon credit programs is expensive, poorly
funded, and rarely performed properly. Most purchasers of carbon
credits are more interested in improved public relations than adequate
monitoring and enforcement.[8]

Critics charge that carbon credits are a distraction from real climate solutions. Carbon offset programs allow polluters to spew carbon into the atmosphere now, because at some future date, trees owned by someone else will recapture that carbon. We need polluters to take responsibility for reducing their emissions dramatically and immediately, not promises of future sequestration that provide polluters cover to continue emitting greenhouse gases.

A carbon offset credit program ought to pay a landowner for sequestration that occurs only because of an offset deal. Many programs pay landowners for not cutting what they had no intention of cutting. Carbon offset credit programs must require carbon be stored indefinitely. Most offset programs require only forty years of storage. Half a human lifetime hardly qualifies as long term, let alone permanent. Carbon offset programs must work in tandem with demand reduction.

Lyme Timber earned $53 million from carbon offsets during 2020–2021. Jim Hourdequin, CEO of Lyme, is the first forest industry executive to acknowledge that carbon offset projects don't change how forests are managed and don't significantly reduce atmospheric carbon levels. His proposed reforms have not, as yet, garnered much support from buyers, sellers, and administrators of offset programs.[9] I am seeing evidence that carbon credits have become the subsidy global capital seeks to reduce the costs of investing in former industrial paper company land. Landowners deserve compensation for the benefits their well-managed and unmanaged forests provide, but current offset programs do not advance us toward a carbon-neutral future. Taxing carbon emissions is a more cost-effective policy.

Public lands serve as the infrastructure for a recreation and tourism economy, northern New England's second most important economic asset. Communities in the vicinity of Baxter State Park and the White Mountain National Forest now rely more on recreation than timbering.

An economy based on recreation and tourism is vulnerable to hard times during economic downturns. A wise northern New England community will view low-impact farming and forestry endeavors that offer a wide variety of high value–added, niche products as its economic main-stays. Recreation and tourism ought to be valued as a bonus, not the foundation, of a vibrant, low-carbon economy.

Forest industry lobbyists bash wilderness as economically worth-less because *they* cannot make money cutting wood. When I advanced the Headwaters proposal in 1995, northern Maine's industrial forest supported roughly one job per 800 acres. A study conducted five years later estimated that one new job is created for every 550 acres of eastern wilderness protected.[10] People do not plan expensive vacations to hike in clear-cuts, nor do they dream of fly-fishing in heated, silted streams. Transforming the Headwaters from an industrial forest to a vast wild-lands could eventually *increase* employment in communities where timber-related jobs have been declining for decades.

Recreation and tourism impose a large carbon footprint. People drive long distances to reach their destinations. Some activities impose a relatively low impact on the land; downhill skiing and motorized recre-ation are high-carbon pursuits. There are conflicts between motorized recreationists and those who value peace, quiet, remoteness, birdsong, and a whiff of fresh air.

Northern New England communities can structure a lower car-bon recreation and tourism economy around their natural and cultural assets. In my town of Stratford, we boast mountains, streams, the Con-necticut River, the Nash Stream State Forest, and Fort Hill State Wild-life Refuge—a wonderful place to encounter otters, skunks, numerous duck species, and a rich variety of migrating birds.

We could establish a natural and cultural history museum to cel-ebrate the presettlement Acadian forest, the Abenaki, colonial-era farm-ing, the great Connecticut River drives, nineteenth-century sawmills, and the regional paper industry. Imagination and wiser use of public funding could elevate our lovely town from the economic doldrums to a gateway into our enchanting natural and human communities.

After the demolition of its pulp mill, Berlin, New Hampshire, turned to conventional economic renewal strategies: subsidized indus-trial biomass, prison construction, and a largely unregulated ATV econ-omy. A decade and a half later, despite more than half a billion dollars of taxpayer and ratepayer funds spent to construct the Burgess biomass plant and two prisons, prosperity has not trickled downtown. Derelict Main Street storefronts face the front steps to Berlin's City Hall.

Lancaster, a forty-five-minute drive from Berlin, offers a more hopeful story. As large box stores moved into the region and the area's mills declined, Lancaster's Main Street began to decay. When the Rialto, a 1930s-era movie theater, closed in 2011 for the third or fourth time, Greg Cloutier, an engineer who had worked at the Groveton mill, brought it back to life: "When we turned the lights of the marquee on," Cloutier told me, "all of a sudden, the compliments: 'Life is coming back to Main Street.' I thought, 'That's not a bad idea.'"[11] Along with new studio releases, the Rialto offers classic movies and regularly sponsors community events, benefits, and concerts.

"To me, downtown is really the heart of the community because people go there," Cloutier said. "If it's closed, and it's boarded up, it permeates how kids think about the community: 'F-that; I'm not going to stay there. It's the armpit.'" In 2014 he purchased and renovated an old, fire-damaged building in the middle of Lancaster's shopping district. Today, one of its attractive storefronts houses the Polish Princess Bakery. The Princess sells fresh bread and baguettes and a delightful variety of pastries, homemade soups, and sandwiches. It has become a popular morning and luncheon gathering place that successfully adapted to the disruptions of the COVID pandemic.

In 2016, Cloutier bought the former bank building that greets visitors entering Lancaster. The William Rugh Art Gallery now occupies the bank's main floor. The old walk-in vault serves as a mini-gallery. Bill Rugh's infectious enthusiasm has benefited local artists and is a popular shopping venue for visitors smitten by the region's natural beauty.

Cloutier also hooked up with a couple of local brewmeisters who had already garnered the backing of several area investors. They renovated the bank basement, and the Copper Pig Brewery opened for business early in 2018. The downstairs walk-in vault is now a climate-controlled storage room for kegs of beer. The brew pub uses the space outside the gallery, overlooking Israel's River, as a warm weather beer garden. These relatively low-cost investments have transformed a declining downtown into a fun place to visit and shop, day and night.

Before the Civil War, agriculture was the mainstay of northern New England's economy. Local farmers focused on producing healthy food and remaining economically viable from generation to generation, not on maximizing return on investment. Farm income recirculated within the community. The demise of the small, family farm has coincided with the marginalization of rural America.

Agribusiness receives massive public subsidies. Small farmers have fallen deep into debt. Agricultural monocultures rely on biocides and petrochemical fertilizers that release more than one-fifth of the world's greenhouse gas. Local agriculture will continue its decline until we redirect subsidies away from land degraders and toward smaller farmers who place soil fertility, water quality, community welfare, and the production of fresh food ahead of maximized profits.

Small farms rely more on human and animal labor; they nurture soil fertility, and they sell in local markets. Purchasers of locally grown fresh food and niche products, such as cheeses, preserves, and a variety of maple sugar products, are happy to pay a higher price because the food is tasty and nutritious, and they know and trust local farmers.

Lancaster has a popular summertime farmers' market on Saturdays. Melissa Grella saw a need for a year-round indoor farmers' market, and she launched the Root Seller in the storefront adjacent to the Polish Princess Bakery. It serves as a central market for people shopping for local food, and it provides local farmers with a venue to sell their produce throughout the week. The Root Seller soon outgrew its storefront, and late in 2022, it moved into a refurbished, larger, venerable downtown Lancaster building.

I asked Greg Cloutier why he thought the entrepreneurs with whom he works could succeed where so many had failed. "Passion," he said. "You can see they have put the commitment into it, and they've got the passion to do it. That means they don't necessarily measure success because [of income]."

Cloutier found that risk-averse building inspectors can complicate the process: "They don't want to be part of making a design. You build something, and then they come in and say, 'That's not right; you've got to do it again.'" Sometimes they pressured Cloutier to hire an architect. "That changes the dynamics of who is investing in your community. That's a developer who's got deep pockets. He's going to be driven by return on investment. Small-town revitalizing has to have a long return—a long view. You fill your Main Street business with young entrepreneurs. Nobody's ever going to be rich being a baker or a farmers' market person. But if they do it right, they can make a fair wage."

The limiting factor in reviving downtowns and developing a diverse local economy is a lack of entrepreneurs with sufficient capital to fix up an aging building or expand a promising small business. When we connect local capital with passionate, local dreamers, our ailing communities begin to revive.

Downtown Lancaster got lucky, but few struggling rural communities have been blessed with a Greg Cloutier. To convert from resource extraction and commodity production to a low-impact, low-carbon economy, northern New England communities need public investment. Redirecting harmful subsidies from bioenergy plants and agribusiness to help revitalize our downtowns is a wise and frugal investment.

The Future Matters

We abuse land because we regard it as a commodity belonging to us. When
we see land as a community to which we belong, we may begin to use it with
love and respect. There is no other way for land to survive the impact of
mechanized man, nor for us to reap from it the esthetic harvest it is capable,
under science, of contributing to culture.

ALDO LEOPOLD, *A Sand County Almanac,* 1948

Steve Blackmer, chairman of the Northern Forest Alliance, offered a generally positive response to the Headwaters idea in
the autumn of 1995: "There is a great deal of good, challenging
thinking behind the proposal to establish a Headwaters Reserve
System in the Northern Forest. I heartily endorse the idea of an explicit
economic transition along the lines proposed, and the establishment
of large wilderness reserves. Yet, the proposal has one disabling flaw:
While espousing low intensity, ecologically based forest management
as a part of the economic strategy, the proposed creation of 16 reserves
leaves little land in the Northern Forest on which to do it."[1]

I believe the termination of logging on degraded industrial lands
is a virtue, not a disabling flaw. *The establishment of the Headwaters
Wilderness Reserve System will increase the ecological value of the former
industry lands and strengthen the economic value of the rural forests of
northern New England.*

Industrial-scale timber harvesting is the number one driver of
carbon loss in New England. Intensive logging over millions of acres

(Copyright © Jon Luoma)

of former industrial forests has dramatically diminished the amount of carbon once stored in the Acadian forest. Our forests will remain net emitters of carbon as long as overcutting continues.

The young, overcut forests of the proposed Headwaters soon will be entering into a period of significant carbon sequestration and storage potential, if they are managed passively as wildlands. Their gradual recovery from half a century of overcutting will steadily increase their ecological value, as habitat for climate-stressed species, and their economic value, as carbon sinks and infrastructure for low-impact recreation.

For decades, industrial forestry has not supplied New England's wood demands. Most of the wood cut in the 8.7-million-acre Headwaters region ends up as wood chips or pulp headed for global commodity markets. Most of the sawlogs cut in northern Maine end up in Canadian mills for processing. Exporting raw logs undermines the development of a local value-adding manufacturing sector.

Establishment of the Headwaters Wilderness Reserve System dramatically shifts the focus of northern New England's timber economy to local timber communities where most of the land is owned by families who live on or near their property. When we develop decent-paying markets for high-quality sawlogs, small woodlot owners will embrace lower impact forestry and relish the opportunity to add value to their wood.

Stumpage payments are a very small percentage of the total value of a healthy forest economy. Ideally, woodlot owners will add value to their own logs *before* they leave the property. When that is not feasible, owners of family forests in a community or region can pool their assets, share equipment, cooperatively operate sawmills, and sell wood in larger quantities to higher paying markets. By cutting out the third party, the landowner receives a higher price, and the buyer pays less for raw materials or finished products.

Local crafters and manufacturers can manufacture boats, bridges, furniture, posts and beams, fencing, musical instruments, toys, bowls, and other useful and beautiful items. The new forest-based economy can build affordable housing with homegrown logs and lumber. Energy-efficient wood houses appreciate in value. Local landowners, loggers, and value-adders recirculate their income and profits within their communities.

To stabilize northern New England's agricultural and timber economies, and preserve and rewild large tracts of undeveloped land, New England needs to function as a healthy organism. If forest owners cut substantially less than growth, and urban and suburban consumers of wood products reduce their demand for wood products by at least 25 percent, we can compensate for the removal of 8.7 million acres of former industrial forest from the wood basket.

The demand for local wood products is no excuse for scrimping on reserve lands, nor should it be used to justify intensive cutting locally or in other regions. Unless there is substantial demand reduction for timber products, overcutting will persist within the region, or elsewhere. We can reduce wood use in a variety of ways:

Paper and packaging: We need to banish the concept of "throwaway forests." Since 2004, the use of newsprint and printed paper has declined dramatically, but the amount of packaging has increased. Paper products account for a quarter of all landfill waste. Decomposing paper releases methane, a vastly more potent greenhouse gas than carbon dioxide. Ending junk mail, the manufacture of paper cups and plates, and most paper packaging would reduce demand for wood fiber and reduce the amount of energy used in the papermaking process.

Wood pallets: Pallets made from hardwoods of low economic value ship commodity goods. Most are thrown away or burned after one use. Reduced production of commodity goods, coupled with reuse of pallets, would lower demand for them.

Home construction: Renounce McMansions, second and third homes, and cheaply constructed housing. Draw upon our vaunted Yankee ingenuity to construct compact, sturdily built, well-insulated homes that are designed for easy deconstruction and salvage so their parts can be reused or recycled. Perform comprehensive energy audits on older buildings, followed by retrofitting and super-insulation. Cellulose insulation, made from shredded paper treated with borax, is fire resistant. Densely packed, it is one of the best insulations commercially available and has much lower embodied energy than foams.

Local mills could utilize small-diameter green poles, lightly milled on one side to construct double-stud walls that allow for thicker insulation. The waste wood is minimal. Small-diameter wood can be used for parallel trusses for long span floors and cathedral ceilings to create large spaces for cellulose insulation. Posts can be constructed from bundles of small, low-value wood. Green poles do not require energy-intensive kiln drying, and wood waste would be modest. This approach pays the landowner, logger, and forester much more than they could earn from commodity wood chips, and it reduces greenhouse gas emissions.

Avoid expensive new products, such as mass timber, that require substantial public subsidies: For decades, the timber industry has been promoting expensive strategies that require massive public subsidies. Mass timber is a manufactured wood product of panels glued together in a crisscross pattern (a layer of vertical grain, a layer of horizontal grain, and another layer of vertical). Proponents say it is strong enough to erect twelve-story wooden structures to replace carbon-intensive concrete and steel structures and reduce the carbon footprint of large buildings.

Northern New England's red and white spruce and balsam fir are superior to southern New England's white pine, hemlock, and northern hardwoods for mass timber manufacture. Mass timber plants require an estimated fifty million board feet of wood a year. Maine produces about five hundred million board feet annually. The mass timber lobby believes Maine could support one or two mass timber plants.[2] There is no guarantee those plants will require cut-less-than-growth forestry, and increasing demand for sawlogs by 10 to 20 percent in a state where more than half of its spruce-fir forest is degraded is hardly a promising solution to the climate crisis.

Mass timber promoters emphasize the large carbon footprints of steel and concrete but gloss over the significant carbon issues of mass timber. Nearly two-thirds of a tree—treetops, branches, and mill waste—is burned, landfilled, or left to rot in the forest. After deducting carbon emissions from logging and transportation, the net long-term carbon storage of a wooden skyscraper would be only about one-fifth of the carbon stored in the trees cut to supply the mass timber.[3] Kiln-drying wood for mass timber to 12 percent moisture for optimal adhesion requires large amounts of energy.

The authors of a study promoting mass timber concede that even under optimistic scenarios, by 2050, mass timber will account for a reduction of only 0.3 percent of New England's expected emissions.[4] This rather trivial gain is insufficient to justify the threat posed by increased demand for commodity wood production from northern New England.

Without subsidies, mass timber is a risky investment. A now-scrapped proposal to build a plant in Maine could have received several million dollars from the state. Subsidizing mass timber undermines efforts to develop a local, low-carbon economy. The profits realized by mass timber investors will leak out of the region. The subsidies coveted by the mass timber lobby could be spent more wisely on reducing demand, building up local value-adding, and acquiring wildlands.

In the mid-1990s, weary of battling corporate foresters and natural resource bureaucrats, Mitch Lansky joined with like-minded Maine loggers, landowners, and foresters to form the Maine Low Impact Forestry Project: "I eventually decided that setting an agenda is more productive than reacting to someone else's." Forester-logger Sam Brown wrote that low-impact logging "is not a specific method of logging, but rather an awareness of the consequences of today's actions on tomorrow's forest values."[5]

Low-impact forestry, Lansky has written, "is multi-generational forestry. It is forestry as if the future mattered. The primary concern is to protect the biological integrity of the forest because the forest is part of the life-support system upon which our society depends. Economic goals are pursued only insofar as they do not interfere with this primary goal."[6]

After experimentation, monitoring, and consultation with other practitioners, the Low Impact Forestry Project developed a series of general guidelines. Every stand is different; no firm guidelines can be applied across the board. There are too many variables, such as site quality, stand type, slope, stocking, age, size, and diversity. If possible, maintain more than 75 percent canopy closure, but if you have an even-aged stand of dying trees, that may not be an option. You have to work with what you have. Rather than prescribing precise stocking standards or cutting cycles for everyone in all circumstances, Lansky hopes landowners will cut significantly less than growth.

To avoid high grading, the logger ought to remove low-vigor and poor-quality trees first. Later cuts will target *some* of the higher quality trees. The logger takes care to avoid or minimize damage to residual

Mitch Lansky in Baxter State Park, 2020. (Photo by author)

trees. Low-impact loggers leave branches and tops in the woods to provide microhabitats and recycle nutrients.

To minimize compacted and rutted soil, logging operations ought
to occur when soil is frozen or dry. Utilizing a forwarder instead of a
conventional skidder reduces the proportion of the stand in logging
trails, roads, and yards. Logging roads can be narrower and farther apart
than those necessary for industrial-scale machinery.[7]

Adopting low-impact guidelines increases the volume, size, and
value of residual trees and decreases the percentage of damaged trees.
It minimizes carbon emissions during logging and allows more trees
to grow old and store substantial carbon for the long term. In time, a
greater proportion of trees will be classed as quality sawtimber.

"Sustainable forestry implies a relationship between society and
forests," Lansky writes. "If the society is not sustainable, neither will be

the forestry. Since forestry is an experiment, we need unmanaged forests as a control. We also need them as an example for how forests are structured and how they function across the landscape. And we need them to protect all the habitats and all the species that would occur naturally on the landscape, including ones sensitive to human encroachment."[8]

Mel Ames of Atkinson, Maine, who died at age ninety-one in 2020, was a charter member of the Low Impact Forestry Project. Stocking on his six hundred acres in the late 1940s averaged about ten to fifteen cords per acre. After more than half a century of careful logging, most of Ames's woodlot boasted twenty to thirty cords per acre. Some stands averaged thirty-five to forty cords; a few, predominately white pine stands, grew fifty to seventy cords to the acre. Lansky has written that Ames had "an inner sense about how to cut."[9]

One hot summer afternoon in 1999, Ames and I toured his woods. He and his son Russ had worked for three hours that morning, cutting three cords worth about $300. In the 1990s, Ames earned $25,000 to $35,000 per year from his part-time logging.

Ames did not conduct clear-cuts or create large openings. When he first entered a stand, he took out the worst trees, and decades later, he cut *some* of the best trees. In contrast to the timber industry, he never disrupted the nutrient cycle: "Industry takes short cuts on everything," he told me. "They have done everything to encourage lousy management. They aren't growing anything now. If you remove all the long-lived trees, you'll only have short-lived trees for the rest of your life."

It makes sense to increase the value of your woods, he said, "*especially if you are going to keep the land.*" Quality trees are worth ten times as much as pulp. In a white pine shelterwood stand he had removed fir and "popple" (poplar) during the budworm era. A quarter century later, he had abundant pine he would not cut until it reached three feet in diameter. Absentee timber investors, with their fixation on short-term ownership and return on investment, have no incentive to increase the value of their land. Ames was content with a patient approach to earning money.

To practice low grading, the woodlot owner needs regular markets for low-value trees, but Ames contemptuously dismissed biomass, saying that it "doesn't pay enough to even take it out of the woods." The paper mills refused to accept small, weekly deliveries of pulpwood from low grading, and when Ames and other woodlot owners formed a co-op in the 1970s, the paper companies discriminated against them. International Paper threatened to take them to court for "monopoly" practices. Ames thought they feared a co-op would be able to force wood prices up. He regretted that he and his fellow woodlot owners did not form an agricultural co-op that is allowed to engage in price fixing.

In an oak stand growing on drier, richer soil, Ames pointed out a five-foot-high tree and tied a branch of this rubbery species into a knot. "That's wicopy," he said. Wicopy (*Dirca palustris*), also known as leatherwood, is a three- to six-foot-tall, dense shrub. It, along with witch hazel, honeysuckle, ferns, and wildflowers, is an important nutrient recycler that performs this service more quickly than trees. "That's why I hate clear-cuts," Ames said, motioning to the wicopy. "If you open up the forest too much, you lose these nutrient recyclers. Also, the forest floor is beautiful."

Ames had removed the diseased, poor-growing hardwoods left behind from a high-grading job conducted by a previous owner. He pointed to a sugar maple measuring twenty-five to thirty inches in diameter at breast height. It was approximately two hundred years old and without branches for thirty to forty feet. Three major branches curved toward the heavens from this arboreal pedestal. About fifteen feet up, one of these branches had broken off years ago, creating a long vertical cavity of the sort favored by the elusive American marten. Ames had once planned to cut that maple, but something told him to leave it. He had recently observed marten tracks leading to it. "I wouldn't take a million dollars for that tree," he said.

He gestured toward a red oak more than three feet in diameter, with no branches for thirty feet. Such an oak grows ten board feet a year and is worth $500, but he is unwilling to cut it. "It is an old friend," he said. "I've known it since I was a little guy." Besides, it has seeded in a lot of good oak he can harvest. "It doesn't owe me anything."

Critics argue that low-impact forestry makes no economic sense. Local, value-adding manufacture and excellent forestry will gain broad acceptance only if they are profitable. I asked David Brynn, founder of Vermont Family Forests: How do we assure the economic viability of his organization and low-impact practitioners? "We must get away from externalities, number one," he replied. "Externalities are cheating."

Low-impact forestry internalizes externalities. Industrial forestry would be an unwise investment if society required the timber industry to pay the costs of carbon emissions and degradation of land, water, and wildlife habitat. Low-impact forestry will become profitable if we tighten and enforce water-quality regulations, set strict requirements for road building, and prohibit cuts greater than growth. The internalization of externalities acts as an invisible tax cut. Public funds currently spent to clean up environmental degradation and provide health care to victims of air pollution and degraded water can be used to build healthy economies and preserve wild lands.

Vermont Family Forests has been creatively implementing a low-exploitation relationship with the land, waters, and forests of Vermont's center-west region since its founding in 1995. Brynn approaches his challenge holistically: "We need to be thinking about the complexity of the system, across all the elements—the water, the soil, the biological diversity, carbon, all those things and more," he told me in 2018.[10]

He continued: "We're really interested in putting forest health first. We're more interested in forest ecosystem conservation than we are in forest resource management. They're different. I'm not saying that forest resource management is bad; it's just not what we're up to."

As with every other state where the timber lobby is powerful, Vermont forest policy focuses primarily on timber production and procurement. Brynn warned the Vermont Agency of Natural Resources Climate Council that increasingly violent, extreme weather events attributable to climate change are "undermining the ecological integrity of Vermont's forests." He urged the state to change direction and focus much more on forest ecosystem integrity and leave timber procurement to the timber industry: "Healthy, intact forests . . . are the most flood and drought resilient of any land uses." He urged the state to focus on forest health and protection of the ecological commons: "Vermont's water, wildlife, and air are unenclosed and are held in Common by the People. . . . The

State of Vermont is Vermont's Trustee of our ecological commons—
water, wildlife, and air. But we the People hold the Ecological Commons." Let family forest owners "pick their own crops and strategies."[11]

Unfortunately, Vermont's current use tax, the Use Value Appraisal
(UVA) program, applies primarily to private forests actively managed
for timber. Clear-cuts qualify for Use Value taxation, but landowners
who manage their forests as wildlands to optimize long-term carbon
storage and provide essential habitat for climate-stressed species do not.
Owners must choose between land health and lower taxes. Brynn argued: "We should tax carbon emissions to fund UVA rather than taxing the healthy, intact forest lands that are the key to mitigating climate
impacts."[12]

Brynn explained to me how wilderness plays an important role in
the Vermont Family Forests landscape:

> We have 700-acres that is Forever Wild. Lester and Mo-
> nique Anderson wanted a piece of land that used to be farmed
> and utilized to be allowed to be self-willed and to just do its
> own thing, and to be monitored for reptiles and amphibians,
> birds, and the like in an on-going way. We have 18 years of data
> now on these re-wilding forests. Adjacent landowners said,
> "What is this? We can't go in there and hike and recreate?"
>
> We said, "This represents [a small fraction] of the town
> of Lincoln. If you hunt only deer and turkey and a couple
> of other things, and you don't trap keystone predators, and
> you pick up trash, and you tell us when there are problems,
> and you help us, we will give you permission to hunt." We
> have 35 hunters going in there, and they are acting as sur-
> rogate wolves, harvesting deer. They have a relationship to
> the place.

On a lovely autumn afternoon, following a walk through one of
Vermont Family Forests' managed stands, Brynn told me:

> I'm trying to tease out an approach to forest ecosystem con-
> servation that says, "Okay, as we look at a landscape that we

David Brynn of Vermont Family Forests.
(Courtesy Vermont Family Forests)

call home, there are going to be ecological reserves, there are
going to be intensively managed areas, and there are going
to be places where we practice what we call *new forestry*."
The land, as [Aldo] Leopold would say, includes the water,
the critters, the soil, the plants, and their interactions. Those
pieces are not all held by the person who has the deed. The
water is held by the people; the critters are held by the people.

Water, Brynn asserts, is a "great indicator of land health." He
shies away from debates over regulating practices such as whole-tree

harvesting and other variants of clear-cutting. He respects the right of landowners to choose to grow what they wish on their private property. In return, he expects them to honor public property rights such as clean air, clean water, and viable wildlife habitat for all species native to the region.

What happens if a logging job degrades water quality? I asked. "You do what it takes to correct the problem," Brynn answered. "*Your timber is not the public good, but the water that's coming off your land is—definitely.* If it's nice, clean, cool, highly oxygenated water, it means that you've got riparian zones that are intact; you don't have too many roads; you have a nice, spongy forest."

Vermont Family Forests devotes as much attention to proper road design and construction as to any other aspect of a logging operation. Roads ought to be narrow, avoid steep slopes, and cover no more than 5 percent of a managed area. "We should be laying these out just like the French lay out terraces for grapes and olives. That's culture," Brynn said. He calls such roads "lines of grace." The group's logging roads had cut neither ditches nor gashes in the landscape. Strategically placed, gravel-filled water bars allowed runoff with minimal impact on roads and streams.

Vermont Family Forests tries to pay loggers roughly 60 percent more than they would earn on a conventional operation. Payment includes the condition of the forest after cutting as well as the value of the logs cut. "We have a contract that says: 'It isn't just the volume; it's also the compliance with these practices.' We always have a cash bond; we don't have a letter of credit. We work with people that we know and trust."

Logging equipment is another huge challenge for low-impact logging. "Equipment is getting larger as treatments are getting smaller," Brynn said. "Grapple skidders, Timbco feller bunchers, chippers often make economic sense, but they often do not make ecological and aesthetic sense." He also avoids conventional skidders: "Why aren't we rolling this wood out of the forest with forwarders or forwarding trailers? Small-scale forwarding is the only way to travel in small woodlots. It saves money in the long run. It takes a little more time, but not a lot more time. A forwarding trailer comes in so handy on small woodlots.

Logger Bill Torrey loading logs onto his forwarder under
frozen winter conditions. (Courtesy Vermont Family Forests)

It allows you to sort, and profits are often all about sorting. [Forwarding trailers] work perfectly with these lines of grace. You're not doing much damage to the soil if you log with forwarding trailers under frozen winter conditions on a preestablished road."

A low-impact logging operation is more costly than a common clear-cut. Mills pay the same price for logs regardless of the condition of the residual stand. "It's really tough for landowners to make money in the undifferentiated commodity market," Brynn said. Biomass at that time fetched the landowner about $2 per ton of chips: "I wouldn't sell anything for $2 a ton."

I wondered whether there are decent-paying markets for wood with low economic value. Brynn said sawmill residues make high-quality insulation materials: "There's a [German] firm called Pavatex that makes the full range of insulating materials that are made out of wood and clay. It has good R-values and great D-values. Once a building has warmed up or cooled down, it stays warm or cool. We ought to be producing a full range of wood and clay products that put our low-grade wood to better uses while sending more value back to the forests that produced them. We need to insulate. We can talk about solar and biomass, but really, we should be using less energy."

He then asked: "How do we move out of the commodity market? To paraphrase Gary Snyder—'Find a place, call it home, take care of it, and hope others are doing the same elsewhere.' That's a key ingredient. It's about loving the place you call home and wanting to take care of it."

Vermont Family Forests' marketing system benefits landowners, loggers, wood purchasers, and the land. Brynn said: "We have found that by being what we call the 'wood shepherd,' just bringing it from forests to finished products, paying the long dollar on all of the value-adding, we're still able to come up with a product that gets delivered at about the same price that you would get at Home Depot or some other place—or slightly more, but never more than 5 percent. Who is it that takes the hit in our model? It's brokers—people who, in two phone calls, make more than landowners do in growing trees for a hundred years."

Vermont Family Forests has modified transaction practices between landowners and wood buyers. Brynn explained:

> When you sell timber, you can sell it "mill-scale." You cut it, you bring it to the mill, and they'll give you what they want to give you based on their scale and their grade. It's a quick way to throw away money. The other way is "lump sum" where you put it out to bid, and you know what you're going to get paid. However, you don't get as much control over the choice of operator who's going to be working the site.
>
> We came up with this thing called "lump sum plus." We mark a sale, come up with the specifications, show it to the loggers that we like to work with, and ask them, "What's it going to take for you to make a living—not a killing, but a living—operating these woods according to our specs?" They'll tell us. Then we say to the big fellows, "What will you pay us to have this logger cut these trees and put them on this landing?" The reason [the mills] are interested is: they don't want to be in the logging business. They're in the procurement business, so if they don't have to fiddle around with all

it takes to get a timber sale out, they're happy. The landowners end up earning about twice what a conventional logging job would pay.

Basically, what we did from the start was to find value-adding building projects, work with the architect if we could—if we couldn't, then it's not a project for us—have them specify what it is our forests are willing to yield, build a local network, and participate in a flexible, ephemeral, value-adding process. That's very labor-intensive, but it's actually a really sweet model.

In the late 1990s Vermont Family Forests supplied the wood to build Bicentennial Hall at Middlebury College: "We provided 135,000 feet of hardwood from local woodlots that were carefully tended with a great logger and a little log-forwarding trailer. Really sweet logging, really sweet forestry. Light, careful stuff."

"[Vermont Family Forests] has completed many building projects that involved procuring wood from carefully tended local forests," Brynn recalled with delight. "In several of these value-adding projects, the participating loggers, landowners, sawmills, and secondary manufacturers were invited to the opening. People love these events because they can see their wood on the walls, and they also know what happened in their forest. They think, 'I'm connected; I'm feeling the love right now.' I don't know how you put a dollar figure on that, but it's tangible as hell."

Natural Democracy

I think I could turn and live awhile with the animals . . .
I stand and look at them sometimes half the day long.

They do not sweat and whine about their condition,
They do not lie awake in the dark and weep for their sins,
They do not make me sick discussing their duty to God,
Not one is dissatisfied . . . . not one is demented
with the mania of owning things,
Not one kneels to another nor to his kind that lived thousands of years ago,
Not one is respectable or industrious over the whole earth.

WALT WHITMAN, "Song of Myself," 1855

I speak the password primeval, I give the sign of democracy,
By God! I will accept nothing which all cannot have their
counterpart of on the same terms.

WALT WHITMAN, "Song of Myself," 1855

One warm March day, when my son Brook was three months old, I bundled him up, and we trekked westward in the deep snow into the forest on a trail to the Gay Brook that terminated at a waterfall with a six-foot drop. When we arrived, I held Brook out to view the thundering falls. Initially, he did not respond. Soon, his arms and legs began kicking and flailing, and he babbled with excitement long after my arms grew weary.

Brook's waterfall vanished one spring when he was about three years old. A logging contractor bought a forest tract upstream and proceeded to liquidate its timber value, leaving behind skidder roads gouged in the steep terrain. After a winter of above-average snowfall, followed by a warm and rainy spring, the forest no longer acted as a sponge that retains and slowly releases water. It could not prevent flooding downstream.

Just above the waterfall, floodwaters slammed into the bank where Gay Brook turns south. Three-foot-high boulders, once perched upon even grander boulders to form the falls, washed into the pool below. Over time, the sharp drop at the falls has smoothed out. What would have taken nature's erosive powers decades, perhaps centuries, to accomplish occurred overnight thanks to someone's quest for quick profits.

The person responsible once had been a three-month-old child. Why do so many of us outgrow our instinctive love for the natural world? Why must our culture turn our natures against nature? How can we nurture and sustain our children's innate, joyful response to wild nature?

What passes today as "self-governance" has failed to mitigate the climate crisis and the sixth extinction event, or ameliorate injustice and misery. The insurrection at the US Capitol on January 6, 2021, designed to overturn the results of the 2020 presidential election, symbolizes the political failure of this failed politics.

To begin the healing, we must acknowledge there has never been true democracy in the United States. The First Nations of North America did not vote for genocide and the enclosure of the indigenous commons. Africans did not elect to be kidnapped and enslaved. Women did not campaign to be disenfranchised. Plants and animals did not cast ballots in support of habitat degradation and persecution of large predators. The unborn have not demanded they inherit an overheated planet.

We need a new politics that willingly, graciously adheres to natural laws and abides by natural limits—a politics that addresses the root causes of our inability to protect land health and the US Capitol

building. As long as corporate cash funneled to low, cunning politicians fuels our politics, the future for all species and future generations
is bleak. We need a Natural Democracy that ensures environmental and
political justice for all.

Wisdom comes from the land. Let us model our politics upon wild
nature. Let us study nature's healing powers that we may restore the
health of our lands and our institutions of self-governance. We must,
as Aldo Leopold advised, save all the parts if we wish to heal the whole.

Gulf of Maine poet Gary Lawless once told me: "A community is
really a conversation, and if you aren't allowing all the voices to be present, then the community is out of balance. It can't heal itself until all
the voices are present, and no one voice is in control." He spoke of our
responsibility to *give voice to place:*

> If you want to speak for trees you have to learn the language
> of interaction because one of the ways the tree is going to
> speak to you is in the way that it interacts with everything else
> within the community. If you deny some of those interac-
> tions, then it's a lot easier to get rid of the trees because you're
> denying [their] interaction with soil microbes, [mycorrhizal
> fungi], or birds, or salamanders, or water. You're not really
> understanding the language of the tree because you're not
> learning about the whole conversation. You're hearing a little
> part of the conversation. Part of the conversation is that tree
> makes good pulp, but there's a whole other community con-
> versation going on.[1]

When I asked Gary how one avoids the trap of *presuming* to speak
for the land and the creatures dwelling in it, he replied, "I think that
if you make the commitment to live in a particular place and educate
yourself as much as you can about that place, that's a commitment of
humility. You're choosing to be a part of, not having power over. I think
that humility comes with respect for the place." He continued:

> I think the whole planet is trying to educate us. . . .
> Everything around you is trying to educate you about how

to be in that place. If you stop to listen to the wind in the trees for a minute, and look down to see what was happening under your feet, or just concentrated on a particular place, even on a sidewalk, there's stuff going on that can educate you about that place. We just have a pretty narrow idea of what education is.

When you start acknowledging your connection to everything, all of a sudden, your language changes, because you have to find a new way of talking about who you are, and where you are, and what you're doing. Once you acknowledge that connection you realize that a lot of what you're doing there isn't so good. And that's okay. You don't have to feel guilt about that, but you have to feel humility about that and start to make changes. We can help each other make changes. Mutual aid isn't such a bad idea, but it isn't just about humans.[2]

The elements of Natural Democracy include the following:

An informed electorate: Former slave Frederick Douglass wryly observed, "Knowledge unfits a child to be a slave."[3] Democracy flourishes when an informed electorate can freely participate in setting the agenda and voting upon it. This requires a human electorate that cherishes wild nature and is well-informed about natural history and atmospheric science. An ecological education, Douglass might agree, unfits a child to be a slave of consumerism and resource exploitation.

Before the advent of civilization, natural selection favored the most competent naturalists. Children of indigenous cultures learned through direct experience with plants and animals, the smells and sounds of forests, plains, deserts, and oceans. Elders taught the young which plants had nutritional or medicinal value and how to hunt successfully. Bugs, worms, birds, ocean waves, and the sounding forest cataract engaged the curiosity of the youngest children. Some children of modern civilization retain their early wonder and awe and grow up to be naturalists.[4] But those who are now in charge of our economy and politics behave as if they have either forgotten, or never enjoyed, an enchanted childhood immersed in nature.

Our schools teach students to read books, but we need citizens who can read the landscape as if their lives depended upon it, as indeed they do. We require regular, direct contact with the workings of everyday nature—to ponder how ecosystems function, what threats they face, or what steps we can take to protect their integrity. For some time, funding for natural history teaching at the college and university level has been shrinking, as budgets for molecular biology and genetic engineering have grown. We need more natural history education at all levels of schooling, not more austerity.

A vote for all: Following emancipation, Douglass wrote, "I looked upon suffrage to the Negro as the only measure which could prevent him from being thrust back into slavery." W. E. B. Du Bois wrote in *The Souls of Black Folk:* "the best arbiters of their own welfare are the persons directly affected; consequently that it is only by arming every hand with a ballot,—with the right to have a voice in the policy of the state,—that the greatest good to the greatest number could be attained."[5]

Land reform: When the Northern capitalists, firmly in control of the US government in the mid-1870s, abandoned Reconstruction, land reform—essential to complete the transition from slave to free person—faltered. Institutionalized racism and mob violence during the Jim Crow era forced former slaves back into virtual slavery. The perpetuation of the status quo plantation economy—minus the formal institution of slavery—stunted economic development throughout the South for decades.

To address today's sixth extinction crisis and climate change, we need more wildlands, more unmanaged lands, and low-impact management on managed lands. Dramatic expansion of the public wild commons is a necessary component of land reform as well as a partial redress of today's unconscionable maldistribution of wealth.

Current ecological and political crises challenge us to enfranchise all who are affected by human decisions. Indigenous cultures speak of "animal people" and "plant people." If we could convene a Congress of Nonhumans, what would the tree and animal people tell us? *Clean air, clean water, and unfragmented habitat that meets the needs of all phases of our lifecycles are essential to our pursuit of life, liberty, and our evolution-*

ary destiny. We need to connect northern New England's unmanaged lands with wild refuges throughout New England and into Canada, the Adirondacks and the rest of North America.

Unborn human generations would answer: *We have a natural right to inherit a low-carbon economy, characterized by low-impact land-use practices. Living within natural limits for the sake of other species and the unborn is an act of grace and reciprocity. To protect physical and mental health, we must begin to heal sacrifice zones and redress the evils of environmental injustice. Everyone, everywhere is entitled to easy access to green spaces.*

Defenders of our failed status quo will object that these changes in human behavior are too abrupt, too radical. During the civil rights struggles of the mid-twentieth century, James Baldwin wrote that only when Blacks are free, will whites be truly free. In 1955, he warned: "People who shut their eyes to reality simply invite their own destruction, and anyone who insists on remaining in a state of innocence long after that innocence is dead turns himself into a monster."[6] We shall never be truly free until we liberate ourselves from speciesism and emancipate the land from resource exploitation.

Baldwin later wrote, "But for power truly to feel itself menaced, it must somehow sense itself in the presence of another power—or, more accurately, an energy—which it has not known how to define and therefore does not really know how to control."[7] Natural Democracy liberates energy that global capital and violent right-wingers are incapable of comprehending or controlling.

Human welfare shall ever be in peril while our voices drown out all other voices. Our pursuit of happiness leads nowhere if we fail to honor the pursuits of others. Their welfare is our only security, fulfillment, and happiness. In wildness, we lose and discover ourselves, and, with gratitude, we shed any conceits that disrupt the harmony of the conversation.

In 1988, I asked the politicians: "Who speaks for the land?" Plants, animals, and even unborn generations are asking us: "Who is listening to the land and its denizens?"

(Copyright © Jon Luoma)

Timeline of Events

21,000 years before present (BP)–13,000 BP:	Glaciers retreat from New England.
2,800 BP–sixteenth century CE:	Woodland Period; Abenaki inhabit greater northern New England region.
Early sixteenth century to early seventeenth century:	Contact between Abenaki and European explorers and traders occurs first along the Maine Coast and, considerably later, inland.
Late seventeenth century–1760:	Abenaki, allied with the French in Canada, prevent English settlements in the interior of northern New England.
1760:	Fall of Quebec (1759) and Montreal (1760) ends the French presence in Canada. New Englanders swarm to interior northern New England.
1783–1860s:	Massachusetts and Maine (after achieving statehood in 1820) sell off most of the undeveloped lands of Maine to land speculators and, in the nineteenth century, to timber barons. New Hampshire completes the sale of its undeveloped lands in 1867.
Ca. 1800:	Logging in Maine moves up major rivers into the interior.
Ca. 1810:	Beginnings of the great logging drives in Maine.

245

1820s–1830s:	Tourists discover the White Mountains.
1846:	Thoreau's first trip to the Maine wilderness.
Ca. 1850:	Maine's old growth white pine are mostly cut; loggers turn to spruce. Old growth spruce is depleted by the end of the nineteenth century.
Ca. 1870:	Railroads and lumbermen reach the White Mountains and intensive logging begins.
1880s–1890s:	New Hampshire Forest Commission documents the extent of forest destruction, especially in the White Mountain region.
1892:	New York establishes the Adirondack Park.
1894:	New York Constitution adopts "Forever Wild" Amendment protecting all state-owned forests.
1897–1898:	Hugh Chisholm merges twenty mills in Maine, New Hampshire, Vermont, New York, and Massachusetts to form International Paper.
1899:	Great Northern breaks ground for a paper mill in Millinocket, Maine, in March. The mill begins to produce paper by the fall of 1900.
1911:	Weeks Act establishes eastern national forests, including the White Mountain National Forest.
1910–1919:	Spruce budworm outbreak kills 27.5 million cords of softwood in northern Maine and 200 million cords in eastern Canada.
1931:	Former Maine governor Percival Baxter completes the first of a series of acquisitions of timberland in northern Maine. By 1962, he had donated more than two hundred thousand acres to the citizens of Maine in the form of Baxter State Park.
1955–1967:	Fortune 500 corporations Scott Paper, Diamond International, and Boise Cascade buy paper mills and hundreds of thousands of acres of uninhabited timberland in Maine. By 1970, absentee corporations have replaced local ownership of most northern New England paper mills.

1972–mid-1980s:	Spruce budworm affects approximately 120 million acres in eastern Canada, Maine, and a portion of northern New Hampshire. Large landowners in Maine, aided by state and federal subsidies, respond with major pesticide spray programs.
October 1975:	Maine Woodsmen Association strikes against paper mills for two weeks.
1978–1982:	Sir James Goldsmith successfully takes over Diamond International. After the completion of the hostile takeover in 1982, Goldsmith sells off Diamond's mills and other nontimberland assets. He retains nearly one million acres of timberland in northern New England and the Adirondack Park until late 1987.
1986–1989:	Maine's timber industry and conservation leaders negotiate a Maine Forest Practices Act that passes in 1989.
June 1987–October 1988:	Strike at International Paper's mill in Jay, Maine.
February 24, 1988:	Diamond land sale in New Hampshire and Vermont becomes public knowledge.
March 10, 1988:	Diamond land sale emergency summit meeting, Concord, New Hampshire.
Late May 1988:	Rancourt Associates buys New Hampshire and Vermont Diamond lands.
Early July 1988:	Rancourt agrees to sell approximately forty-five thousand acres in New Hampshire to state and federal governments. Subsequently, the US Forest Service acquires a conservation easement from New Hampshire for the forty-thousand-acre Nash Stream Forest.
September 27, 1988:	Congress establishes the Northern Forest Lands Study (NFLS).
October 4, 1988:	Senators Patrick Leahy (Vermont) and Warren Rudman (New Hampshire) secure Maine's participation in the NFLS by writing, "The current landownership and management patterns have served the people and the forests of the region well."

October 1988 – September 1989:	NFLS conducts research.
August 1989:	NFLS releases a preliminary draft report.
September 1989:	Publication of *The End of Nature,* by Bill McKibben, which warns of threats to the spruce-fir forest posed by climate change.
October 1989:	NFLS releases its draft report for public comment.
Late October 1989:	Georgia Pacific announces a hostile takeover bid for Great Northern Nekoosa, owner of 2.1 million acres of forestland in northern Maine. It completes the takeover in February 1990.
November 1989 and January 1990:	NFLS convenes numerous public comment sessions on its draft report.
December 1989 – December 1990:	Nash Stream Advisory Committee develops a progressive management plan for the Nash Stream Forest.
April 1990:	*Northern Forest Lands Study* is released.
May 1990:	Governors' Task Force to the NFLS releases its recommendations.
October 1990:	Northern Forest Lands Council (NFLC) formally begins.
November 1990:	Senator Patrick Leahy (Vermont) secures $1 million to fund the four-year NFLC.
December 1990:	Approximately fifteen state, regional, national, and grassroots conservation groups form the Northern Forest Alliance to monitor and lobby the NFLC.
Winter – spring 1991:	Senator Leahy drafts the Northern Forest Lands Act.
Spring 1991:	NFLC hires the former executive director of the New Hampshire Timberland Owners Association, Charles Levesque, as executive director.
July 1991:	Property rights groups storm Senate hearings on the Northern Forest Lands Act held in Lyndonville, Vermont, and Bangor, Maine.

August 1991:	Adirondack Park property rights activists shut down the NFLC's meeting at Ray Brook, New York. The council conducted the meeting without incident the following day.
October 1991:	Georgia Pacific sells former Great Northern mills, hydropower, and 2.1 million acres to Bowater for approximately $380 million.
October 1991:	NFLC releases its work plan at its bimonthly meeting in Bangor.
December 1991:	Northern Forest Alliance forces the NFLC to add biological diversity protection to its work plan; the council continues to refuse to address forest practices.
September 1992:	Publication of Mitch Lansky's *Beyond the Beauty Strip,* the most comprehensive critique of industrial forestry in Maine.
September 1992:	First of fifty-two bimonthly issues of the *Northern Forest Forum* is published.
September 1992:	Preliminary report of the Land Conversion Committee refutes the NFLC's operating assumptions that rampant development poses the greatest threat to industrial northern forests.
December 1992:	Conservation scientists at the NFLC's Biodiversity Forum in Manchester, New Hampshire, recommend the establishment of ecological reserves.
September 1993:	NFLC releases *Findings and Options;* 64 percent of the 406 letters commenting on the findings call for a stronger NFLC conservation agenda.
Early March 1994:	NFLC releases its *Draft Recommendations.*
Mid-March to early May 1994:	NFLC sponsors twenty listening sessions. Seven hundred forty-one people testify and six hundred submit written comments; the public again offers strong support for the conservation agenda of the Northern Forest Alliance.

June 1994:   RESTORE announces a 3.2-million-acre Maine
                       Woods National Park proposal.

September 1994:   NFLC issues its final report, *Finding Common
                       Ground,* and disbands after concluding
                       there is "no imminent crisis" in northern
                       New England's paper industry.

October 1994:   Scott Paper, in the process of being
                       dismembered by "Chainsaw Al" Dunlap,
                       sells its Maine mills and more than nine
                       hundred thousand acres of forestland to
                       South African Pulp and Paper Industries
                       (Sappi).

1995:   Senator Judd Gregg (New Hampshire)
                       introduces the Family Forestland Protection
                       Act to implement federal tax cuts proposed
                       by the NFLC; the bill fails.

1995:   Senator Patrick Leahy (Vermont) introduces
                       the Northern Forest Stewardship Act to
                       carry on the legacy of the NFLC; it never
                       passes.

Summer 1995:   *Northern Forest Forum* proposes the
                       8.7-million-acre Headwaters Wilderness
                       Reserve System for northern Vermont, New
                       Hampshire, and Maine.

November 1995:   Green Party in Maine secures more than fifty-
                       two thousand signatures to place the Ban
                       Clearcutting in Maine Referendum on the
                       November 1996 ballot.

1995–1998:   New Hampshire Ecological Reserves Steering
                       Committee recommends the state establish
                       a network of ecological reserves, with a goal
                       of ecosystem integrity, not representation of
                       ever-shifting natural communities. Concord
                       insiders bury the report.

1996:   Year-long campaign for the Ban Clearcutting
                       in Maine Referendum. Maine's large
                       landowners spend millions to defeat the
                       referendum, with considerable assistance
                       from Maine's largest conservation
                       organizations and Governor Angus King.

1997–2004:   Champion International sells lands in
                               New York, Vermont, and some in New
                               Hampshire, but not those in Maine or
                               Connecticut Lakes in New Hampshire.
                               Great Northern–Bowater and Sappi sell
                               large tracts. When International Paper sells
                               its last holdings in 2004, all timberlands
                               owned by US paper companies in northern
                               New England in 1988 have been sold one or
                               more times.

Ca. 2000:   Roxanne Quimby, owner of Burt's Bees, joins
                               RESTORE's board and begins to buy
                               wildlands in Maine for an eventual national
                               park. In 2016, she donates 87,500 acres
                               to the National Park Service as Katahdin
                               Woods and Waters National Monument.

1997–2016:   Seventeen large and small paper mills in
                               northern New England cease making paper.
                               The mill in Groveton, New Hampshire (see
                               Chapter 14) shuts down in December 2007.

Notes

One: The Education of a Tree-Hugger

1. William D. Newmark, "Legal and Biotic Boundaries of Western North American National Parks: A Problem of Congruence," *Biological Conservation* 33 (1985): 197–208; Jared M. Diamond, "The Island Dilemma: Lessons of Modern Biogeographic Studies for the Design of Natural Reserves," *Biological Conservation* 7 (1975): 129–146; Reed F. Noss and Allen Y. Cooperrider, *Saving Nature's Legacy: Protecting and Restoring Biodiversity* (Washington, DC: Island Press, 1994), 138–139.

2. Jamie Sayen, "The Appalachian Mountains: Vision and Wilderness," *Earth First!* 7, no. 5 (1987): 26–30.

3. John Harrigan, "Two Giants of the Forest, Locked in Death's Embrace," *Coös County Democrat*, November 11, 1987; "Beaver Fells Tree; 3 Towns Lose Power," *Coös County Democrat*, September 14, 1988.

4. Jamie Sayen, "Diamond to Sell 90,000 Acres for $19 Million," *Coös County Democrat*, February 24, 1988.

5. Jamie Sayen, "Conservationists and Politicians Hold 'Emergency' Forest Meeting," *Coös County Democrat*, March 16, 1988; Martha Carlson, "North of the Notches," *Forest Notes* 173 (1988): 7; "Finding Common Ground: An Interview with Hank Swan," *Northern Forest Forum* 1, no. 6 (1993): 8.

6. Sayen, "Conservationists and Politicians"; "Conservation Digest: Diamond Land: 'We'll Go All Out on This One,'" *Forest Notes* 172 (spring 1988): 28.

7. John Harrigan, "We Must Be Realistic About Our North Country Woodlands," *Coös County Democrat*, March 16, 1988.

8. Peter Riviere, "Conservationists Stumped on Diamond's Forest Sale," *Coös County Democrat*, May 11, 1988.

Two: A Force Not Bound to Be Kind to Man

1. Robert Marshall and Althea Dobbins, "Bob Marshall's 1936 Roadless Area Inventory," in Dave Foreman and Howie Wolke, *The Big Outside: A Descriptive Inventory of the Big Wilderness Areas of the United States,* rev. ed. (New York: Harmony Books, 1992), 464–469.

2. Andrew M. Barton, Alan S. White, and Charles V. Cogbill, *The Changing Nature of the Maine Woods* (Durham: University of New Hampshire Press, 2012), 34–38.

3. An excellent film, *The Lost Forests of New England,* available on YouTube (New England Forests), provides an informative introduction to old growth forests of southern and central New England; https://www.youtube.com/watch?v=Vi12xaJxA5U. Last accessed September 27, 2022.

4. New Hampshire Forest Sustainability Standards Work Team, *Good Forestry in the Granite State: Recommended Voluntary Forest Management Practices for New Hampshire* (Concord: New Hampshire Division of Forests and Lands, DRED, and the Society for the Protection of New Hampshire Forests, 1997), 57.

5. Paul Catanzaro and Tony D'Amato, *Forest Carbon: An Essential Natural Solution for Climate Change* (Amherst: University of Massachusetts Amherst, 2019), 7.

6. Craig G. Lorimer, "The Presettlement Forest and Natural Disturbance Cycle of Northeastern Maine," *Ecology* 58 (1977): 139–148.

7. David R. Foster, Glenn Motzkin, and Benjamin Slater, "Land-Use History as Long-Term Broad-Scale Disturbance: Regional Forest Dynamics in Central New England," *Ecosystems* 1 (1998): 115.

8. William A. Haviland and Marjory W. Power, *The Original Vermonters: Native Inhabitants, Past and Present* (Hanover, NH: University Press of New England, 1981), 177; Gary Snyder, "The Place, the Region, and the Commons," in *The Practice of the Wild* (New York: North Point Press, 1990), 42.

9. Marshall Sahlins, "The Original Affluent Society," in Jacqueline Solway, ed., *The Politics of Egalitarianism: Theory and Practice* (New York: Berghahn Books, 2006), 79–98.

10. John F. Richards, *The Unending Frontier: An Environmental History of the Early Modern World* (Berkeley: University of California Press, 2003), 506.

11. Robert J. Naiman, Jerry M. Melillo, and John E. Hobbie, "Ecosystem Alteration of Boreal Forest Streams by Beaver (*Castor Canadensis*)," *Ecology* 67, no. 5 (1986): 1254–1269; Robert J. Naiman, Carol A. Johnston, and James C. Kelley, "Alteration of North American Streams by Beaver," *BioScience* 38, no. 11 (1988): 753–762.

12. New Hampshire Forest Sustainability Standards Work Team, *Good Forestry,* 45.

13. Naiman, Melillo, and Hobbie, "Ecosystem Alteration."

14. William Bradford, *Of Plymouth Plantation,* ed. Harvey Wish (New York: Paragon, 1962), quoted in Carolyn Merchant, *Ecological Revolutions: Nature, Gender, and Science in New England* (Chapel Hill: University of North Carolina Press, 1989), 101.

15. Gordon G. Whitney, *From Coastal Wilderness to Fruited Plain: A History of Environmental Change in Temperate North America from 1500 to the Present* (New York: Cambridge University Press, 1994), 150.

16. Virginia DeJohn Anderson, *Creatures of Empire: How Domestic Animals Transformed Early America* (New York: Oxford University Press, 2004), 38–42; William Cronon, *Changes in the Land: Indians, Colonists, and the Ecology of New England* (New York: Hill & Wang, 1983), 127–156.

17. Quoted in John Putnam Demos, *Entertaining Satan: Witchcraft and the Culture of Early New England* (Oxford: Oxford University Press, 1982), 344.

18. Carolyn Merchant, *Ecological Revolutions: Nature, Gender, and Science in New England* (Chapel Hill: University of North Carolina Press, 1989), 102.

19. Snyder, "The Etiquette of Freedom," in *Practice of the Wild*, 7; Jill Lepore, *The Name of War: King Philip's War and the Origins of American Identity* (New York: Alfred A. Knopf, 1998), 164–165.

20. Brian Donahue, *Reclaiming the Commons: Community Farms and Forests in a New England Town* (New Haven: Yale University Press, 1999), 118–119.

21. Gordon G. Whitney and William C. Davis, "From Primitive Woods to Cultivated Woodlots: Thoreau and the Forest History of Concord, Massachusetts," *Journal of Forest History* 30, no. 2 (1986): 73–75.

22. Henry D. Thoreau, *The Maine Woods: A Fully Annotated Edition*, ed. Jeffrey S. Cramer (New Haven: Yale University Press, 2009), 71–72, 256.

23. Thoreau, *Maine Woods*, 140.

24. Henry D. Thoreau, *I to Myself: An Annotated Selection from the Journal of Henry D. Thoreau*, ed. Jeffrey S. Cramer (New Haven: Yale University Press, 2007), 261–262.

25. Thoreau, *Maine Woods*, 62–63.

Three: Over the Hump

1. Edwin A. Churchill, "English Beachheads in Seventeenth-Century Maine," in Richard W. Judd, Edwin A. Churchill, and Joel W. Eastman, eds., *Maine: The Pine Tree State from Prehistory to the Present* (Orono: University of Maine Press, 1995), 67.

2. Charles F. Carroll, *The Timber Economy of Puritan New England* (Providence: Brown University Press, 1973), 110; Charles E. Clark, *The Eastern Frontier: The Settlement of Northern New England 1610–1763* (New York: Alfred A. Knopf, 1970), 55.

3. Joseph J. Malone, *Pine Trees and Politics: The Naval Stores and Forest Policy in Colonial New England 1691–1775* (Seattle: University of Washington Press, 1964), 86.

4. Richard G. Wood (*A History of Lumbering in Maine, 1820–1861* [Orono: University of Maine Press, 1935], 48, 78) says 17 cents an acre. Philip T. Coolidge (*History of the Maine Woods* [Bangor, ME: Furbish–Roberts, 1963], 553) cites Forest Commissioner Edgar Ring in 1900 at 22¾ cents per acre, but says he calculates it at "a little more than 21 cents per acre."

5. John S. Springer, *Forest Life and Forest Trees*, rev. ed. (Somersworth: New Hampshire Publishing Co., 1971 [1851]), 20. The quotation at the start of the chapter is from page 71.

6. Springer, *Forest Life*, 70, 36, 51, 206, 50, 126.

7. Springer, *Forest Life*, 97–98.

8. Springer, *Forest Life*, 22, 35.

9. Springer, *Forest Life,* 27–28.

10. Springer, *Forest Life,* 39, 65.

11. Springer, *Forest Life,* 53–54.

12. Andrew Egan, *Haywire: Discord in Maine's Logging Woods and the Unraveling of an Industry* (Amherst: University of Massachusetts Press, 2022), 10–14.

13. Robert E. Pike, *Tall Trees, Tough Men* (New York: W. W. Norton, 1967), 90–101, 139.

14. Fannie Hardy Eckstorm and Mary Winslow Smyth, *Minstrelsy of Maine: Folk-Songs and Ballads of the Woods and the Coast* (Boston: Houghton Mifflin, 1927), 118, Version A, verse 2.

15. Henry D. Thoreau, *The Maine Woods: A Fully Annotated Edition,* edited by Jeffrey S. Cramer (New Haven: Yale University Press, 2009), 212.

16. Springer, *Forest Life,* 168–169.

17. David C. Smith, *A History of Lumbering in Maine, 1861–1960* (Orono: University of Maine Press, 1972), 432–434, 438–439; Glenn A. Hodgkins, Ivan C. James II, and Thomas G. Huntington, "Historical Changes in Lake Ice-Out Dates as Indicators of Climate Change in New England, 1850–2000," *International Journal of Climatology* 22 (2002): 1819–1827.

18. Eckstorm and Smyth, *Minstrelsy of Maine,* 82–83.

19. Thoreau, *Maine Woods,* 2–3.

20. Springer, *Forest Life,* 227.

21. Wood, *History of Lumbering, 1820–1861,* 135. The average pine log driven to Bangor in 1833 had produced 343 board feet. In 1857, as spruce was eclipsing pine, the average log driven to Bangor was 192 board feet. By 1892 it had declined to 105 board feet. At the end of the era of big timber, in 1915, the average log produced only 58 board feet. Smith, *History of Lumbering, 1861–1960,* 88, 293.

22. Smith, *History of Lumbering, 1861–1960,* 20.

23. Stewart Holbrook, *Holy Old Mackinaw: A Natural History of the American Lumberjack* (Sausalito, CA: Comstock, 1938), 69–72, 145.

24. Drew McCoy, *The Elusive Republic: Political Economy in Jeffersonian America* (New York: W. W. Norton, 1982), 252; Patricia Nelson Limerick, *The Legacy of Conquest: The Unbroken Past of the American West* (New York: W. W. Norton, 1987), 94.

25. Thoreau, *Maine Woods,* 143, 110–112.

26. Thoreau, *Maine Woods,* 213–214.

27. Thoreau, *Maine Woods,* 144–145.

Four: A Marriage of Morality and Capability

1. Frederick Jackson Turner, "The Significance of the Frontier in American History" (1893), in Frederick Jackson Turner, *The Frontier in American History* (New York: Dover, 1996), 1, 3, 30.

2. Frederick Jackson Turner, "The Problem of the West" (1896), in Turner, *Frontier in American History,* 206–207; Frederick Jackson Turner, "The West and American Ideals" (1914), in Turner, *Frontier in American History,* 293.

3. Frederick Jackson Turner, "Contributions of the West to American Democracy" (1903), in Turner, *Frontier in American History,* 261; Frederick Jackson Turner, "Social Forces in American History" (1910), in Turner, *Frontier in American History,* 320–321; Frederick Jackson Turner, "Middle Western Pioneer Democracy" (1918), in Turner, *Frontier in American History,* 343.

4. Christopher Johnson, *This Grand and Magnificent Place: The Wilderness Heritage of the White Mountains* (Hanover, NH: University Press of New England, 2006), 130, 167–168.

5. Ernest Russell, "The Wood Butchers," *Colliers,* March 1908. Quoted in C. Francis Belcher, *Logging Railroads of the White Mountains* (Boston: Appalachian Mountain Club, 1980), 131–132.

6. Bill Gove, *J. E. Henry's Logging Railroads: The History of the East Branch and Lincoln and Zealand Valley Railroads* (Littleton, NH: Bondcliff Books, 1998), 37–39, 47–50.

7. Fannie Hardy Eckstorm and Mary Winslow Smyth, *Minstrelsy of Maine: Folk-Songs and Ballads of the Woods and the Coast* (Boston: Houghton Mifflin, 1927), 111–112, verses 3–6; Gove (*J. E. Henry's Logging Railroads,* 30–31) offers a longer, different version that appeared in Edward. D. Ives, *Larry Gorman: The Man Who Made Songs* (Bloomington: Indiana University Press, 1964).

8. George Perkins Marsh, *Man and Nature* (Cambridge, MA: Belknap Press of Harvard University Press, 1965), 187, 36.

9. *Report of the Forestry Commission of New Hampshire,* June Session, 1885 (Concord: Parsons B. Cogswell, Public Printer, 1885), 19.

10. Joseph B. Walker, "The White Mountain Region," *Second Annual Report of the New Hampshire Forestry Commission, 1894,* Volume I, Part II, Appendix C (Concord: Edward N. Pearson, Public Printer, 1894), 102–103, available at https://extension.unh.edu/resources/files/Resource006141_Rep8773.pdf.

11. Second Report of the Forestry Commission of New Hampshire, January Session 1893 (Concord: Ira C. Evans, Public Printer, 1893), 10, available at https://babel.hathitrust.org/cgi/pt?id=uc1.$b6693;view=1up;seq=11.

12. David C. Smith, *A History of Lumbering in Maine, 1861–1960* (Orono: University of Maine Press, 1972), 357, quoted from the *Bangor Daily Commercial,* February 18, 1899.

13. Philip W. Ayers, "Forest Problems in New Hampshire," *Forestry Quarterly* 1, no. 4 (1903): 123–124.

14. "Alfred Knight Chittenden, 1879–1930," *Journal of Forestry* 29, no. 2 (1931): 259; Alfred K. Chittenden, *Forest Conditions of Northern New Hampshire,* Bulletin No. 55 (Washington, DC: USDA Bureau of Forestry, 1905), 15, 20, available at https://archive.org/details/forestconditions55chit/page/20/mode/2up.

15. Christopher Johnson and David Govatski, *Forests for the People: The Story of America's Eastern National Forests* (Washington, DC: Island Press, 2013), 21–22.

16. Chittenden, *Forest Conditions,* 50–51.

17. Chittenden, *Forest Conditions,* 64–67, 92, 98.

18. Johnson and Govatski, *Forests for the People,* 99; William G. Robbins, *Lumberjacks and Legislators: Political Economy of the U.S. Lumber Industry, 1890–1941* (College Station: Texas A&M University Press, 1982), 42.

19. Johnson, *This Grand and Magnificent Place*, 184–187. The Judiciary Committee ruling reflected a European tradition by which the Crown claimed ownership of fishing rights on navigable waters; private owners, such as feudal lords, retained fishing rights to nonnavigable waters. Bonnie J. McCay, "The Culture of the Commoners: Historical Observations on Old and New World Fisheries," in Bonnie J. McCay and James M. Acheson, eds., *The Question of the Commons: The Culture and Ecology of Communal Resources* (Tucson: University of Arizona Press, 1987), 198; Johnson and Govatski, *Forests for the People*, 103–104.

20. Paul Bruns, *A New Hampshire Everlasting and Unfallen* (Concord: Society for the Protection of New Hampshire Forests, 1969), 11.

21. Johnson and Govatski, *Forests for the People*, 109.

22. David Publicover and Tom Steinbach, "Public Land Acquisition—A Greater Bargain Than Ever," *Northern Forest Forum* 3, no. 5 (1995): 15; George Henry to Billy Boyle, July 24, 1912, in Gove, *J. E. Henry's Logging Railroads*, 121–122, 180.

23. Richard W. Judd, *Common Lands, Common People: The Origins of Conservation in Northern New England* (Cambridge, MA: Harvard University Press, 1997), 110–120.

24. John Clayton, *Natural Rivals: John Muir, Gifford Pinchot, and the Creation of America's Public Lands* (New York: Pegasus Books, 2019), 215.

25. Theodore Roosevelt, "Address at Leland Stanford Junior University, May 12, 1903," in Theodore Roosevelt, *Addresses and Presidential Messages of Theodore Roosevelt, 1902–1904* (New York: G. P. Putnam's Sons, 1904), 193.

26. Gifford Pinchot, *Breaking New Ground* (New York: Harcourt Brace, 1947), 505; Samuel P. Hays, *Conservation and the Gospel of Efficiency: The Progressive Conservation Movement, 1890–1920* (Cambridge, MA: Harvard University Press, 1959), 41–42.

27. John Muir, *A Thousand-Mile Walk to the Gulf* (Boston: Houghton-Mifflin, 1916), 136–139.

28. Hays, *Conservation and the Gospel of Efficiency*, 41–42.

29. Henry D. Thoreau, "Resistance to Civil Government" ["Civil Disobedience"], in Henry D. Thoreau, *Essays: A Fully Annotated Edition,* edited by Jeffrey S. Cramer (New Haven: Yale University Press, 2013), 147, 150.

30. Thoreau, "Civil Disobedience," 156.

31. James Forten Jr., "An Address Delivered Before the Ladies' Anti-Slavery Society of Philadelphia, on the Evening of the 14th of April, 1836," in Schomburg Center for Research in Black Culture, Michelle D. Commander, ed., *Power Concedes Nothing Without a Demand* (New York: Penguin, 2021), 106, 112.

Five: The Paper Plantation

1. Quoted in Mitch Lansky, "Deja Vu All Over Again: Maine Forestry Controversies at the Turn of the Century," *Northern Forest Forum* 4, no. 1 (1995): 11.

2. Michael G. Hillard, *Shredding Paper: The Rise and Fall of Maine's Mighty Paper Industry* (Ithaca, NY: Cornell University Press, 2020), 83.

3. David C. Smith, *A History of Lumbering in Maine, 1861–1960* (Orono: University of Maine Press, 1972), 247–250.

4. Lloyd C. Irland, "Maine's Natural Resources," *Sun-Journal* (Lewiston, ME), October 31, 1999.

5. Smith, *History of Lumbering, 1861–1960*, 252–255.

6. Philip T. Coolidge, *History of the Maine Woods* (Bangor, ME: Furbish–Roberts, 1963), 411.

7. Hillard, *Shredding Paper*, 8–9, 21.

8. Richard W. Judd, *Common Lands, Common People: The Origins of Conservation in Northern New England* (Cambridge, MA: Harvard University Press, 1997), 118–120.

9. Judd, *Common Lands*, 90, 113–114.

10. Richard W. Judd, *Aroostook: A Century of Logging in Northern Maine* (Orono: University of Maine Press, 1989), 213.

11. Smith, *History of Lumbering, 1861–1960*, 371.

12. The court's verdict is quoted in Mitch Lansky, *Beyond the Beauty Strip: Saving What's Left of Our Forests* (Gardiner, ME: Tilbury House, 1992), 360; Smith, *History of Lumbering, 1861–1960*, 373.

13. Craig G. Lorimer, "The Presettlement Forest and Natural Disturbance Cycle of Northeastern Maine," *Ecology* 58 (1977): 146.

14. J. R. Blais, "Trends in the Frequency, Extent, and Severity of Spruce Budworm Outbreaks in Eastern Canada," *Canadian Journal of Forest Research* 13 (1983): 542.

15. Lansky, *Beyond the Beauty Strip*, 204–205.

16. Baxter quoted in John W. Hakola, *Legacy of a Lifetime: The Story of Baxter State Park* (Woolwich, ME: TBW Books, 1981), 53, 55.

17. Neil Rolde, *The Baxters of Maine: Downeast Visionaries* (Gardiner, ME: Tilbury House, 1997), 222.

18. Hakola, *Legacy of a Lifetime*, 101.

19. *Portland Press Herald*, June 14, 1969, quoted in Rolde, *Baxters of Maine*, 311. For profiles of some of the most significant examples of wildlands philanthropy, see Tom Butler, *Wildlands Philanthropy: The Great American Tradition* (San Rafael, CA: Earthaware, 2008).

20. William C. Osborn, *The Paper Plantation: Ralph Nader's Study Group Report on the Pulp and Paper Industry in Maine* (New York: Grossman, 1974), 56–62; Lansky, *Beyond the Beauty Strip*, 60.

21. Paul Hawken, *The Ecology of Commerce: A Declaration of Sustainability* (New York: HarperCollins, 1993), 82–83.

22. Hillard, *Shredding Paper*, 204–206.

23. Hillard, *Shredding Paper*, 188.

24. *Northern Forest Forum* 5, no. 5 (1997): 19.

25. Osborn, *Paper Plantation*, 139, 177–178.

26. Osborn, *Paper Plantation*, 160–161; Pan Atlantic Consultants and the Irland Group, *Maine Logging Industry and the Bonded Labor Program: An Economic Analysis* (Augusta: Maine Department of Labor, 1999), 31, 74, 176, 185.

27. Lansky, *Beyond the Beauty* Strip, 74–84; Hillard, *Shredding Paper,* 140–162.

28. Bill Butler, personal communication, June 26, 2001.

29. Mitch Lansky, "The Canadian Connection: Background on the Job Import Log Export Issues," *Northern Forest Forum* 7, no. 6 (1999): 6.

Six: The Budworm Made Me Do It

1. Robert S. Seymour and Ronald C. Lemin Jr., *Timber Supply Projections for Maine 1980–2080,* Bulletin 7, Maine Agricultural Forestry Experiment Station, Misc. Report 337 (Orono: University of Maine Cooperative Forestry Research Unit, 1989), 18.

2. Mitch Lansky, *Beyond the Beauty Strip: Saving What's Left of Our Forests* (Gardiner, ME: Tilbury House, 1992), 145–146. Researchers at the Penobscot Experimental Forest tested Westveld's strategy. In 1986, when the budworm epidemic had subsided, they found that budworms had caused only 2 percent of the mortality of fir, spruce, and hemlock on their selectively managed stands. On stands that had been commercially clear-cut, budworms caused 99 percent of the mortality.

3. J. R. Blais, "Trends in the Frequency, Extent, and Severity of Spruce Budworm Outbreaks in Eastern Canada," *Canadian Journal of Forest Research* 13 (1983): 542; Shawn Fraver, Robert S. Seymour, James H. Speer, and Alan S. White, "Dendrochronological Reconstruction of Spruce Budworm Outbreaks in Northern Maine, USA," *Canadian Journal of Forest Research* 37 (2007): 526; Neil Rolde, *The Interrupted Forest: A History of Maine's Wildlands* (Gardiner, ME: Tilbury House, 2001), 348.

4. Lansky, *Beyond the Beauty Strip,* 211–212, 264–269.

5. Lansky, *Beyond the Beauty Strip,* 8, 233

6. Lansky, *Beyond the Beauty Strip,* 221.

7. Maine Public Employees for Environmental Responsibility, *Losing Paradise: The Allagash Wilderness Waterway Under Attack,* 2nd ed. (Millinocket, ME: Public Employees for Environmental Responsibility, 2002), 35–36, available at https://www.peer.org/wp-content/uploads/attachments/losing_paradise2001.pdf.

8. David Brower, with Steve Chapple, *Let the Mountains Talk, Let the Rivers Run: A Call to Those Who Would Save the Earth* (New York: HarperCollinsWest, 1995), 29; Suzanne Simard, *Finding the Mother Tree: Discovering the Wisdom of the Forest* (New York: Alfred A. Knopf, 2021), 232–233; Merlin Sheldrake, *Entangled Life: How Fungi Make Our Worlds, Change Our Minds and Shape Our Futures* (New York: Random House, 2020), 145.

9. D. A. Perry, M. P. Amaranthus, J. G. Borchers, S. L. Borchers, and R. E. Brainerd, "Bootstrapping in Ecosystems," *BioScience* 39, no. 4 (1989): 230–237; Nicholas C. Dove and William S. Keeton, "Structural Complexity Enhancement Increases Fungal Species Richness in Northern Hardwood Forests," *Fungal Ecology* 13 (2015): 181–192, available at https://doi.org/10.1016/j.funeco.2014.09.009.

10. David A. Patrick, Malcolm L. Hunter Jr., and Aram J. K. Calhoun, "Effects of Experimental Forestry Treatments on a Maine Amphibian Community," *Forest Ecology and Management* 234 (2006): 323–332.

11. Nicholas V. L. Brokaw and Richard A. Lent, "Vertical Structure," in Malcolm L. Hunter Jr., ed., *Maintaining Biodiversity in Forest Ecosystems* (Cambridge: Cambridge University Press, 1999), 373–399.

12. Robert S. Seymour, Alan S. White, and Philip G. deMaynadier, "Natural Disturbance Regimes in Northeastern North America—Evaluating Silvicultural Systems Using Natural Scales and Frequencies," *Forest Ecology and Management* 155 (2002): 360, 365.

13. Seymour, White, and deMaynadier, "Natural Disturbance Regimes," 363.

14. David R. Foster and David A. Orwig, "Preemptive and Salvage Harvesting of New England Forests: When Doing Nothing Is a Viable Alternative," *Conservation Biology* 20, no. 4 (2006): 966–968.

15. Forests for the Future Program and Citizens' Forestry Advisory Council, "Forest for the Future: A Report on Maine's Forest to the Legislature, the Governor, and the People of Maine" (1988), 9–12, *Department of Agriculture, Conservation, and Forestry (ACF), University of Southern Maine Digital Commons,* https://digitalcommons.usm.maine.edu/maine-acf-docs/1.

16. Kim Clark, Dennis Bailey, and Bob Cummings, "Forests in Crisis: Maine Woods Enter Era of Decline," *Maine Sunday Telegram,* July 20, 1986.

17. Clark, Bailey, and Cummings, "Forests in Crisis."

18. Lansky, *Beyond the Beauty Strip,* 324.

19. Randy Wilson, "The Perils of Success," *Maine Times,* March 13, 1987, 2–5.

20. Lansky, *Beyond the Beauty Strip,* 354–355.

21. Martin Leighton, "Maine Woodsman Laments Destruction of North Woods," *Northern Forest Forum* 2, no. 5 (1994): 24–25.

Seven: The Sum of the Parts

1. "We Need Your Help: RARE II Position Update," *Forest Notes,* 135 (winter 1978–1979): 16–18; Paul Bofinger, "Case for a White Mountain Wilderness Bill or How to Avoid RARE III," *Forest Notes* 153 (summer 1983): 1; Paul Bofinger, "A Plague o' Both Your Houses!" *Forest Notes* 155 (winter 1984): 1; Christopher McGrory Klyza, "Public Lands and Wild Lands in the Northeast," in Christopher McGrory Klyza, ed., *Wilderness Comes Home: Rewilding the Northeast* (Hanover, NH: University Press of New England, 2001), 92.

2. Klyza, "Public Lands," 94.

3. The following section on Goldsmith's takeover of Diamond draws from Jamie Sayen, *You Had a Job for Life* (Hanover, NH: University Press of New England, 2018).

4. Ivan Fallon, *Billionaire: The Life and Times of Sir James Goldsmith* (Boston: Little Brown, 1992), 359.

5. Stephen C. Harper, Laura L. Falk, and Edward W. Rankin, *The Northern Forest Lands Study of New England and New York* (Rutland, VT: Forest Service, US Department of Agriculture, 1990), 10; Thomas Michael Power, *Lost Landscapes and Failed Economies: The Search for a Value of Place* (Washington, DC: Island Press, 1996), 137–138.

6. Perry Hagenstein, *A Challenge for New England: Changes in Large Forest Land Holdings* (Boston: Fund for New England, 1987).

7. "Paul Bofinger Retires After 35 Years at Society for the Protection of NH Forests: A *Forum* Interview," *Northern Forest Forum* 4, no. 6 (1996): 22–23.

8. Nash Stream Advisory Committee, *Nash Stream Forest Management Plan* (Concord: State of New Hampshire, Department of Resources and Economic Development, 1995), 3–4.

9. Paul A. Doscher and Richard Ober, "Easements Ensure Good Forestry," *Northern Forest Forum* 8, no. 5 (2000): 4–5.

10. Conservation Easement Deed Between the State of New Hampshire and the United States of America, August 4, 1989, 1.

11. *American Forests,* "Act Stirs Controversy Beyond New Hampshire," Free Library, 1989, available at https://www.thefreelibrary.com/Act+spurs+controversy +beyond+New+Hampshire.-a07502471; Christopher McGrory Klyza, "The Northern Forest: Problems, Politics, and Alternatives," in Christopher McGrory Klyza and Stephen C. Trombulak, eds., *The Future of the Northern Forest* (Hanover, NH: University Press of New England, 1994), 40.

12. "North Woods Farce," editorial, *Sun-Journal* (Lewiston, ME), August 4, 1989.

13. Martha Carlson, "North of the Notches," *Forest Notes* 173 (summer 1988): 4–5; John G. Mitchell, "Mountain Views, Bargain Prices," *Harrowsmith* (July–August 1989): 39.

14. Hagenstein, *Challenge for New England,* 12–15.

15. "Paul Bofinger Retires," 23.

16. Harper, Falk, and Rankin, *Northern Forest Lands Study,* 89.

17. "Legislative Direction," Appendix A, in Harper, Falk, and Rankin, *Northern Forest Lands Study,* 89.

18. The following account of the strike draws upon the Jay-Livermore Falls Working Class History Project, *Pain on Their Faces: Testimonies on the Paper Mill Strike Jay, Maine, 1987–1988* (New York: Apex, 1998).

19. Mitch Lansky, *Beyond the Beauty Strip: Saving What's Left of Our Forests* (Gardiner, ME: Tilbury House, 1992), 59–60, cites Scott Allen, "Days of Living Dangerously: Two Poisonous Leaks in Nine Days Put a Town on Edge," *Maine Times,* February 19, 1988, 12–14.

20. Letter from Senator Patrick Leahy and Senator Warren B. Rudman to F. Dale Robertson, chief of US Forest Service, October 4, 1988, reprinted in Harper, Falk, and Rankin, *Northern Forest Lands Study,* 90–91.

Eight: Ignoring the Problem Will Not Make It Go Away

1. Stephen C. Harper, Laura L. Falk, and Edward W. Rankin, *The Northern Forest Lands Study of New England and New York* (Rutland, VT: Forest Service, US Department of Agriculture, 1990), x.

2. Harper, Falk, and Rankin, *Northern Forest Lands Study,* 2–3.

3. John G. Mitchell, "Mountain Views, Bargain Prices," *Harrowsmith* (July–August 1989): 44.

4. Carl Reidel, "The Political Process of the Northern Forest Lands Study," in Christopher McGrory Klyza and Stephen C. Trombulak, eds., *The Future of the Northern Forest* (Hanover, NH: University Press of New England, 1994), 102–103.

5. Harper, Falk, and Rankin, *Northern Forest Lands Study*, 76–79, 84–87, 160–162; Norman Boucher, "Whose Woods These Are," *Wilderness* (fall 1989): 34; Reidel, "Political Process," 102.

6. "International Paper Harvests 1926 to 2001," prepared by RSM of the New Hampshire Division of Forests and Lands, September 2001, in the author's possession. Note: IP took over Champion in 2000. Quotations here and following are transcribed by the author from a tape-recording that Peter Riviere made of the Northern Forest Lands Study and Governors' Task Force hearing, Lancaster, NH, January 30, 1989.

7. Henry D. Thoreau, *The Maine Woods: A Fully Annotated Edition*, ed. Jeffrey S. Cramer (New Haven: Yale University Press, 2009), 139.

8. Andrew M. Barton, Alan S. White, and Charles V. Cogbill, *The Changing Nature of the Maine Woods* (Durham: University of New Hampshire Press, 2012), 72.

9. Unpublished draft of *The Northern Forest Lands Study of New England and New York*, September 1, 1989, I-1, II-6, VIII-51; in the author's possession. Note: page 1 gives the date July 31, 1989, which clearly is the correct date of release because John Dillon wrote articles in the *Rutland Herald* on August 13 and 14, 1989, that critiqued this draft. John Dillon, "States Divided in Criticism of Report on Northern Forest," *Rutland Herald*, August 14, 1989.

10. Governors' Task Force on Northern Forest Lands and USDA Forest Service, *Draft of the Northern Forest Lands Study Report*, October 5, 1989, 91–92, 9; Jeff Elliott and Jamie Sayen, *The Ecological Restoration of the Northern Appalachians: An Evolutionary Perspective* (North Stratford, NH: Loose Cannon, 1990), 43.

11. Jamie Sayen, "Unrepentant, *Erratic* Editor Responds to TNC Criticisms," *Glacial Erratic* 2, no. 4 (1990): 21.

12. Society for the Protection of New Hampshire Forests, "Response and Recommendations for Action: *Northern Forest Lands Study*," November 2, 1989, unpublished draft in the author's possession, 5; Richard Ober, "First Word," *Forest Notes* 180 (January–February 1990): 7; Richard Ober, "Time to Move: Report: The Northern Forest," *Forest Notes* 183 (July–August, 1990): 9.

13. Steven A. Wolf and Jeffrey A. Klein, "Enter the Working Forest: Discourse Analysis in the Northern Forest," *Geoforum* 38 (2007): 985–998, available at https://doi.org/10.1016/j.geoforum.2007.03.009.

14. Preserve Appalachian Wilderness, "The Working Forest Is Not Working: A Critique of the Northern Forest Lands Study," January 1990, in the author's possession. Tom Butler, later editor of *Wild Earth*, performed heroic service as editor in whittling my sprawling one-hundred-plus-page critique to a mere sixteen pages.

15. Harper, Falk, and Rankin, *Northern Forest Lands Study*, 166.

16. Harper, Falk, and Rankin, *Northern Forest Lands Study*, 3, 164.

17. Harper, Falk, and Rankin, *Northern Forest Lands Study,* 8. Robert Whitney, vice president of LandVest, told the NFLS in May 1989 that there was no evidence that large ownerships are likely to be developed soon. Robert H. Whitney, "Forces for Change in Forest Land Ownership and Uses: The Large Landowner's Situation," in Clark S. Binkley and Perry R. Hagenstein, eds., *Conserving the North Woods* (New Haven: Yale School of Forestry and Environmental Studies, 1989), 72–96. The NFLS hired Lloyd Irland to evaluate recent development trends. He concluded that not much industrial land was going into development. The Irland Group, "Case Studies in Land Use Change: Overview of the Northern Forest Lands," in Harper, Falk, and Rankin, *Northern Forest Lands Study,* Appendix D, 104–115; Harper, Falk, and Rankin, *Northern Forest Lands Study,* 42. For Existing Use Zoning, the NFLS referenced John A. Humbach, "Law and a New Land Ethic," *Minnesota Law Review* 74, no. 2 (1989): 339–370.

18. Harper, Falk, and Rankin, *Northern Forest Lands Study,* 49–50.

19. Harper, Falk, and Rankin, *Northern Forest Lands Study,* 18, 49.

20. Governors' Task Force on Northern Forest Lands, *The Northern Forest Lands: A Strategy for Their Future,* May 1990, 4.

21. Jamie Sayen, "*Northern Forest Lands Study* Contains Some Surprises," *Glacial Erratic* 2, no. 2 (1990): 20.

22. Bill McKibben, *The End of Nature* (New York: Random House, 1989), 14.

23. McKibben, *End of Nature,* 32–33.

24. Harper, Falk, and Rankin, *Northern Forest Lands Study,* 21, 84, 166.

Nine: Intellectually Valid but Not Very Useful

1. Jeffrey St. Clair and Joshua Frank, "Dave Foreman and the First Green Scare Case," *Counterpunch,* September 22, 2022, available at https://www.counterpunch.org/2022/09/22/dave-foreman-and-the-first-green-scare-case/.

2. Gene Ehlert, "Dead Diamond Denizens Dumped on Department Desk," *Coös County Democrat,* September 20, 1989.

3. Gene Ehlert and Charles J. Jordan, "The Uncompromising World of Jeff Elliott and Jamie Sayen," *Coös Magazine* 1, no. 8 (1990): 7.

4. Unsigned, but authored by Jamie Sayen, "Intellectually Valid," *Glacial Erratic* 1, no. 4 (1990): 3.

5. Jeff Elliott and Jamie Sayen, "Will Management Plan Protect Nash Stream?," *Glacial Erratic* 2, no. 3 (1990): 9.

6. State of New Hampshire Department of Resources and Economic Development, "Nash Stream Forest Management Plan—Draft Revision," January 2017, 8, 45, online document in the author's possession.

7. State of New Hampshire, "Nash Stream Forest Management Plan," 2; Elliott and Sayen, "Will Management Plan Protect Nash Stream?" 9.

8. State of New Hampshire, "Nash Stream Forest Management Plan," 129; see Chapter 15, "Nightmare of the North."

9. Jamie Sayen, "NH Fish & Game 'Biology'—A Disgrace," *Glacial Erratic* 2, no. 3 (1990): 11.

10. State of New Hampshire, "Nash Stream Forest Management Plan," 61–63.

11. "Finding Common Ground: An Interview with Hank Swan," *Northern Forest Forum* 1, no. 6 (1993): 8–9.

12. Letter from William S. Bartlett Jr. to Members of the Nash Stream Advisory Committee, January 15, 1996, in the author's possession.

13. John David Delehanty, "Application to Bail After Commitment by Local Justice Court: The People of the State of New York Against James R. Sayen and Jeffrey W. Elliott," November 1, 1990, in the author's possession; Andy Molloy, "Adirondack Pond Assaulted, PAW Protesters Arrested," *Glacial Erratic* 2, no. 4 (1990–1991): 11.

14. The state groups most active during the Northern Forest Lands Council years were the Maine Audubon Society, the Natural Resources Council of Maine, the Forest Society (Society for the Protection of New Hampshire Forests), the Audubon Society of New Hampshire, the Vermont Natural Resources Council, and the Adirondack Council. The Appalachian Mountain Club and Conservation Law Foundation were regional groups. National groups included the National Wildlife Federation, the Wilderness Society, the National Audubon Society (not affiliated with either New Hampshire or Maine Audubon), and the Sierra Club. Grassroots groups included RESTORE: The North Woods, the Northern Appalachian Restoration Project, New York Rivers United, and the Environmental Air Force. Half a dozen other conservation organizations were affiliated but less active.

15. Carl Reidel, "The Political Process of the Northern Forest Lands Study," in Christopher McGrory Klyza and Stephen C. Trombulak, eds., *The Future of the Northern Forest* (Hanover, NH: University Press of New England, 1994), 108.

16. Jamie Sayen, "Blueprint for Cooperation Among Northern Appalachian Enviros," *Glacial Erratic* 3, no. 1 (1991): 9.

Ten: Government-Financed Lobbyist Group

1. Stephen C. Harper, Laura L. Falk, and Edward W. Rankin, *The Northern Forest Lands Study of New England and New York* (Rutland, VT: Forest Service, US Department of Agriculture, 1990), 86.

2. Carl Reidel, "The Political Process of the Northern Forest Lands Study," in Christopher McGrory Klyza and Stephen C. Trombulak, eds., *The Future of the Northern Forest* (Hanover, NH: University Press of New England, 1994), 106.

3. Robert B. Beattie, "Finding Uncommon Ground: Sustainable Development Conflicts in the Northern Forest of New England and New York," PhD diss., Massachusetts Institute of Technology, 1998, 174.

4. Reidel, "Political Process," 105; Phyllis Austin, "The Northern Forest Lands Council Is the Lightning Rod for Debate," *Maine Times*, August 23, 1991, 7; Charles Levesque, *Northern Forest Lands Council NEWS* 5, June 27, 1991 (all unpublished materials related to the Northern Forest Lands Council are in the possession of the author).

5. Gary Fournier, "Protest, Press Conference Staged by John Birch Society," *Caledonian Record* (St. Johnsbury, VT), July 16, 1991; Levesque, *NEWS* 8, July 19, 1991; Levesque, *NEWS* 37, February 28, 1992.

6. Levesque, *NEWS* 11, August 16, 1991; Northern Forest Lands Council, Minutes of Meeting, Ray Brook, NY, August 13–14, 1991; Phyllis Austin, "Emotions Are High as Old Adversaries Confront the Northern Forest," *Maine Times*, August 23, 1991, 4.

7. Levesque, *NEWS* 14, September 6, 1991.

8. Mitch Lansky, *Beyond the Beauty Strip: Saving What's Left of Our Forests* (Gardiner, ME: Tilbury House, 1992), 20–21. Lansky cited Phyllis Austin, "A Rare Deal: Bowater Paid Bargain-Basement Prices for Georgia-Pacific's Holdings," *Maine Times*, November 8, 1991.

9. Northern Forest Lands Council, Ray Brook Minutes, 7–8.

10. Levesque, *NEWS* 21, October 25, 1991.

11. Levesque, *NEWS* 44, April 17, 1992.

12. Levesque, *NEWS* 35, February 14, 1992; Matthew Simonton, *Classical Greek Oligarchy: A Political History* (Princeton, NJ: Princeton University Press, 2017), 80–84; Wendy Brown, *Undoing the Demos: Neoliberalism's Stealth Revolution* (Brooklyn, NY: Zone Books, 2015), 127.

13. Gary Lawless, Letter, *Northern Forest Forum* 1, no. 1 (1992): 3.

14. Mitch Lansky, "Faulty Assumptions of Northern Forest Lands Council," *Northern Forest Forum* 1, no. 1 (1992): 23–25.

15. Jamie Sayen, "Bleak Paper Industry Future," *Northern Forest Forum* 1, no. 2 (1992): 5.

16. Mitch Lansky, "Northern Forest Lands Council Credibility Undermined by Refusal to Study Forest Practices," *Northern Forest Forum* 1, no. 6 (1993): 10; Land and Water Associates and Market Decisions, *A Summary of the Commission's Current Land Use Policies and Their Net Effects After 20 Years of Development in Maine's Unorganized Territories* (Augusta, ME: Use Regulation Commission, Department of Conservation, 1994).

17. James W. Sewall Company, Market Decisions, Inc., "Northern Forest Lands Council: Land Conversion Study," April 9, 1993, 33, 41–43, in section 2 of Northern Forest Lands Council, *Technical Appendix: A Compendium of Technical Research and Forum Proceedings from the Northern Forest Lands Council* (Concord, NH: February 1994).

18. Beattie, "Finding Uncommon Ground," 155.

19. Andrew Whittaker, "The Economics of Place," *Northern Forest Forum* 1, no. 6 (1993): 23.

20. John Harrigan, "Editorial: Every Load of Logs Sent Out Means Lots of Local Jobs Lost," *News & Sentinel* (Colebrook, NH), January 22, 1992; Timberlands Staff, Champion International Corporation, "Changing the Landowners' Economic Conditions: A New Hampshire/Vermont Case Study of Champion International Corporation," in Clark S. Binkley and Perry R. Hagenstein, eds., *Conserving the North Woods* (New Haven: Yale School of Forestry and Environmental Studies, 1989), 104–105.

21. "Finding #7," Northern Forest Lands Council, *Findings and Options: For Public Policy Changes Affecting the 26 Million-Acre Northern Forest of Maine, New Hampshire, New York and Vermont*, September 1993, 28.

22. Finding #2C, Northern Forest Lands Council, *Findings and Options*, 27.

23. Northern Forest Lands Council, *Finding Common Ground: The Draft Recommendations of the Northern Forest Lands Council* (Concord, NH: 1994), 78–82 and A-63; "Finding Common Ground: An Interview with Hank Swan," *Northern Forest Forum* 1, no. 6 (1993), 8–9.

24. Beattie, "Finding Uncommon Ground," 152.

25. Northern Forest Lands Council, *Finding Common Ground*, 53; Mitch Lansky, "Council Treatment of Forest Practices—Too Little, Too Late," *Northern Forest Forum* 2, no. 4 (1994): 11.

26. David Dobbs and Richard Ober, *The Northern Forest* (White River Junction, VT: Chelsea Green, 1995), 302–303, 310.

27. "Council Listening Sessions Demonstrate Broad Support for Strengthening Conservation Measures," *Northern Forest Forum* 2, no. 6 (1994): 2, 3, 13; Fife Hubbard, "Public Demands Land Acquisition, Ecological Reserves, and Good Forestry," *Northern Forest Forum* 2, no. 5 (1994): 26.

28. Letter to the Northern Forest Lands Council from Robert Matthews, Houlton, ME, May 8, 1994.

29. Beattie, "Finding Uncommon Ground," 125, 192.

30. Northern Forest Lands Council, *Finding Common Ground*, 9, 18.

31. Jamie Sayen, "Northern Forest Lands Council Promotes Regional Dialogue," *Northern Forest Forum* 1, no. 4 (1993): 6.

32. Bill McKibben, "Why Was Council Afraid to Investigate Adirondacks?" *Northern Forest Forum* 3, no. 1 (1994): 8.

33. Northern Forest Lands Council, *Finding Common Ground*, 11–12; Lloyd C. Irland, "Papermaking in Maine: Economic Trends 1894–2000," *Maine History* 45, no. 1 (2009): 59; Jym St. Pierre, "Maine Woods Up for Grabs—Again! Scott Paper Wants to Unload 910,000 Acres and Two Mills in Maine," *Northern Forest Forum* 2, no. 6 (1994): 7.

34. Michael G. Hillard, *Shredding Paper: The Rise and Fall of Maine's Mighty Paper Industry* (Ithaca, NY: Cornell University Press, 2020), 197–199.

35. Jamie Sayen, "NFL Council's Final Report Fails to Address Regional Crisis," *Northern Forest Forum* 3, no. 1 (1994): 23.

36. Northern Forest Lands Council, *Finding Common Ground*, 11.

Eleven: A Fork in the Road

1. Monte Burke, "The Yellowstone of the East? A Bold Proposal for a National Park Has Stubborn Mainers Divided," *Sports Afield*, March 2000, 13, 16.

2. "Maine Audubon Society Press Release Opposes National Park Proposal," *Northern Forest Forum* 2, no. 6 (1994): 13; the press release was dated June 7, 1994. "Editorial," *Maine Times*, June 17, 1994, quoted in "What They're Saying About the Maine Woods National Park Proposal," *Northern Forest Forum* 2, no. 6 (1994): 12.

3. Memo from Jerry Bley to Northern Forest Alliance, November 15, 1994, in the author's possession.

4. Jamie Sayen, "'Family' Forestland Preservation Tax Act May Cost $800 Million a Year," *Northern Forest Forum* 4, no. 1 (1995): 17.

5. Patrick Leahy, "Protecting the Traditions of the Northern Forest: The Northern Forest Stewardship Act," *Northern Forest Forum* 4, no. 1 (1995): 16; Jamie Sayen, "Northern Forest Stewardship Act Reflects Failures of Council," *Northern Forest Forum* 4, no. 1 (1995): 19.

6. James D. Petersen, "War in the North Country: The Battle for Control of the Northeast's New Forest," *Evergreen,* the Magazine of the Evergreen Foundation, September 1998, 33.

7. Letter to the Northern Forest Lands Council from Kenneth A. Colburn, vice president, Business and Industry Association of New Hampshire, May 13, 1994; Charles A. Levesque, "Forests for Today, Forests for Tomorrow," Keynote Address, Northern Forest Alliance Conference, Dixville Notch, NH, March 22, 1997, 8, in the author's possession.

8. "Love Canal, Dioxin, Environmental Justice and Rebuilding Democracy: A Conversation with Lois Marie Gibbs," *Northern Forest Forum* 4, no. 4 (1996): 23.

9. Charles Niebling, Society for the Protection of New Hampshire Forests, testimony to New Hampshire House Committee on Environment and Agriculture RE: HB 1431, January 21, 1998.

10. For instance, Pamela Prodan, "The Legal and Economic Obstacles to a Sustainable Energy Policy," *Northern Forest Forum* 3, no. 2 (1994): 12–15.

Twelve: No Jobs on a Healthy Planet

1. Jonathan Carter, "Referendum to Promote Forest Rehabilitation and Eliminate Clear-Cutting Makes Maine Ballot for 1996," *Northern Forest Forum* 4, no. 2 (1995): 3; Jamie Sayen, "Mud Season: A Time of Renewal and Hope," *Northern Forest Forum* 4, no. 4 (1996): 2; Jym St. Pierre, "Maine Woods Watch," *Northern Forest Forum* 4, no. 3 (1996): 9; Randall D. Snodgrass, "Maine Ban Clear-Cutting Campaign: A Prop Watch Case Study for Americans for the Environment," April 1, 1996, 8, in the author's possession.

2. Jamie Sayen, "Ban Clear-Cutting in Maine Referendum Updates"; Memo from Susan J. Bell to Governor Angus King, January 12, 1996, both in *Northern Forest Forum* 4, no. 6 (1996): 8. Bell meant that opponents should portray themselves as environmentally sensitive, not as corporate shills. The ban clear-cutting campaign secured these documents in the summer of 1996 via the Maine Freedom of Access Act.

3. Memo from William Vail to Governor Angus King, "Talking Points for Governor King Regarding the Green Party's Forestry Referendum," undated, but early January 1996, in the author's possession.

4. Jamie Sayen, "Thwarting the Public Interest—Public Relations and Clear-Cuts," *Northern Forest Forum* 4, no. 4 (1996): 27.

5. Kathleen Fitzgerald, "Maine Woods National Park: A Seductive Idea," *Northern Forest Forum* 4, no. 5 (1996): 27.

6. "NRCM Will Endorse Clear-Cut Referendum Unless Stronger Alternative Is Enacted by July 1," *Northern Forest Forum* 4, no. 4 (1996): 26; Jym St. Pierre, "Maine Woods Watch," *Northern Forest Forum* 4, no. 4 (1996): 16.

7. Jamie Sayen, "Timber Industry and MaineStream Enviros Cut Deal Designed to Scuttle 'Ban Clear-Cutting Referendum,'" *Northern Forest Forum* 4, no. 5 (1996): 4; Conrad Heeschen, "Maine Legislator: Forest Compact Damages Democracy," *Northern Forest Forum* 5, no. 1 (1996): 2. The 1989 Forest Practices Act was negotiated by many of the same people.

8. Mitch Lansky, "The Forest Compact: A Happy Day for Cynics," *Northern Forest Forum* 5, no. 1 (1996): 9–10; Sayen, "Timber Industry and MaineStream Enviros," 4.

9. Mitch Lansky, "Sustaining Forests Through Certification, Regulation, or Rhetoric?" *Northern Forest Forum* 5, no. 5 (1997): 22.

10. Maine Forest Service and State Planning Office, *Economic Impact of the Citizens' Initiative to Promote Forest Rehabilitation and Eliminate Clear-Cutting*, July 3, 1996, iii.

11. Greg Gerritt, *A Campaign for the Forest: The Campaign to Ban Clear-Cutting in Maine in 1996* (Raymond, ME: Leopold Press, 1997), 125.

12. Sara Rimer, "In Clear-Cutting Vote, Maine Will Define Itself," *New York Times*, September 25, 1996.

13. Notes by Jamie Sayen at Maine Forest Products Council PAC Press Conference, Augusta, Maine, March 18, 1996; Jym St. Pierre, "Maine Woods Watch," *Northern Forest Forum* 5, no. 2 (1996): 30; Jym St. Pierre, "Maine Woods Watch," *Northern Forest Forum* 5, no. 3 (1997): 19; Jym St. Pierre, "Maine Woods Watch," *Northern Forest Forum* 6, no. 1 (1997) 11; Jym St. Pierre, "Maine Woods Watch," *Northern Forest Forum* 6, no. 2 (1997): 24–25; Maine Department of Labor Data: NAICS Code 321 (wood product manufacturing), NAICS Code 322 (paper manufacturing), and NAICS Code 113 (forestry and logging); Alec Giffen, "Thoughts on a Coordinated Regional Effort to Reinvigorate the Rural Economies of the Northern Forest," September 13, 2004.

14. Mitch Lansky, "Maine Forest Compact: Endorsing Mediocrity?" *Northern Forest Forum* 5, no. 6 (1997): 8.

15. Lansky, "Sustaining Forests?," 22; *Northern Logger*, December 1995, quoted in Jym St. Pierre, "Maine Woods Watch," *Northern Forest Forum* 4, no. 3 (1996): 11; Letter from Catherine B. Johnson, "Label Assures Quality," December 16, 2000, in the author's possession.

16. Scientific Certification Systems, *Public Summary of the Certification Report* [of Irving's Woodlands], May 2000; Mitch Lansky, *Grade Inflation? SCS Certification of Irving's Allagash Timberlands: A Report for Sierra Club*, May 2002, in the author's possession. On page 4, Lansky quoted from page 10 of SCS's *Forest Conservation Plan Operating Manual*: "scores should be based strictly upon observed conditions ('what is') rather than upon intentions, plans, and assurances. Specifically, the scores should not reflect anticipated compliance with any stipulated conditions."

17. Robert Seymour and David Sherwood, "Assessing Maine's Certified Sustainable Timber Harvest," Northeastern States Research Cooperative, 2013, available at

https://nsrcforest.org/project/assessing-maine's-certified-sustainable-timber-harvest;
Mitch Lansky, "Double Bottom Line: Managing Maine's Forests to Increase Carbon Sequestration and Decrease Carbon Emissions," March 2016, available at http://
planetmaine.net/meepi/lif/; Greenpeace, *Destruction: Certified,* March 10, 2021, con-
firms what Lansky was saying twenty years earlier, available at https://www.greenpeace
.org/international/publication/46812/destruction-certified/.

18. Scientific Certification Systems, *Public Summary,* 43. See Lansky, *Grade Inflation?,* 30–33.

19. Mitch Lansky, "The Canadian Connection: Background on the Job Import
Log Export Issues," *Northern Forest Forum* 7, no. 6 (1999): 6.

20. "Challenging the Paper Plantation: An Interview with Hilton Hafford, July 13,
1999, Allagash, Maine," *Northern Forest Forum* 7, no. 6 (1999): 7–13. Faye O'Leary Hafford (*The Fall of the Forest: Tales of the Last Generation* [Allagash Plantation, ME: 2002])
tells the story of a score or more of Hafford's Allagash neighbors. Almost all have quit
logging, moved away, or are disabled from injuries.

Thirteen: Alternative to Federal Ownership

1. Jamie Sayen, "Champion's 300,000 Acres Sold to Conservation Fund," *Northern Forest Forum* 7, no. 2 (1998): 3.

2. Jamie Sayen, "SAPPI to sell 911,000 Acres in Western Maine," *Northern Forest
Forum* 6, no. 5 (1998): 3.

3. Phyllis Austin, "The West Branch Project: Are Economic Interests Outweighing Conservation Goals?" *Maine Environmental News,* September 25, 2002, http://
planetmaine.net/meepi/files02/pa092602.htm.

4. The poll by Abacus Associates ("Creating a National Park in Maine's North
Woods," Poll Commissioned by the Sierra Club, May 2000) found that support for the
park was stronger in southern Maine, where 66 percent supported it and 18 percent
were opposed. In northern Maine, 55 percent supported the park and 32 percent opposed it. Urban and rural dwellers and men and women supported the park by wide
majorities. The weakest support came from men (55 percent supported, 29 percent opposed), and people older than sixty (53 percent supported, 23 percent opposed). The
poll found that native Mainers supported the park by an impressive 62 percent, with
23 percent opposed. Nonnative Mainers supported the park by 64 percent, to 20 percent
opposed.

5. Jamie Sayen, "Council Supports Land Acquisition????," *Northern Forest Forum* 1, no. 2 (1992): 9. The statement was lifted from the Report of the Governors' Task
Force on Northern Forest Lands, *The Northern Forest Lands: A Strategy for Their Future,* May 1990, 4; David Carle and Jamie Sayen, "Easements: Advantages and Disadvan-
tages," *Northern Forest Forum* 1, no. 2 (1992): 7.

6. Letter to the NFLC from Stephen W. Schley, Pingree Associates, Inc., Bangor,
Maine, May 3, 1994; New England Forestry Foundation, "Conservation Achievements:
Pingree Forest Partnership," available at https://newenglandforestry.org/learn/land

-conservation/conservation-achievements/; Jeff Pidot, *Reinventing Conservation Easements: A Critical Examination and Ideas for Reform* (Cambridge, MA: Lincoln Institute of Land Policy, 2005), 16.

7. Bret Ladine, "Yale Embroiled in Conservation Fight: University, Maine at Odds over Land," *Yale Daily News,* September 20, 2001; Phyllis Austin, "The West Branch Project: Are Economic Interests Outweighing Conservation Goals?" *Maine Environmental News,* September 25, 2002, available at http://planetmaine.net/meepi/files02/pa092602.htm.

8. Lloyd Irland, "Maine Forests: A Century of Change, 1900–2000 . . . and Elements of Policy Change for a New Century," *Maine Policy Review* 9 (winter 2000): 76.

9. Memorandum, Comments on Draft Conservation Easement, from Jeff Pidot, Chief, Natural Resources Division, Office of the Attorney General, State of Maine, to Ralph Knoll, Director of Planning and Land Acquisition, Bureau of Parks and Lands, June 14, 2001; Memorandum, Comments on Draft Conservation Easement for West Branch Project, from Jeff Pidot, Chief, Natural Resources Division, Office of the Attorney General, State of Maine, to Ralph Knoll, Director of Planning and Land Acquisition, Bureau of Parks and Lands, and Mark DesMeules, Director, Land for Maine's Future Program, August 3, 2001; both in the author's possession.

10. See Phyllis Austin, "Federal Investigators Weigh in on West Branch Project," *Maine Environmental News,* August 2, 2002, available at http://www.meepi.org/files02/pa080202.htm; anonymous, "West Branch Maine," *Forest Legacy Update* (November 2002): 2, 4.

11. Lloyd C. Irland, "Maine's Public Estate and Conservation Lands: Brief History and Assessment," *Maine Policy Review* 27, no. 2 (2018): 11–29; Scott Stewart, "West Branch Project Closes" and "Total Acres Protected to Date," *Forest Legacy Update* 3, no. 1 (2005): 1–3.

12. David Foster, Emily Johnson, Brian Hall, Elizabeth Thompson, Brian Donahue, Jon Leibowitz, Edward Faison, et al., "Wildlands in New England: Past, Present and Future," Harvard Forest Paper 35 (Petersham, MA: Harvard Forest, 2023).

13. Jamie Sayen, "Champion Pursuit of Forest Legacy Money in NH Exposes Misuse of Easements," *Northern Forest Forum* 8, no. 3 (2000): 6.

14. Richard Cooksey, "House Appropriations Completes Investigation of Forest Legacy Program," *Forest Legacy Update* (November 2002): 1, 3; Austin, "Federal Investigators Weigh in."

15. Jerry Jenkins, *Conservation Easements and Biodiversity in the Northern Forest Region,* Open Space Institute and the Wildlife Conservation Society (2008), iii, available at https://s3.us-east-1.amazonaws.com/osi-craft/Conservation_Easements_Biodiversity_2008-sm.pdf.

16. Jenkins, *Conservation Easements and Biodiversity,* 81–83.

17. Jenkins, *Conservation Easements and Biodiversity,* 3.

18. Rick Weyerhaeuser, "An Introduction to Timberland Investment," Lyme Timber Company, May 2005, 15, available at http://osi.convio.net/site/DocServer/Weyehauser_TimberPrimer.pdf?docID=2442.

19. Jonathan Thompson of Harvard Forest, personal communication with the author, April 25, 2022.

20. John S. Gunn, Mark J. Ducey, and Ethan Belair, "Evaluating Degradation in a North American Temperate Forest," *Forest Ecology and Management* 432 (2019): 421.

21. Jym St. Pierre, "Doing Deals in Maine," *Northern Forest Forum* 7, no. 4 (1999): 25.

22. Author interview with Robert Seymour, November 12, 2018.

23. Irland, "Maine's Public Estate and Conservation Lands," 19.

24. Aaron Miller, "Quimby Buys T5-R8," *Katahdin Times,* December 2, 2003; Gene Conlogue, "Maine Woods Coalition Chairman Expresses Concerns About Quimby," Letter to *Moosehead Messenger,* December 17, 2003.

25. Renee E. Batchelder, "Quimby Draws a Full House at Controversial Vision Unveiling," *Community Press,* December 9, 2003.

26. Phyllis Austin, "Quimby Purchases 24,000-Acre Township East of Baxter Park," *Moosehead Messenger,* December 3, 2003; Misty Edgecomb, "Quimby Speaks on Land Deal," *Bangor Daily News,* December 5, 2003.

27. "A Bee of a Different Stripe," Editorial, *Bangor Daily News,* December 8, 2003.

28. Murray Carpenter, "Park Proposal Stays Afloat, an Acre at a Time," *Christian Science Monitor,* September 20, 2001; Edie Clark, "The Most Controversial Woman in Maine," *Yankee Magazine,* March/April 2008, 128.

29. Deirdre Fleming, "Trust for Public Land Acquires 31,000 Acres Next to National Monument," *Portland Press Herald,* December 21, 2022.

Fourteen: Uncontrollables

1. Rachel Ohm, "Two Years After Madison Mill Closed, Town Faces Uncertain Future," *Portland Press Herald,* May 20, 2018; Mitch Lansky, "Maine Paper Industry Changes by Year 1985–1993," *Northern Forest Forum* 2, no. 3 (1994): 12.

2. The following section is adapted from, and quotations are from, Jamie Sayen, *You Had a Job for Life* (Hanover, NH: University Press of New England, 2018).

3. Dave Atkinson, "Ready, Set, Go!!!," *Wausau Happenings,* September–October 2002, 2. See Sayen, *Job for Life,* 220.

4. "Public Utility Regulatory Policy Act (PURPA)," Union of Concerned Scientists, Reports & Multimedia/Explainer, July 15, 2002, last updated October 26, 2002, available at https://www.ucsusa.org/resources/public-utility-regulatory-policy-act.

5. Peter Riviere, "Biomass: What's It All About," *Coös County Democrat,* April 6, 1988; Peter Riviere, "Biomass Power Plants: How They Work," *Coös County Democrat,* April 13, 1988.

6. Peg Boyles, "No Fuel like an Old Fuel," *Forest Notes* 167 (winter 1987): 4–10.

7. Mary S. Booth and Brett Leuenberger, *The Bioenergy Boom from the Federal Stimulus: Outcomes and Lessons,* Partnership for Policy Integrity, October 2018, 5, available at https://www.pfpi.net/wp-content/uploads/2018/10/PFPI-Bioenergy-and-the

-Stimulus-Oct-24.pdf; Suzanne Barlyn, "U.S. Energy Company, Founder Must Pay $3.1 Million in Fraud Suit: Court," Reuters, March 31, 2016, available at https://www
.reuters.com/article/us-sec-insidertrading-microcap/u-s-energy-company-founder
-must-pay-3-1-million-in-sec-fraud-suit-court-idUSKCN0WX2A1.

8. Chris Jenson, "Berlin Biomass Plant Fully Operational, But at What Cost to Rate Payers?," New Hampshire Public Radio, August 21, 2014; Chris Jenson, "Feds Fine Original Developer of Berlin Biomass Plant," New Hampshire Public Radio, April 4, 2016, available at https://www.nhpr.org/post/feds-fine-original-developer-berlin-bio mass-plant-3-million#stream/0.

9. Jenson, "Berlin Biomass Plant Fully Operational"; Mary S. Booth, *Trees, Trash, and Toxics: How Biomass Energy Has Become the New Coal,* Partnership for Policy Integrity, April 2, 2014, 5–11, 76, available at http://www.pfpi.net/wp-content/uploads/2014/04/PFPI-Biomass-is-the-New-Coal-April-2-2014.pdf.

10. Anna M. Mika and William S. Keeton, "Net Carbon Fluxes at Stand and Landscape Scales from Wood Bioenergy Harvests in the US Northeast," *GCB-Bioenergy,* March 8, 2014, available at https://onlinelibrary.wiley.com/doi/full/10.1111/gcbb.12143.

11. Jane Difley, "Support Wood Energy, Support NH Forests," *Concord Monitor,* August 28, 2018.

12. Society for the Protection of New Hampshire Forests, "A Healthy Biomass Industry Helps Forest Owners Sustainably Manage Their Forests," first accessed August 28, 2018, a screenshot is in the author's possession. As of November 30, 2022, the SPNHF site read: "Maintaining the markets for all grades of wood is essential to the practice of sustainable forestry. . . . On Forest Society land, about seventy percent of the standing timber is 'low grade,' meaning it is not suitable for sale as saw logs to a commercial sawmill that makes lumber." "Wood Markets and Sustainably Managed Forest Land," available at https://forestsociety.org/advocacy-issue/low-grade-wood-markets-help -landowners-sustainably-manage-forest-land.

13. Interview with Robert Seymour, November 12, 2018.

14. John S. Gunn, Mark J. Ducey, and Ethan Belair, "Evaluating Degradation in a North American Temperate Forest," *Forest Ecology and Management* 432 (2019): 421–423.

15. Jamie Sayen, Letter to New Hampshire Forest Advisory Board, July 8, 2015, in the author's possession.

16. New Hampshire Division of Forests and Lands, *New Hampshire Forest Action Plan—2020* (Concord, NH: Department of Natural and Cultural Resources, 2020), 104–115.

Fifteen: Nightmare of the North

1. Minutes of the Nash Stream Advisory Committee, September 29, 1998, in the author's possession.

2. Minutes of the Nash Stream Advisory Committee, September 25, 2001, in the author's possession.

3. Minutes of the Nash Stream Advisory Committee, November 8, 2001, in the author's possession; "ATV Use in New Hampshire's Nash Stream Forest: Opponents Call for State to Stand by Its Plan; Supporters Say Give Us a Try," *Northern Forest Forum* 9, no. 2 (2002): 24–26.

4. New Hampshire Legislature, "ATV Study Committee, Attachment One: Conclusions," December 19, 2001; ATV Study Committee, "Attachment Two: Recommendations," December 28, 2001, in the author's possession.

5. Memo from Thomas Wagner, Forest Supervisor, White Mountain National Forest, to Paul Stockinger, Director, Lands and Minerals, Eastern Region, Forest Service, September 25, 2001, in the author's possession.

6. Nash Stream Forest Conservation Easement: State of New Hampshire to US Forest Service, August 4, 1989, Section II-C.

7. Memo from Phil Bryce, Director of Division of Forests and Lands, to George Bald, Commissioner of DRED, November 5, 2001; Minutes of the Nash Stream Advisory Committee, November 8, 2001, both in the author's possession.

8. Minutes of the Nash Stream Advisory Committee, February 13, 2002, in the author's possession.

9. Peter Benson and David Publicover, "Minority Report," to the Nash Stream ATV Study Committee, February 7, 2002, in the author's possession.

10. State of New Hampshire, Department of Resources and Economic Development, "Nash Stream Forest Management Plan Updates and Revisions," 2002, 50.

11. Minutes of the Nash Stream Advisory Committee, February 13, 2002, and May 16, 2002, both in the author's possession.

12. Letter from George Bald, Commissioner of DRED, to Representative Fred King, Chairman of Nash Stream Forest Citizens Committee, March 21, 2007, in the author's possession.

13. Minutes of the Nash Stream Forest Citizens Committee, January 25, 2007, in the author's possession.

14. Carol R. Foss, "A Preliminary Investigation of Impacts of ATV Activity on Breeding Birds in the Nash Stream State Forest, Coos County, New Hampshire," August 2006, 7, 2, in the author's possession.

15. Minutes of the Nash Stream Forest Citizens Committee, March 7, 2012; DRED, "Response to CORD Management Concerns Pursuant to RSA 163-C:6," prepared for CORD's meeting of April 11, 2013; Minutes of the Nash Stream Forest Citizens Committee, November 13, 2012, all in the author's possession.

16. Jim Oehler, New Hampshire Department of Fish and Game, to "State of New Hampshire Department of Resources and Economic Development Division of Forests and Lands State Lands Management Team—Request for Review," January 28, 2013; State of New Hampshire Department of Resources and Economic Development, "Nash Stream Forest Management Plan," December 2017, 286–289, both in the author's possession.

17. Memo from John Magee, Fish Habitat Biologist, to Glenn Normandeau, Director of New Hampshire Department of Fish and Game, August 2, 2016, in the author's possession.

18. Minutes of the Nash Stream Forest Citizens Committee, November 2, 2017, in the author's possession.

19. Letter from the Appalachian Mountain Club, The Nature Conservancy, and the Society for the Protection of New Hampshire Forests to Council on Resources and Development, May 5, 2016; in the author's possession; "Nash Stream Forest Management Plan Updates and Revisions," 2002, 50; State of New Hampshire, "Nash Stream Forest Management Plan," December 2017, page 309 of 340 (pages are unnumbered).

20. Jeffrey Rose, Commissioner of New Hampshire Department of Resources and Economic Development, to Council on Resources and Development, July 6, 2016, in the author's possession.

21. State of New Hampshire, "Nash Stream Forest Management Plan," December 2017, 329–337; Minutes of the Nash Stream Forest Citizens Committee, January 25, 2007; CORD, "Findings Regarding ATV/UTV Use in the Nash Stream Forest Adopted by CORD on December 8, 2016," December 14, 2016, all in the author's possession.

22. Kelsey Notch Trail Environmental Compliance Report to CORD, December 2020, in the author's possession.

23. Kelsey Notch Trail Environmental Compliance Report to CORD, December 2020; "Probable Carcinogenicity of Glyphosate," *British Medical Journal,* April 8, 2019, available at https://www.bmj.com/content/365/bmj.l1613; Tom Hals and Tina Bellon, "Bayer Reaches $2 Million Deal over Future Roundup Cancer Claims," Reuters, February 3, 2021, available at https://www.reuters.com/article/us-bayer-glyphosate/bayer-reaches-2-billion-deal-over-future-roundup-cancer-claims-idUSKBN2A32MX.

24. Kelsey Notch Trail Environmental Compliance Report to CORD, December 2020.

25. Department of Resources and Economic Development RSA 215:A-42 and A-43; "ATV and Trail Bike Operation on State Land Coarse and Fine Filter Worksheet: Kelsey Notch ATV/UTV Trail," n.d., but probably 2017; Kelsey Notch Trail Environmental Compliance Report to CORD, December 2021; Kelsey Notch Trail Environmental Compliance Report to CORD, December 2022, all in the author's possession.

26. Letter from the Appalachian Mountain Club, The Nature Conservancy, and the Society for the Protection of New Hampshire Forests to CORD, August 20, 2020; in the author's possession.

27. Appalachian Mountain Club, The Nature Conservancy, and the Society for the Protection of New Hampshire Forests to CORD, November 11, 2020; Memo from Ryan S. Duerring to R. Newcomb Stillwell, Ropes and Gray LLC, to Appalachian Mountain Club, The Nature Conservancy, and the Society for the Protection of New Hampshire Forests, September 21, 2020; Minutes of CORD, January 14, 2021, all in the author's possession.

28. Letter from the Appalachian Mountain Club, The Nature Conservancy, and the Society for the Protection of New Hampshire Forests to Sarah Stewart, Commissioner of DNCR, February 7, 2022; Letter from Derek Ibarguen, Superintendent of WMNF, to Kris Pastoriza, March 8, 2022, both in the author's possession.

29. DRED, "Response to CORD Management Concerns Pursuant to RSA 163-C:6," prepared for CORD's meeting of April 11, 2013.

30. Daniel Lee, "The Economic Contributions of OHRV Riders in New Hampshire," New Hampshire Off Highway Vehicle Association, September 2021, 9–11.

Sixteen: Bid the Tree Unfix His Earthbound Root

1. Elizabeth Kolbert, *Under a White Sky: The Nature of the Future* (New York: Crown, 2021), 147; Maria K. Janowiak, Anthony W. D'Amato, Christopher W. Swanston, Louis Iverson, Frank R. Thompson III, William D. Dijak, Stephen Matthews, et al., "New England and Northern New York Forest Ecosystem Vulnerability Assessment and Synthesis: A Report from the New England Climate Change Response Framework Project," Gen. Tech. Rep. NRS-173 (Newtown Square, PA: USDA Forest Service Northern Research Station, 2018), 26, 37, available at https://doi.org/10.2737/NRS-GTR-173.

2. Janowiak et al., "New England and Northern New York Forest Ecosystem," 56–60.

3. Susan C. Gawler, John J. Albright, Peter D. Vickery, and Frances C. Smith, *Biological Diversity in Maine: An Assessment of Status and Trends in the Terrestrial and Freshwater Landscape* (Augusta: Maine Natural Areas Program, 1996), 53; Gawler et al. cite R. T. Eckert, "Genetic Variation in Red Spruce and Its Relation to Forest Decline in the Northeastern United States," in H. B. Bucher and I. Bucher-Wallin, eds., *Air Pollution and Forest Decline,* 14th International Meeting for Specialists in Air Pollution Effects on Forest Ecosystems, IUFRO P2.05, Interlaken, Switzerland, 1989, and T. A. Hullenberg and R. T. Eckert, "Genetic Variation in Old-Growth Red Spruce," Abstract in *Conservation and Working Landscapes: Proceedings of the 20th Annual Natural Areas Association Conference, Orono, Maine,* 1993.

4. N. L. Rodenhouse, S. N. Matthews, K. P. McFarland, J. D. Lambert, L. R. Iverson, A. Prasad, T. S. Stillett, and R. T. Holmes, "Potential Effects of Climate Change on Birds of the Northeast," *Mitigation and Adaptation Strategies for Global Change* 13 (2008): 523–528.

5. Janowiak et al., "New England and Northern New York Forest Ecosystem," 30, 26, 35, 48, 73; Andrew Whitman, Andrew Cutko, Phillip deMaynadier, Steve Walker, Barbara Vickery, Sally Stockwell, and Robert Houston, *Climate Change and Biodiversity in Maine: A Climate Change Exposure Summary for Species and Key Habitats,* rev. ed. (Brunswick, Maine: Manomet Center for Conservation Sciences, in collaboration with Maine Beginning with Habitat Climate Change Adaptation Working Group, 2013), 22.

6. Janowiak et al., "New England and Northern New York Forest Ecosystem," 228–229, 98.

7. Whitman et al., *Climate Change and Biodiversity,* 26.

8. Janowiak et al., "New England and Northern New York Forest Ecosystem," 29; Katharine Hayhoe, Cameron P. Wake, Thomas G. Huntington, Lifeng Luo, Mark D. Schwartz, Justin Sheffield, Eric Wood, et al., "Past and Future Changes in Climate and Hydrological Indicators in the US Northeast," *Climate Dynamics* 28 (2007): 402.

9. Peter O. Dunn and David W. Winkler, "Climate Change Has Affected the Breeding Date of Tree Swallows Throughout North America," *Proceedings of the Royal Society of London B* 266 (1999): 2487–2490; James P. Gibbs and Alvin R. Breisch, "Climate Warming and Calling Phenology of Frogs Near Ithaca, New York, 1900–1999," *Conservation Biology* 15 (2001): 1175–1178.

10. Janowiak et al., "New England and Northern New York Forest Ecosystem," 229, 104; Whitman et al., *Climate Change and Biodiversity*, 69–72.

11. Whitman et al., *Climate Change and Biodiversity*, 65.

12. Janowiak et al., "New England and Northern New York Forest Ecosystem," 80–82.

13. Janowiak et al., "New England and Northern New York Forest Ecosystem," 82–83.

14. Paul Catanzaro and Tony D'Amato, *Forest Carbon: An Essential Natural Solution for Climate Change* (Amherst: University of Massachusetts Amherst, 2019), 4.

15. Chad Hanson and John Talberth, *Running Backwards: Logging Provisions in the Infrastructure and Budget Reconciliation Packages Would Worsen the Climate Crisis and Threaten Public Health* (Bear City, CA: John Muir Project, 2021), 3, 8. The report cites Chad Hanson, *Smokescreen: Debunking Wildfire Myths to Save Our Forests and Our Climate* (Lexington: University Press of Kentucky, 2021), 95.

16. John S. Gunn, Mark J. Ducey, and Ethan Belair, "Evaluating Degradation in a North American Temperate Forest," *Forest Ecology and Management* 432 (2019): 421–423; Megan Graham MacLean, Matthew J. Duveneck, Joshua Plisinski, Luca L. Morreale, Danelle Laflower, and Jonathan R. Thompson, "Forest Carbon Trajectories: Consequences of Alternative Land-Use Scenarios in New England," *Global Environmental Change* 69 (2021): 13, available at https://harvardforest1.fas.harvard.edu/sites/harvardforest.fas.harvard.edu/files/publications/pdfs/MacLean_GEC_2021.pdf.

17. Catanzaro and D'Amato, *Forest Carbon*, 6; Charles Canham, "Forest Carbon Credits: Too Good to Be True?," Cary Institute of Ecosystem Studies, November 12, 2021, available at https://www.caryinstitute.org/news-insights/lecture-video/forest-carbon-offsets-too-good-be-true-video?mc_cid=8171185918&mc_eid=d00febaed6&utm_campaign=8171185918-EMAIL_CAMPAIGN_2020_butterfly_followup_COPY_01&utm_medium=email&utm_source=Public Event Registrants&utm_term=0_ca04886 74e-8171185918–387855342.

18. William S. Keeton, Andrew A. Whitman, Gregory C. McGee, and Christine L. Goodale, "Late Successional Biomass Development in Northern Hardwood-Conifer Forests of the Northeastern United States," *Forest Science* 57 (2011): 489–505.

19. Jared S. Nunery and William S. Keeton, "Forest Carbon Storage in the Northeastern United States: Net Effects of Harvesting Frequency, Post-Harvest Retention, and Wood Products," *Forest Ecology and Management* 259 (2010): 1374.

20. Catanzaro and D'Amato, *Forest Carbon*, 12, 63, 68; New Hampshire Division of Forests and Lands, *New Hampshire Forest Action Plan—2020* (Concord, NH: Department of Natural and Cultural Resources, 2020), 66–67.

Seventeen: Fierce Green Fire

1. Michael Soulé and Reed Noss, "Rewilding and Biodiversity: Complementary Goals for Continental Conservation," *Wild Earth* 8, no. 3 (1998): 18–28, quotations at 23, 22.

2. Soulé and Noss, "Rewilding," 26.

3. Daniel J. Harrison and Theodore B. Chapin, "An Assessment of Potential Habitat for Eastern Timber Wolves in the Northeastern United States and Connectivity with Occupied Habitat in Southeastern Canada," Wildlife Conservation Society Working Paper No. 7, 1997, 6, available at https://global.wcs.org/Resources/Publications/Publications-Search-II/ctl/view/mid/13340/pubid/DMX548900000.aspx; Memo from Gerry Lavigne, Maine Department of Inland Fisheries and Wildlife Deer Biologist, June 28, 1999, see Kristen DeBoer, "North Woods Riddle: How Does Weakening Protection for Wolves Help Them Recover?," *Northern Forest Forum* 8, no. 2 (2000): 8.

4. Bill McKibben, "Epilogue," in Christopher McGrory Klyza, ed., *Wilderness Comes Home: Rewilding the Northeast* (Hanover, NH: University Press of New England, 2001), 276.

5. Northern Forest Lands Council, *Finding Common Ground: The Draft Recommendations of the Northern Forest Lands Council* (Concord, NH: 1994), 45–47.

6. Stephen C. Trombulak, "Why Recommendation 13 Won't Protect Biotic Integrity and What Must Be Done to Fix It," *Northern Forest Forum* 2, no. 5 (1994): 6–7.

7. Northern Forest Lands Council, *Finding Common Ground*, 61–63.

8. Susan C. Gawler, John J. Albright, Peter D. Vickery, and Frances C. Smith, *Biological Diversity in Maine: An Assessment of Status and Trends in the Terrestrial and Freshwater Landscape* (Augusta: Maine Natural Areas Program, 1996), 10, 30, 31, 35–36, 38, 71, 26.

9. Press Release from Maine Department of Conservation, January 9, 2001, "Department of Conservation Establishes Maine's First Ecological Reserves," *Northern Forest Forum* 8, no. 6 (2001): 11; Mitch Lansky, "An Ecological Reserve System for Maine: Are We Really Making Progress?," *Northern Forest Forum* 9, no. 1 (2001): 18–20; Christopher S. Cronan, Robert J. Lilieholm, Jill Tremblay, and Timothy Glidden, "An Assessment of Land Conservation Patterns in Maine Based on Spatial Analysis of Ecological and Socioeconomic Indicators," *Environmental Management,* April 6, 2010.

10. Steering Committee of the New Hampshire Ecological Reserve System Project, "Protecting New Hampshire's Living Legacy: A Blueprint for Biodiversity Conservation in the Granite State" (Concord: New Hampshire Ecological Reserves System Project, 1998), 3; Scientific Advisory Group, New Hampshire Ecological Reserve System Project, "An Assessment of the Biodiversity of New Hampshire with Recommendations for Conservation Action" (Concord: New Hampshire Ecological Reserves System Project, 1998), 28.

11. New Hampshire Division of Forests and Lands, *New Hampshire Forest Action Plan—2020,* available at https://www.nh.gov/nhdfl/documents/nh-stateforestaction plan_2020.pdf.

12. See *Northern Forest Forum* 3, no. 5 (1995), available at https://harvardforest1 .fas.harvard.edu/sites/harvardforest.fas.harvard.edu/files/publications/nff/ V3N5.pdf. In 1995, I estimated that the size of the Headwaters was 8 million acres. More precise measurements put the figure at 8.7 million acres.

13. John S. Gunn, Mark J. Ducey, and Ethan Belair, "Evaluating Degradation in a North American Temperate Forest," *Forest Ecology and Management* 432 (2019): 421– 423; Matthew J. Duveneck and Jonathan R. Thompson, "Social and Biophysical Deter- minants of Future Forest Conditions in New England: Effects of a Modern Land Use Re- gime," *Global Environmental Change* 55 (2019) 125, available at https://harvardforest1.fas .harvard.edu/sites/harvardforest.fas.harvard.edu/files/publications/pdfs/Duveneck _GlobEnvChange_2019.pdf.

Eighteen: Frugal Prosperity

1. Corinne Le Quéré, Robert B. Jackson, Matthew W. Jones, Adam J. P. Smith, Sam Abernethy, Robbie M. Andrew, Anthony J. De-Gol, et al., "Temporary Reduction in Global CO_2 Emissions During the COVID-19 Forced Confinement," *Nature Climate Change,* May 19, 2020, available at https://www.nature.com/articles/s41558-020-0797-x.

2. Aldo Leopold, "The Land Ethic," in Aldo Leopold, *A Sand County Almanac and Sketches Here and There* (New York: Oxford University Press, 1987), 201–226.

3. Trust for Public Land, "Parks and the Pandemic: A TPL Special Report," 2020, available at https://www.tpl.org/parks-and-the-pandemic.

4. Katharine R. E. Sims, Lucy G. Lee, Neenah Estrella-Luna, Margot R. Lurie, and Jonathan R. Thompson, "Environmental Justice Criteria for New Land Protection Can Inform Efforts to Address Disparities in Access to Nearby Open Space," *Environmental Research Letters* 17, no. 6 (2022): 4014, available at https://iopscience.iop.org/article/10 .1088/1748-9326/ac6313.

5. Josef Settele, Sandra Díaz, Eduardo Brondizio, and Peter Daszak, "COVID-19 Stimulus Measures Must Save Lives, Protect Livelihoods, and Safeguard Nature to Re- duce the Risk of Future Pandemics," IPBES Guest Expert Article, April 22, 2020, avail- able at https://ipbes.net/covid19stimulus.

6. Marshall Sahlins, "The Original Affluent Society," in Jacqueline Solway, ed., *The Politics of Egalitarianism: Theory and Practice* (New York: Berghahn Books, 2006), 96; Henry D. Thoreau, *Walden: A Fully Annotated Edition,* ed. Jeffrey S. Cramer (New Haven: Yale University Press, 2004), 79.

7. Mitch Lansky, "Demand Reduction: A Brief History of the Ups & Downs of Maine's Forest," *Northern Forest Forum* 4, no. 1 (1995): 8–11; Mitch Lansky, "Double Bottom Line: Managing Maine's Forests to Increase Carbon Sequestration and Decrease Carbon Emissions," March 2016, available at http://planetmaine.net/meepi/lif/.

8. Alia al Ghussain, "The Biggest Problem with Carbon Offsetting Is That It Doesn't Really Work," Greenpeace UK, May 26, 2020, available at https://www .greenpeace.org.uk/news/the-biggest-problem-with-carbon-offsetting-is-that-it -doesnt-really-work/; "Interview with Larry Lohman, The Corner House: 'Carbon

Markets Do Not Need to Be "Fixed"; They Need to Be Eliminated,'" REDD-Monitor, October 22, 2020, available at https://redd-monitor.org/2020/10/22/interview-with -larry-lohmann-the-corner-house-carbon-markets-do-not-need-to-be-fixed-they -need-to-be-eliminated/; G. Cornelis van Kooten, "Forest Carbon Offsets and Carbon Emissions Trading: Problems of Contracting," *Forest Policy and Economics* 75 (February 2017): 83–88; Josh Keefe, "Maine Stands to Gain from Carbon Offsetting but Whether It Fights Climate Change Is Complicated," *Bangor Daily News,* January 16, 2021.

9. Ben Elgin, "This Timber Company Sold Millions of Dollars of Useless Carbon Offsets," *Bloomberg Green,* March 17, 2022, available at https://www.bloomberg.com/ news/articles/2022-03-17/timber-ceo-wants-to-reform-flawed-carbon-offset-market. Jim Hourdequin served as an intern for the Northern Appalachian Restoration Project and *Northern Forest Forum* in the late 1990s.

10. John B. Loomis and Robert Richardson, *Economic Values of Protecting Roadless Areas in the United States* (Washington, DC: Wilderness Society, 2000), 13.

11. Author interview with Greg Cloutier, September 3, 2019.

Nineteen: The Future Matters

1. Stephen Blackmer, "A Critique of the HEADWATERS Reserve Proposal," *Northern Forest Forum* 4, no. 1 (1995): 20–21.

2. Catherine Schmitt, "Against the Grain," *Northern Woodlands* (spring 2020): 66, 68.

3. Chad Hanson and John Talberth, *Running Backwards: Logging Provisions in the Infrastructure and Budget Reconciliation Packages Would Worsen the Climate Crisis and Threaten Public Health* (Bear City, CA: John Muir Project, 2021), 13.

4. Spencer R. Meyer, Kavita Kapur Macleod, Jonathan R. Thompson, David R. Foster, Robert Perschel, Nicole St. Clair Knobloch, Jon Leibowitz, et al., "New England's Climate Imperative: Our Forests as a Natural Climate Solution: A Highstead Report," Highstead Foundation, September 2022, 29, available at https://highstead.net/library/ forests-as-a-natural-climate-solution/.

5. Mitch Lansky, "*Beyond the Beauty Strip* Revisited: Another Decade of Industrial Forestry," *Northern Forest Forum* 9, no. 3 (2002): 11; Sam Brown, "Wood Harvesting Technologies and Low-Impact Logging," in Mitch Lansky, ed., *Low-Impact Forestry: Forestry as if the Future Mattered* (Hallowell: Maine Environmental Policy Institute, 2002), 47.

6. Mitch Lansky, "As If the Future Mattered . . . ," in Lansky, ed., *Low-Impact Forestry,* 129.

7. Mitch Lansky, "Principles, Goals, Guidelines and Standards for Low-Impact Forestry," in Lansky, ed., *Low-Impact Forestry,* 22–34.

8. Lansky, "As If the Future Mattered . . . ," 133.

9. Mitch Lansky, "Mel Ames Proves You Can Get There from Here," in Lansky, ed., *Low-Impact Forestry,* 102.

10. Author interview with David Brynn, October 3, 2018. Quotations from Brynn in the following are from this interview unless otherwise noted.

11. David Brynn, "Weighing in on Vermont's Climate Action Plan," September 2021, digital copy in the author's possession.

12. Brynn, "Weighing in."

Epilogue

1. "Conversation with Poet Gary Lawless," *Northern Forest Forum* 5, no. 2 (Solstice 1996): 18–21.

2. "Conversation with Poet Gary Lawless."

3. Frederick Douglass, "The Life and Times of Frederick Douglass, Written by Himself," in Frederick Douglass, *Autobiographies,* ed. Henry Lewis Gates Jr. (New York: Library of America, 1994), 527.

4. Reed F. Noss, "Does Conservation Biology Need Natural History?," *Wild Earth* 8, no. 3 (1998): 10–14.

5. Douglass, "Life and Times," 834; W. E. B. Du Bois, *The Souls of Black Folk* (Boston: St. Martin's, 1997), 117.

6. James Baldwin, *The Fire Next Time* (New York: Dial, 1963), 111; James Baldwin, *Notes of a Native Son* (Boston: Beacon, 1955), 174–175.

7. James Baldwin, *No Name in the Street* (New York: Dial, 1972), 88.

Acknowledgments

I have been involved in the events recounted in *Children of the Northern Forest* for more than three decades. Long before I began to write, I received inspiration, guidance, and assistance from many wonderful people. I regret I have failed to include the names of all whose kindness and wisdom enriched my life as I explored the northern forest.

Dave Foreman, who passed away as this book neared completion, changed my life. He cofounded Earth First! He was a visionary who had a profound impact upon the late twentieth-century reawakening to the value of—and necessity for—Big Wilderness in North America. Dave was an erudite, wild force of nature. He understood that the defense of wild nature required no-compromise citizen activists informed by the work of cutting-edge conservation science. Dave challenged me to take responsibility for transforming my visions into realities. Thank you, Dave.

Dave introduced me to Bill McKibben, who has been a friend and inspiration ever since. Dave evolved from being an activist to being a great conservation writer. Bill, one of our time's most important literary voices, has become a leading citizen activist in the fight to reverse climate change. He also witnessed the arrest of Jeff Elliott and me in the Adirondacks many years ago. I am certain Bill's testimony before an Adirondack grand jury contributed to its refusal to bring trumped-up charges against us that would have led to jail time. Most of all, Bill is a generous, wise, and funny friend.

When I met David Brower in 1991, I described the potential for rewilding the industrial forestlands of northern New England. He loved the idea, and over the next decade, he offered me wise advice, encouragement, material support, and friendship. For several years, I served as chauffeur on his visits to New England. Dave entertained and educated me with stories from his extraordinary conservation career. He helped me launch the *Northern Forest Forum*. Dave's faith in my work imbued me with both confidence and humility.

I met Gary Lawless at one of the legendary Earth First! Round River Rendezvous in 1985. I believe Gary is the poet laureate of the Gulf of Maine. His gift for seeing the world through the eyes of others— whales, caribou, the homeless, the forest—opened my eyes to the notion of "giving voice to place"—not speaking for a place, but serving as a modest conduit for a particular place to tell its own story on its own, nonhuman terms. Gary and his wife, Beth Leonard, have run Gulf of Maine Books in Brunswick, Maine, for more than four decades— the best bookstore I know. Their commitment to community and their sense of humor have helped me keep things in perspective all these years.

Dave Foreman wisely turned over the editorship of the *Earth First! Journal* to John Davis. A few years later Dave, John, and John's lifelong friend Tom Butler launched *Wild Earth,* an extraordinary journal of serious conservation activism and conservation science. Tom later succeeded John as editor. Tom and John are valued colleagues and dear friends. Their work for wildlands preservation is important and effective. They have been sounding boards for me for decades, and from time to time they invite me along for a canoe ride. In the evening we sit around the campfire and reminisce and dream and plot a more effective path to rewilding Earth.

Around the time I transitioned from news reporter to full-time wildlands activist, I hooked up with Jeff Elliott, a natural born activist and trained biologist. For three years we challenged conventional wisdom that alleged wilderness was a wasteland. When insiders excommunicated us for dreaming of a society willing to coexist with wild nature, we fought back. Jeff came up with one hilarious response after another to status quo, anti-wildlands conventional wisdom. I was delighted to tag along. We got into a lot of trouble, but our persistence slowly earned us some respect, and more importantly, challenged thoughtful conservationists to question conventional wisdom. I regret that eventually we burned out and became estranged. After our collaboration ended, we both persisted, and if cancer had not cut short Jeff's life, there would have been a reconciliation.

I met Michael Kellett at the March 10, 1988, Emergency Conservation Summit in Concord, convened to discuss the impending Diamond land sale. He and I have been great friends and close collaborators ever since. Michael envisions a dramatic expansion of the National Park System, and he and cofounder of RESTORE, David Carle, proposed a 3.2-million-acre Maine Woods National Park in 1994. Michael is now leading the charge for new national parks throughout the fifty states. David Carle made himself unpopular with entrenched interests with his comprehensive appeals of Forest Service logging proposals and his championship of endangered species status for the Atlantic salmon in the mid-1990s. Dave's role in securing protection for the Maine population of salmon in 2000 has not been properly acknowledged.

Jym St. Pierre and Michael Kellett began to collaborate in the late 1980s. Jym, witty and soft-spoken, has been RESTORE's Maine representative since the early 1990s. He knows more about Maine conservation issues and the state's wildlands than anyone I know. He has endured more abuse from anti–public lands ideologues, and has done more for Maine's wild nature, than anyone in the northeastern United States. He is a wonderful friend and a most reliable personal reference library for Maine conservation history.

After the first issue of the *Northern Forest Forum* appeared in the fall of 1992, Andrew Whittaker contacted me to discuss ideas for economic revitalization. He contributed an article to the second issue of the *Forum* and soon assumed the role of assistant editor. When I stepped down, he became the editor and injected a fresh perspective into the *Forum*. (Online, search for "Northern Forest Forum" to view digitized copies of the *Forum*.) He also assumed the thankless role of executive director of the Northern Appalachian Restoration Project. Happily, our friendship survived and thrives.

The Northern Appalachian Restoration Project provided meagre stipends to a talented group of activists scattered throughout northern New England. I wish we had enjoyed stronger financing so that activists' monthly checks could have more accurately reflected the value of their work. I have provided brief profiles of Northern Appalachian Restoration Project activists Barbara Alexander, Bill Butler, Daisy Goodman, Ron Huber, and Pamela Prodan in Chapter 11.

Over the decades, I have benefited from the work and support of many people. I especially thank Middlebury College professors Steve Trombulak, now retired, and Chris Klyza, who edited the most important contemporary book on the issues investigated by the Northern Forest Lands Study: *The Future of the Northern Forest.* Chris also edited *Wilderness Comes Home: Rewilding the Northeast.* Steve contributed numerous articles to the *Forum* on rewilding, preservation, and ecological integrity. I owe both so much and am grateful for their friendship.

Kathleen Fitzgerald, with *Wild Earth* and the Wildlands Project (now Wildlands Network), and Kristen Deboer, with RESTORE, raised our awareness of the need for and potential to restore viable populations of wolves to the region. Their energy, commitment, and thoroughness on a variety of additional issues made them effective and inspiring colleagues.

Lloyd Irland's original research and reports on the forest products industry, largely but not exclusively in Maine, have been invaluable. I am grateful for his patient responses to my many queries.

Dave Publicover of the Appalachian Mountain Club has always provided me with deep insights into mystifying ecological, land-management, and ownership issues. I continue to be inspired by the great work he has done to preserve and conserve forestland.

Pilot Rudy Engholm flew me and other activists over the Maine woods on numerous occasions to observe industrial logging practices. Rudy also generously supported the work of the Northern Appalachian Restoration Project and the *Forum.*

Aerial photographer Alex Maclean documented the extent of the industrial clear-cutting in Maine in the 1980s and 1990s. His shocking photographs transformed the public debate about industrial forest practices. He kindly shared many of them with me.

During the later stages of writing this book, Kris Pastoriza supplied me with a wealth of documents from governmental agencies regarding the management of the Nash Stream Forest, New Hampshire's collaboration with the ATV lobby, and much more. I would ask Kris a question, and soon a pile of important documents would arrive in my inbox.

Several people have performed special work to help bring *Children of the Northern Forest* to fruition:

Barbara Robarts, the amazing librarian at Weeks Memorial Library, unfailingly has the answers to my questions and often to questions I did not know to ask.

Brian Hart of the Harvard Forest designed seven maps for the book. They are simple, clear, essential, and elegant. His patience with my never-ending requests and changes of mind qualify him for sainthood.

Jon Luoma's artwork graced the pages of the *Northern Forest Forum* almost from its inception. I am delighted that he permitted the use of his wonderful drawings in *Children of the Northern Forest*.

Fletcher Manley, an artist with the camera and a wizard on the production end of graphics, prepared the artwork and photographs in *Children of the Northern Forest* to meet Yale University Press's high standards. Fletch displayed patience and good humor as we worked through many technical problems far beyond my comprehension.

I am deeply grateful to the following people for granting me permission to use their artwork or photographs: Charles Jordan, Kitty Kerner, Jon Luoma, Rachel O'Meara, and Barbara Tetreault. Carol Riley of the Upper Pemigewasset Historical Society, with an invaluable assist from Mike Dickerman, publisher of Bondcliff Books, provided me with the photograph of nineteenth-century loggers cutting old growth forests in the White Mountains.

Robert Beattie, Jerry Bley, David Brynn, Bob Matthews, and Robert Seymour kindly permitted me to quote them. Jeffrey S. Cramer, Curator of Collections at the Walden Woods Project's Thoreau Institute Library, patiently clarified certain matters regarding the writings of Henry David Thoreau.

Brandeis University Press has assumed the catalogue of the University Press of New England. Its director, Sue Berger Ramin, graciously granted me permission to adapt a few sections of my *You Had a Job for Life* for inclusion in *Children of the Northern Forest.*

I am gratified that Yale University Press is publishing *Children of the Northern Forest.* James C. Scott accepted it for publication by the Yale Agrarian Studies Series. Jean Thompson Black, senior executive editor, life sciences, physical sciences, environmental sciences, and medicine, has been a tough, fair, and superb editor. It has been a joy working with her and her editorial assistant Elizabeth Sylvia, whose conscientious attention to my many questions and requests is greatly appreciated. Jessie Dolch's thorough, sensitive copy editing has greatly improved my manuscript. My experiences with Yale University Press have been challenging and rewarding.

Highstead Foundation provided critical support for the production of this book through the Wildlands, Woodlands, Farmlands and Communities initiative.

Rachel O'Meara, my wife, has been supportive and patient throughout. With Rachel, life is wonderful.

David Foster, longtime director of the Harvard Forest, now retired, has made so many contributions to *Children of the Northern Forest,* and to my conservation work, that I shall simply say, Thank you, David, for everything. David has orchestrated important forest research through Harvard Forest's Long Term Ecological Research Program. He is a gifted writer, author of *Thoreau's Country,* among other works. About twenty years ago, he brought together a diverse group of conservationists, scientists, and others to launch the important New England–wide conservation initiative Wildlands and Woodlands that has evolved into the Wildlands, Woodlands, Farmlands and Communities initiative for all of New England.

When I began to write these acknowledgments, Rachel asked me to whom I planned to dedicate *Children of the Northern Forest.* I said Mitch Lansky. She smiled and replied, "Of course." For more than a third of a century, Mitch and I have worked together on nearly all the issues discussed in this book. His knowledge of Maine forestry issues, already voluminous when I arrived on the scene, is unparalleled, and he has generously shared it all with me. Mitch's 1992 book *Beyond the Beauty Strip* remains essential reading for anyone who would understand why and how Maine's industrial forest has been degraded. Forest activists across the continent will immediately recognize their own stories in Mitch's tale of Maine deforestation. He edited a pioneering work on low-impact forestry in 2002, *Low-Impact Forestry: Forestry as If the Future Mattered.* Mitch's thinking and writing on subjects such as demand reduction and low-impact economic revitalization will be read for many years to come. I believe he contributed one, or several, articles to every issue of the *Northern Forest Forum.*

I also dedicate *Children of the Northern Forest* to Mitch because of his great heart, and in gratitude for our friendship, and his mordant and whimsical sense of humor.

Thank you, Mitch, my alter ego.

Index

Gadzik, Charles, 143–144, 153
Gamache, Chris, 184, 189
Gammie, Anthony, 133
Gardner, William T., 163
Gay Brook, 238–239
genetic variability, 196, 210
Georgia Pacific, 68, 99–100, 121, 148, 248, 249
Gerritt, Greg, 146
Gibbs, Lois Marie, 140
Glacial Erratic, 109–110, 111–112, 117
global economy, 21, 27, 30, 127–128
GMO Renewable Resources, 155–156
Goldsmith, James, 83–85, 153, 167, 247
Goodman, Daisy, 141
Gorman, Larry, 49
Governors' Task Force on Northern Forest Lands (GTF), 94–96, 118, 119, 248; establishment of, 89–91; Lancaster information session, 96–98; Lyndonville information session, 98; public comment sessions, 96–98, 101–102. *See also* Northern Forest Lands Study (NFLS)
Great Northern, 5, 61–62, 66, 78, 98, 99–100, 121, 167, 246
Great Northwoods, LLC, 155, 156, 157
green certification, 148–150
green line, 96
Green Mountain National Forest, 82, 89
Green Party, 143, 250
Gregg, Judd, 7, 110, 134, 138, 250
Grella, Melissa, 220
Groveton, New Hampshire, 83, 84, 167–173, 251
Groveton Papers, 5

habitat fragmentation, 183, 193, 207
Hafford, Hilton, 150–152
Hagenstein, Perry, 85, 88
Hanson, James, 104
Harper, Steve, 89, 94, 102, 118, 122
Harrigan, Dave, 109, 111, 116, 117

Harrigan, John, 4, 9–10, 108, 126–127
Hatfield, Meredith, 175
Hathaway, William, 71
Haviland, William, 20
Haynes, Herb, 163
Headwaters Wilderness Reserve System, 208–211, 212, 218, 222, 224, 250
Helmbolt, Krista, 111
Henry, George, 47, 54–55
Henry, James Everell, 47–49, 54
herbicide spraying, 72–74, 141–142, 247
high-grading, 79, 144, 227
Holbrook, Stewart, 42
Hollingsworth & Whitney Company, 68
Hourdequin, Jim, 217
Howatt, Tom, 171
Huber, Ron, 142
Humphrey, Gordon, 7, 8
Hunter, Malcolm, 206

Ibarguen, Derek, 191
Immigration and Naturalization Act (1952), 70, 150
indigenous peoples, 19–21, 25–26, 245
industrial bioenergy, 173–177, 179
Inexcon, 155
intensive logging, 18, 47, 49–50, 55, 65, 66, 76, 222–223. *See also* clear-cutting
International Brotherhood of Firemen and Oilers, 91, 92
International Paper, 79, 85, 230; formation of, 61, 246; lands of, 62, 155, 251; strike at, 91–92, 93, 247
invasive species, 189
Irland, Lloyd, 157

J. D. Irving Corporation, 149, 155, 163
"The Jam at Gerry's Rock," 40
James River Corporation, 84, 133, 167
Jay, Maine, 67, 91–92, 247
Jefferson, New Hampshire, 15
Jenkins, Jerry, 160–161
Johnson, Cathy, 130